MILTON STUDIES

XX

MILTON STUDIES

XX *Edited by*

James D. Simmonds

UNIVERSITY OF PITTSBURGH PRESS

MILTON STUDIES

is published annually by the University of Pittsburgh Press as a forum for Milton scholarship and criticism. Articles submitted for publication may be biographical; they may interpret some aspect of Milton's writings; or they may define literary, intellectual, or historical contexts — by studying the work of his contemporaries, the traditions which affected his thought and art, contemporary political and religious movements, his influence on other writers, or the history of critical response to his work.

Manuscripts should be upwards of 3,000 words in length and should conform to the *MLA Style Sheet*. Manuscripts and editorial correspondence should be addressed to James D. Simmonds, Department of English, University of Pittsburgh, Pittsburgh, Pa. 15260.

Milton Studies does not review books.

Within the United States, *Milton Studies* may be ordered from the University of Pittsburgh Press, Pittsburgh, Pa. 15260.

Overseas orders should be addressed to Feffer and Simons, Inc., 100 Park Avenue, New York, N.Y. 10017, U.S.A.

Library of Congress Catalog Card Number 69-12335

ISBN 0-8229-3497-3

US ISSN 0076-8820

Published by the University of Pittsburgh Press, Pittsburgh, Pa. 15260

Feffer & Simons, Inc., London

Manufactured in the United States of America

CONTENTS

MILTON STUDIES

XX

MILTON NATURANS, MILTON NATURATUS: THE DEBATE OVER NATURE IN *A MASK PRESENTED AT LUDLOW*

James Andrew Clark

I N W O R K S of literature, perhaps more often than in life, seduction finds time for irrelevance. Especially in the Renaissance, literary temptation proceeds by digression toward its ends. Thus in Milton's *Mask Presented at Ludlow*, when Comus offers the Lady a charmed and tempting drink from his cup, it is not surprising that while the overtones may be sexual, the words he ventures are not. Instead, for nearly two hundred lines (659–813), the Lady follows her captor into an apparent irrelevance: a debate over the nature of nature. Some readers have found the dramatic inconsequence of this debate troublesome. For example, John Carey argues that the more the Lady attends to the subject of nature, the less she can remain wary of the threat Comus poses to her own natural chastity. On more formal grounds, John G. Demaray finds "not the slightest indication that either Comus or the Lady will be swayed by the other's arguments," making this whole interlude in the masque — between Comus' offer of the potent cup and its spilling by the Lady's brothers — an aimless, if pleasing, indulgence.[1]

Yet however implausible the dramatic action afforded by this debate over nature, surely other readers are justified in finding there central and plausible themes. Samuel Johnson, who objected on principle to the long speeches in Milton's masque, nevertheless calls this debate "the most animated and affecting scene in the drama." E. M. W. Tillyard goes further, calling this debate the very center of *A Mask*.[2] Following these illustrious Miltonists, I wish to suggest why readers find this apparently irrelevant debate both affecting and central: it is because two understandings of nature and hence two attitudes toward human life stand systematically opposed there, defying and yet demanding reconciliation. I would argue that Milton, in fact, does reconcile the attitudes of Comus and the Lady in the figure of Sabrina, who rises from the Severn toward the end of *A Mask* in order to ease all manner of tensions. Hence in its upshot, if not in its own moment, the debate over nature is highly dramatic.

3

By calling the action of *A Mask* a reconciliation of opposing attitudes rather than, say, the suppression of evil by good, I attribute to Milton, of course, a preference for reason over flogging. Not all interpreters have held this view, however. For many — the study by William G. Madsen, "The Idea of Nature in Milton's Poetry," is exemplary of the type — the Lady's notions are to be promoted as truly Christian, while Comus is flunked as a notorious libertine.[3] Certainly, Comus is unruly. Milton chastizes him for it, perhaps even rusticates him (as the record suggests the poet himself had been rusticated), but the poet allows Comus' delight in disorder to suffuse the Lady's stricter ideals — Faith, Hope, and Chastity. Milton had no need to expel this scapegrace from the state of nature.

A debate needs first not a topic but speakers to take the *pro* and *contra*, and, in the manner of a Cambridge disputation, Comus and the Lady as soon as they take each other's measure stand ready to fulfill these functions. Philip Brockbank has shown in "The Measure of 'Comus'" how their instinctive opposition touches points of style. Calling these two Milton's "largest figures of contrast" in *A Mask*, Kathleen M. Swaim has more recently added that "the two differ nearly as much in their views and voices as in the moral positions underlying their language." Swaim outlines suggestively particular differences in the disputants' views of light and nature.[4] I wish to consider the latter topic more fully here.

It may be helpful first to review what Comus and the Lady actually say. Apart from the framing action, the scene of their debate consists of four speeches formally alternating as thesis and rebuttal. The first sallies are important but preliminary. In his (666–90), Comus tries to banish the Lady's frowning reluctance to drink from his cup. He praises the "cordial Julep" (672) and asserts that nature — a hint of what will come later — lent flesh to the Lady only "For gentle usage and soft delicacy" (681), not for solemn scowls.[5] In her response (690–705), the Lady expresses her disgust at the "grim aspects" and "ugly-headed Monsters" (694–95) that surround her. Answering the tempter's appeal to final causes with an appeal of her own to formal necessities, she refuses the proffered cup because

none

> But such as are good men can give good things,
> And that which is not good, is not delicious
> To a well-govern'd and wise appetite.   (702–05)

These first speeches in the debate thus outline each speaker's premises. Comus begins from the demands of nature, the Lady from the duties of men and women.

The speeches in the second exchange, the more formal dispute over the nature of nature, build upon these premises. Comus delivers in his speech (706–55) what Louis Martz has called "a great aria of temptation," but the operatic gestures support an argument in this case or sustain the illusion of one.[6] In two stages Comus protests memorably against the binding of desire by unnatural caution. First (706–36), he decries the "foolishness of men" (706) who follow outmoded philosophies and praise "lean and sallow Abstinence" (709). If, in "a pet of temperance" (721), he argues, everyone were to follow the Lady's abstemious example, the world would soon suffocate in its own lap, for, given the *physis* of Aristotle or the *ratio seminalis* of Augustine — that sort of continuously productive nature which W. C. Curry has discerned behind Shakespeare's *Macbeth* — appetite will lag and strangle if desire is artificially curbed.[7]

To drive home this argument Comus employs the strategies of *copia rerum*, as Erasmus taught, miming in words what he claims nature, unharvested, would do in her medium of things. He works his rhetoric through all the elements. He crams the fiery core of the earth with "all-worshipt ore and precious gems" (719), crowds its surface with "odors, fruits, and flocks" (712), fills the trees — "green shops" (716) — with "millions of spinning Worms" (715), brims the waters with "spawn innumerable" (713), and burdens the air with plumes (730). Thus Comus presents to the Lady an image of herself as heiress, one so fantastically ladened by nature, her benefactress, that she must allow her demands to grow lest she be swamped by perennial supplies.

After this titanic fanfare, Comus modulates into the real key of seduction. Confident address marks the turn: "List Lady, be not coy, and be not cozen'd / With that same vaunted name Virginity" (737–38). Having set forth his major premise (706–36), Comus may feel so confident and confidential here because his minor premise, now to be advanced, seems so inevitable. He has argued powerfully that nature's bounty must be accepted, harvested, used. Obviously, he says, the Lady herself has certain natural gifts: "a vermeil-tinctur'd lip . . . Love-darting eyes . . . tresses like the Morn" (752–53). These gifts form part of the natural abundance, he contends. Hence it follows that the Lady's beauty

> must not be hoarded,
> But must be current, and the good thereof
> Consists in mutual and partak'n bliss,
> Unsavory in th'enjoyment of itself.   (739–42)

The Lady, "but young yet" (755), must harvest what nature has planted.

This conclusion of Comus' enthymeme has been called by Balachandra Rajan a moment of "enormous triviality," and the descent from the mode of Lucretius to that of Lovelace is certainly bathetic.[8] Yet the effect can be seen as deliberate. Comus appears to take the Cavalier truisms — among others that beauty is a rose that "withers on the stalk" (744) — and to slip them in among his vaster generalizations about the way things are. Such a strategy might lend inevitability to his solicitations, and like other imperialists Comus is ready to appeal to manifest destiny. Even if that appeal fails logically, it may succeed rhetorically.

The Lady's reply to Comus (756–99), of comparable length and structure, repulses the "dazzling fence" (791) of his rhetoric. High claims have been made for her argumentative power.[9] At the very least, she addresses the point. After a brief prologue (756–61), in which she reluctantly decides that speech is required, the Lady turns directly to the issue of natural abundance:

> Imposter, do not charge most innocent nature,
> As if she would her children should be riotous
> With her abundance; she, good cateress,
> Means her provision only to the good
> That live according to her sober laws
> And holy dictate of spare Temperance:
> If every just man that now pines with want
> Had but a moderate and beseeming share
> Of that which lewdly-pamper'd Luxury
> Now heaps upon some few with vast excess,
> Nature's full blessings would be well dispens't
> In unsuperfluous even proportion,
> And she no whit encumber'd with her store,
> And then the giver would be better thank't,
> His praise due paid, for swinish gluttony
> Ne'er looks to Heav'n amidst his gorgeous feast,
> But with besotted base ingratitude
> Crams, and blasphemes his feeder.   (762–79)

Thus the Lady denies Comus' major premise, which held that universal temperance would lead to ingratitude and superfetation. On the contrary, she affirms that indulgence, "swinish gluttony," is what stifles thanksgiving; it is only unrestrained accumulation of stores by a few, she holds, that could provoke the fear of natural strangulation. Like Hooker, she holds that "The works of Nature are all behoveful, beautiful, without superfluity or defect."[10]

Her opponent's major premise thus rebutted, the Lady does not feel required to address his other assertion linking her beauty to the necessary fruition of nature's bounty.[11] Rather, picking up his image of "shameless brows" that grow "inur'd to light" (735–36), she rebukes Comus for daring to speak contemptuously against "the Sun-clad power of Chastity" (782). Finally, at considerable length (792–99), she refuses to continue the debate, instead warning that her "pure cause" could move nature itself to shake until Comus' "magic structures rear'd so high, / Were shatter'd into heaps" (798–99) like another Bower of Bliss or Philistine banqueting hall.

Having reviewed these speeches, one may now attempt to state more abstractly the opposing positions of Comus and the Lady with respect to the nature of nature. The terms *libertine* and *Christian*, applied by Madsen, have already been mentioned. To them he adds pairs linking Comus with Epicureanism and nominalism, the Lady with Stoicism and idealism.[12] But such terms are perhaps too general. In his essay on *A Mask* for the *Variorum Commentary*, Douglas Bush provides a more satisfactory statement of the sides. In his view, the Lady finds Comus' understanding of "prolific nature" more incomplete than wrong. Bush writes, "Nature is a rational as well as a vital scale of being; if nature the vital and prolific furnishes the provisions among which one must choose, nature the rational furnishes the principle of choice."[13] Swaim offers much the same distinction by saying of Comus and the Lady, "His nature is rife and ready; her human nature aspires to the divine it incorporates."[14] These categories, natural vitality and human or divine rationality, perhaps descend ultimately from the Cartesian dualism of substances, *res extensa* and *res cogitans*. But Milton's mature understanding of nature is not dualistic, as Bush himself says.[15] For this reason, what the debate over nature in *A Mask* involves will perhaps become clearer if for vitality and rationality are substituted the more unified terms *natura naturans* and *natura naturata*, drawn from the monistic metaphysics of Descartes's critic and inheritor Spinoza.

Although Spinoza was only five years old, and living in Amsterdam, when Milton's Ludlow masque was printed in London in 1637, the metaphysical categories that he would develop already lay to hand. In particular the distinction between *natura naturans* and *natura naturata*, according to Richard McKeon's *The Philosophy of Spinoza*, had arisen long before in forms of scholasticism.[16] Perhaps on account of this origin of his terms, Spinoza gives them a theological cast in his *Ethics*. In a note to Book 1, proposition 29, *natura naturans* is defined as

that which is in itself and is conceived through itself, or those attributes of substance which express eternal and infinite essence, that is to say . . . God in so far as He is considered as a free cause.

By *natura naturata*, on the other hand, Spinoza means

> everything which follows from the necessity of the nature of God or any one of
> God's attributes in so far as they are considered as things which are in God, and
> which without God can neither be nor can be conceived.[17]

Because Spinoza's famous equation, *Deus seu Natura,* merges theology
with natural philosophy, Stuart Hampshire can explain this distinction
as between "Nature actively creating herself and deploying her essential
powers in her infinite attributes," that is, *natura naturans,* and nature "in
its passive capacity, as an established system," that is, *natura naturata.*[18]

For Spinoza these opposed concepts represent dual aspects of a single
substance or whole, but that partisans should champion one or the other
aspect of nature as single truth is not surprising. On some points the two
sides will agree, of course. As Madsen says of Comus and the Lady, "they
agree that Nature is abundantly fertile."[19] But such agreement is largely
illusory. Like Comus, enthusiasts for *natura naturans* will stress the
energetic, transitive, generative qualities of the world. Plenitude for them
appears to spring from the shifting motions of atoms in a void. *Natura
naturata,* however, is static and reflexive. Its partisans understand the
world, perhaps without much reference to generation or decay, in the
nominative case and the perfective aspect. It, too, can contain abundance,
but its plenitude will be expressed as a crystallized system of natural law.

Alfred North Whitehead, for one, has noted the importance of some
such distinction as this for Milton's poetry. In *Process and Reality* he adduces a similar contrast between the cosmologies of Plato and Newton,
especially between the *Timaeus* and the famous *Scholium* prefatory to
the opening definitions of *Principia:* "The *Scholium* betrays its abstract-
ness by affording no hint of that aspect of self-production, of generation,
of [*physis*], of *natura naturans,* which is so prominent in nature. For the
Scholium, nature is merely, and completely, *there,* externally designed
and obedient. The full sweep of the modern doctrine of evolution would
have confused the Newton of the *Scholium,* but it would have enlightened
the Plato of the *Timaeus.*"[20] As Whitehead suggests here, the distinction
between these two interpretations of nature is parallel to that between
evolutionary biology and classical physics. Milton "wavers" between these
two cosmologies in *Paradise Lost,* Whitehead writes, though a more ap-
proving verb might be chosen.[21] In any case, as both natural and theological categories, *natura naturans* and *natura naturata* participate in
a contrast between self-making and obedience which is full of implication for much of Milton's poetry.

In *A Mask* these contrasting cosmologies produce the debate I have been discussing. Hence one may use a tidy formula: Comus *naturans*, Lady *naturata*. Energy, motion, and proliferation all typify Comus' view of the world. "Nature's coin," he says, "must be current" (739–40), and the modern reader's momentary association of the phrase with electricity, while anachronistic, captures the antimasquer's spirit. The Lady, however, favors a world in which things stay put, each in its coordinates of time and space, as "sober laws" (766) require. Though she threatens to become vehement she never surrenders her capacity to think integrally. Her seducer, by contrast, thinks through continua. All limiting membranes of law or flesh seem permeable to him.

A surprising number of details in *A Mask* reflect the light of this distinction between *natura naturans* and *natura naturata*, that is, between the dynamic processes of generation and motion and the stative realities of plenitude and order.[22] For instance, the contrast gives salience to some curious parallels between the first speeches of Comus and the Attendant Spirit. The famous lines that open the published masque allow the Spirit to set up several oppositions between sky and earth that reveal his cosmology:

> Before the starry threshold of *Jove's* Court
> My mansion is, where those immortal shapes
> Of bright aerial Spirits live inspher'd
> In Regions mild of calm and serene Air,
> Above the smoke and stir of this dim spot,
> Which men call Earth, and with low-thoughted care
> Confin'd and pester'd in this pinfold here,
> Strive to keep up a frail and Feverish being,
> Unmindful of the crown that Virtue gives
> After this mortal change, to her true Servants
> Amongst the enthron'd gods on Sainted seats. (1–11)

In this interpretation of nature, the sky is "bright," "starry," and "serene," while the earth is "dim" and smoky, a perfect scene for a caucus of "Feverish" mortals. The verbs apportioned here to gods and spirits allow them only to "live inspher'd" and to keep their seats (as the Lady later keeps hers perforce), albeit "Sainted" ones. Earthly verbs, by contrast, involve living things in stir and strife. Thus change, to the Attendant Spirit, is "mortal."

While in these opening lines the Spirit clearly avails himself of the old distinction between the unmoved *primum mobile* and the turning spheres it drives, later in the speech imagery of teeming motion returns in more mudane ways. First, it touches the Spirit's description of the earl of Bridgewater's "fair offspring" (34), now journeying

> through the perplex't paths of this drear Wood,
> The nodding horror of whose shady brows
> Threats the forlorn and wand'ring Passenger.   (37–39)

When the Spirit turns next to describe Comus, such imagery of motion finds its source. The son of Bacchus and Circe, he says, "Ripe and frolic of his full grown age," has been "Roving the *Celtic* and *Iberian* fields" (59–60) before moving north and west to sojourn in "this ominous Wood" (61) between England and Wales. Thus the Spirit marks Comus with signs of both fertility and progress. His influence, as *A Mask* opens, is threatening to become pandemic.

The Spirit's own charms, however, are largely inhibitory. He characterizes Thyrsis, the persona he is about to adopt, as a placid swain

> Who with his soft Pipe and smooth-dittied Song
> Well knows to still the wild winds when they roar,
> And hush the waving Woods.   (86–88)

A two-fold allusion here precisely identifies the type of musical magic that Thyrsis will employ. First, his music will be like the words of Jesus, "Peace, be still" (Mark iv, 39), that hushed a tempest on the Sea of Galilee. Secondly, his song will reverse the effect of Orpheus' notes, which, according to Ovid, brought all the trees running to hear.[23] Thus the Attendant Spirit virtually dissociates himself from motion and, to a lesser extent, from generation, ceding these vital principles to Comus.

The first speech of Comus (93–169), which follows immediately, accepts what the Spirit has ceded. Readers often feel that the irruption of Comus into the masque breaks off the Spirit's solemn cadences with something both cruder and more lively, what Martz politely calls "the lyric form of the Anacreontic."[24] It is less often noted that Comus works not only disruption but also thorough parody of the Spirit's prologue. In fact, the two speeches, like the debating tactics later of Comus and the Lady, are almost systematically opposed. It is for this reason that Comus also begins with astronomy, echoing his precursor's diction of stars, shepherds, and folds:

> The Star that bids the Shepherd fold
> Now the top of Heav'n doth hold,
> And the gilded Car of Day
> His glowing Axle doth allay
> In the steep *Atlantic* stream,
> And the slope Sun his upward beam
> Shoots against the dusky Pole,
> Pacing toward the other goal
> Of his Chamber in the East.   (93–101)

John Hollander's *Figure of Echo* has demonstrated the tendency of echo songs toward puns and satire, and Comus' opening speech is no exception.[25] Where the Attendant Spirit concerns himself with the hierarchical cosmos, ever the same at any moment, Comus joins post-Ptolomaic cosmographers in speaking of a system of transient members at a given moment. Hesperus "now" (94) holds the zenith of this diurnal universe, but that "now" is a necessary qualification. Comus' system of nature is one where the sun constantly paces; where the heavens are mapped by thwart angles, the trines and oppositions of planets in motion; where things heat and cool; where "the top" is defined as a place which may be attained but must be relinquished.

The rest of his speech continues the parody. Rejecting "Rigor," "Advice," "Strict Age, and sour Severity" (107–09), Comus proclaims to his followers his cosmological creed:

> We that are of purer fire
> Imitate the Starry Choir,
> Who in their nightly watchful Spheres,
> Lead in swift round the Months and Years.   (111–14)

Three words in just four lines here — "purer," "Starry," and "Spheres" — are slightly disguised thefts from the Attendant Spirit's prologue (cf. 1, 3, and 16). Moreover, the "cloudy Ebon chair" (134) of Cotytto, whom Comus invokes as "Goddess of Nocturnal sport" (128), transposes into a darker register the Spirit's image of "Sainted seats" (11). Where those seats are stationary, however, Cotytto rides with Hecate in hers (135). Aware of such universal motions, Comus continually punctuates his verse with temporal adverbs: meanwhile, now, when, till, ere.

In the concluding lines of his speech, while his antimasquers whirl like monstrous planets about him, Comus multiplies the imagery of fertility and motion:

> The Sounds and Seas with all their finny drove
> Now to the Moon in wavering Morris move,
> And on the Tawny Sands and Shelves
> Trip the pert Fairies and the dapper Elves;
> By dimpled Brook and Fountain brim,
> The Wood-Nymphs deckt with Daisies trim,
> Their merry wakes and pastimes keep:
> What hath night to do with sleep?   (115–22)

Along with temporal pressures and spiritual parodies in such lines, one may feel the kinetic, nervous abundance of Comus' nature, a *natura naturans* "actively creating herself and deploying her essential powers in her infinite attributes."

If we consider the thematic oppositions in these opening speeches, together with those that later characterize the debate between Comus and the Lady, Milton seems to make possible a pair of coordinate distinctions, expressible in this form: in *A Mask* virginity is to fecundity as the "eternal" model of the cosmos is to the "diurnal" alternative. It is possible, in turn, to abstract these pairs to the level of Spinoza's more general distinction between *natura naturans* and *natura naturata*. As briefly suggested already, these terms appear at first to be aligned with the two sets of characters in *A Mask*, grouped around the Lady and Comus. If this alignment should hold, Milton's drama would become a legend of chastity in the fullest sense, and one can indeed point to many places which support such a reading.

One can hardly doubt that the Elder Brother owes allegiance to the perfective aspects of *natura naturata*. His very first words appeal to the stars and moon as the Attendant Spirit, not Comus, has described them:

> Unmuffle ye faint stars, and thou fair Moon
> That wont'st to love the traveller's benison,
> Stoop thy pale visage through an amber cloud,
> And disinherit *Chaos*, that reigns here
> In double night of darkness and of shades.   (331–35)

Disorder, redundancy, liquefaction, or what he calls "the various bustle of resort" (379): these chaotic expressions of nature hold no delight for the Elder Brother, whose terms of aesthetic value are rather words like "faint," "fair," and "pale." He reveals his dislike for energetic liquidity again later by identifying sin as a "lavish act" (465), pouring down, as expressed by the Old French etymon *lavasse*, in torrents. He favors ice instead and the gruesome shield of Minerva, "Wherewith she freez'd her foes to congeal'd stone" (449). Nor does motion fare any better. In "From Chaos to Community" Gale H. Carrithers, Jr., has noted the Elder Brother's use of words as "static counters."[26] Stasis also characterizes his ethical notions. He imagines his sister's virginity as a "constant mood of her calm thoughts" which "single want of light and noise" cannot "stir" (369–71). "Stir," in fact, becomes a leitmotif of evil in both *A Mask* and *Paradise Lost*.

It is the Elder Brother who expresses most resonantly the opposition I am tracing. After Thyrsis reveals to the boys that their sister is in danger, the Elder Brother must justify his confidence in her safety. He does so by irreconcilably separating pleasure from virtue:

> this I hold firm;
> Virtue may be assail'd but never hurt,

> Surpris'd by unjust force but not enthrall'd,
> Yea even that which mischief meant most harm
> Shall in the happy trial prove most glory.
> But evil on itself shall back recoil,
> And mix no more with goodness, when at last
> Gather'd like scum, and settl'd to itself,
> It shall be in eternal restless change
> Self-fed and self-consum'd; if this fail,
> The pillar'd firmament is rott'nness,
> And earth's base built on stubble.   (588–99)

Thus the brother, wishing to undo the mixture of good and evil that now constitutes the world, divides sharply the "restless change" of "Self-fed and self-consum'd" generation and decay from virtue, resting calm above the "pillar'd firmament."

The early speeches of the Lady resemble her brother's, but they leave behind a larger residue of uncertainty. Most of the time she espouses the still plenitude of *natura naturata*, turning away from stir or revolution. Her first act in the masque is to interpret the sound of Comus' revelry as "noise" of "Riot and ill-manag'd Merriment,"

> Such as the jocund Flute or gamesome Pipe
> Sitrs up among the loose unletter'd Hinds,
> When for their teeming Flocks and granges full
> In wanton dance they praise the bounteous *Pan*,
> And thank the gods amiss.   (172–77)

"I should be loath," she adds, "To meet the rudeness and swill'd insolence / Of such late Wassailers" (177–79). Bush may be entirely correct to assert that "the Lady does not deny the truth of Comus' picture of prolific nature," but some of her disapprobation of the "loose" shepherds here, before she has met Comus, may represent a deeper ambivalence toward the plentiful flocks and full granges, if not toward "bounteous *Pan*" himself.[27] At the least, she wishes the god could be satisfied by seemlier worship.

The Lady's song to Echo, answered instead by Comus, also leaves behind traces of paradox. Echo is a "Daughter of the Sphere" (241), and this song is a child of the Spirit's opening speech. As she sings, the Lady translates to earth his celestial language. Just as his mansion is pitched "Before the starry threshold" (1) of heaven, so the Lady situates Echo's "airy shell / By slow *Meander's* margent green" (231–32), both liminal dwellings. Similarly, her "violet embroider'd vale" (233) recalls his "Regions mild of calm and serene Air" (4). Again, the "flow'ry Cave" (239), in which the Lady thinks Echo may have confined the brothers, performs, if more gently, the same function as the "pinfold" (6) of earth in the Spirit's cosmology. Both are dim spots. Thus the Lady's song neatly reproduces the Spirit's view of nature.

Later, I will review evidence that the Lady's true echo is Sabrina, whose epiphany perfects the greening of virtuous nature anticipated in this song. For the moment, however, it must be said that although the Echo song posits firm structures and assured responses, its own formal structures make it, in Geoffrey Hartman's formulation, "a lyric tour de force woven out of the substantial nothingness of sound effects and the redundant harmonics of literary allusion."[28] Indeed, the energy of the Lady's technique may cause her solid notions to tremble. Moreover, if her brothers are like Narcissus and his reflection, then their principles, the principles of *natura naturata*, may become open to the boy's paradox, expressed in Ovid's famous tag *inopem me copia fecit* (abundance has made me poor).[29]

This paradox of a wealth that impoverishes is borne out by the dramatic action of *A Mask*. Well-stocked as the lady may be with understanding of the moral system that follows from the nature of things, the datum of the masque forces her into accommodation with revelry, energy, and the free form of *natura naturans*. "Late Wassailers" (179), she confesses, are better help than none at all. Like her brother the Lady disapproves of *stir*, yet she herself is embarked upon a problematic motion or stirring through the woods. As Carrithers has put it, "She has moved out of the study into a world of 'Riot' and conversation and summons."[30]

Appearances may be saved, of course, by reconciling facts and principles. One may demonstrate apparent deviations to be in reality unvarying epicycles of a rational course. But even when the Lady justifies or trues the providence of nature, the demonstration imposes a sadness such as we hear in her account of how "the gray-hooded Ev'n / Like a sad Votarist in Palmer's weed / Rose from the hindmost wheels of *Phoebus'* wain" (188–90) as her brothers left her side. Technically, these lines tell the same time as Comus' talk of the "gilded Car" and "glowing Axle" (95–96). Yet that technical identity exposes all the more distinctively the differences between Comus and the Lady. Although she has not overheard his speech, a dramatic irony like those Hollander has found in *Paradise Lost* lets the Lady unconsciously strain away from Comus in her metaphors.[31] Because she cannot deny the diurnal passage of the sun, her image of "*Phoebus'* wain" accords with Comus' of the "gilded Car." In the same way, the tread of her "sad Votarist" must keep in step with the pacing of Comus' sun toward his "Chamber in the East" (101). Her metaphors seem virtually to deny such identities of time and motion, however. The tonal difference between her chronology and his—as though George Eliot had set out to revise Walter Scott—reveals Milton's antithetical art as ideology swerves under pressure.[32]

Such swervings in the poetry of *A Mask* make it unsatisfying to say that Milton entirely disowns Comus' views as unbefitting to a Christian humanist. To assign Milton to either camp, in fact, especially with respect to nature, and to establish a *cordon sanitaire* around the other position is itself unsatisfactory. It is also common in Milton criticism. At least since F. R. Leavis's *Revaluation*, aesthetically oriented interpretations of *A Mask* have accorded what Carey calls "poetic fluency" to Comus, the artistic laureate. Quite justifiably, in turn, Christian interpreters have given the laurel to the Lady, arguing that Milton prefers virtue to fluency. Moral and aesthetic readings alike, however, leave Milton little room to maneuver. Instead, even temperate critics report Comus' utter defeat (or, in the case of Leavis, his total victory). Thus William J. Grace finds in the masque "a strong sense of humanistic order imposed on the fertile and fecund." Likewise, Martz's magisterial *Poet of Exile* contains the judgment that the Attendant Spirit, singing for Milton, "brings imagery of music to bear upon the riot and disorder of Comus."[33]

Few would deny that, in the debate over nature and in the whole masque, Milton ultimately sides with the Lady and her allies against Comus and his. "Milton of course takes sides," as Tillyard writes, "and the Lady is made to win."[34] Winning, however, need not imply total elimination of one's foes. If for Milton, as Martz claims, the *imperium* of virtue is sustained by the gentle agencies of imagery and music, then they, not appraisal of Milton's other commitments, should guide interpretation of *A Mask*. The poetic agencies involve almost every character in paradox and suggest that Milton's view of nature is equally paradoxical.

The first step toward establishing these paradoxes is not, as one might think, to show where Milton aligns himself with Comus' view of nature, though there are hints of *natura naturans* in such Latin poems of this period as *Elegia Quinta* and *Naturam Non Pati Senium*. It is more helpful rather to loosen Comus' connection with the vitality of *natura naturans*. One may consider first his real attitude toward natural abundance. In debate with the Lady he speaks of the brimming over of nature as pure, impartial event that proceeds without respect to her interests or his own. This attitude toward *natura naturans* is impersonal in a way that Spinoza would approve.

Elsewhere, however, Comus views the generative processes of nature with more pragmatic interest. When the Lady first enters, interrupting the antimasque, his hope for a new minion betrays his real outlook

on abundance. "Now to my charms," he exults, "And to my wily trains;
I shall ere long / Be well stock't with as fair a herd as graz'd / About my
Mother *Circe*" (150–53). In Latin word-formation, a fixing or abstraction of the vitality in *pecus* ("flock," "herd") leaves behind the more self-
interested noun *pecunia* ("wealth," "money"). Hoping to stock his herd
by any means, Comus allows here just such another conceptual harden-
ing. He stands on the no longer pastoral ground between the copulation
of cattle and the accumulation of capital. Thus his affiliation with the
"purer fire" (111) of *natura naturans* is compromised already. If Comus
is to preserve his magical investment, it turns out, his "fair herd" will
require a restraining pinfold.

As Leslie Brisman has shown in *Milton's Poetry of Choice and Its
Romantic Heirs*, manic Comus turns out to have deeply vested interests
in stasis.[35] Again and again, Milton underscores the fixation that Comus'
charms produce in place of the liberation they promise. The Attendant
Spirit, for instance, tells the brother how "great *Comus*"

> here to every thirsty wanderer,
> By sly enticement gives his baneful cup,
> With many murmurs mixt, whose pleasing poison
> The visage quite transforms of him that drinks,
> And the inglorious likeness of a beast
> Fixes instead, unmoulding reason's mintage
> Character'd in the face.   (522, 524–30)

The Spirit's account gives a local name to the more general process described by the Elder Brother a moment before. The desires of a chaste
spirit, the brother says, gradually convert flesh into "the soul's essence"
(462), but

> when lust
> By unchaste looks, loose gestures, and foul talk,
> But most by lewd and lavish act of sin,
> Lets in defilement to the inward parts,
> The soul grows clotted by contagion,
> Imbodies and imbrutes, till she quite lose
> The divine property of her first being.   (463–69)

It should not be thought that these images of ghastly fixation are mere
propaganda, misrepresenting a genuine vitality. If anything, the Elder
Brother and the Attendant Spirit limit their warnings unduly.

How right they are about Comus is suggested by the dramatic irony
that undercuts his pronouncements about the generative powers of nature. This spokesman for change and proliferation gains time for his part

in the debate only by threatening the Lady with sterile fixation. As she attempts to rise from her chair, he threatens,

> Nay Lady, sit; if I but wave this wand,
> Your nerves are all chain'd up in Alabaster,
> And you a statue; or as *Daphne* was,
> Root-bound, that fled *Apollo*.   (659–62)

Thus even before the debate begins, Comus, in effect, replaces the openness of *natura naturans* with close confinement. In his speech echoes and anticipations of other binding tempters, Acrasia and Satan, are therefore predictable.[36] His final act is similarly predictable: to leave the Lady "In stony fetters fixt" (819), even though she has refused the offered cup. One cannot, therefore, identify Comus in any simple way with the abundant generative and motive powers of *natura naturans*. Like Milton's Satan, he only claims self-generation, Circe and Bacchus being rather aspects of his nature than true parents. Comus exemplifies the paradoxes of Zeno the Eleatic, making the most astonishing mental leaps in order ultimately to deny the possibility of motion.

That similarly the Lady's side in the debate cannot be linked simply with *natura naturata* is also part of Milton's paradox. Certain images in *A Mask* loosen the connection of virtue with stasis, even as the entropaic cast of Comus' magic is being shown. Thus, in spite of his ideological commitments, the Elder Brother at one point reverses his normal imagery and contrasts *wandering* good with *fixed* evil. Virtue, he says, "May trace huge Forests and unharbor'd Heaths" (423), but wickedness, a "very desolation," "dwells / By grots and caverns shagg'd with horrid shades" (428–29). Thus the Lady's stirring through the woods is rationalized, if not adequately explained. True, chastity remains a calm virtue, but the Lady is associated with both chastity and virginity, only the latter of which, as Angus Fletcher notes in *The Transcendental Masque*, requires "absolute stasis."[37] Thus virtue need not always sit still, even though the Lady, like Spenser's Britomart, first adopts the style of knight-errantry only as an accommodation with the world, not as a fulfillment of primary desire.

Imagery of generation associated with the Lady lets virtue burgeon even more. One may find hints of *natura naturans* in the parallel appreciations of her Echo song by Comus and the Attendant Spirit. The Spirit describes her song by way of telling her brothers how he discovered their sister in the woods (an account that forms part of his disguise as Thyrsis):

> At last a soft and solemn-breathing sound
> Rose like a stream of rich distill'd Perfumes,

And stole upon the Air, that even Silence
Was took ere she was ware, and wish't she might
Deny her nature, and be never more,
Still to be so displac't. I was all ear,
And took in strains that might create a soul
Under the ribs of Death.   (555–62)

That its song should give birth to a soul allows virtue to approach *natura
naturans*, for even in the Spirit's realm the Lady's natural and moving
strains continuously displace silence and, to that extent, defer stasis.

In his *Anatomy of Milton's Verse*, W. B. C. Watkins has argued for
a "subtle differentiation" in Comus' response to the Echo song. That response, however, reveals even more the potential energy in the Lady's
nature. True, in the narcotic image that Hartman has analyzed, Comus
speaks of her song "At every fall smoothing the Raven down / Of darkness till it smil'd" (251–52).[38] But this image of stillness is followed by
lines that contrast the effects of the Lady's singing with those wrought
by Circe's dark lullabies. "I have oft heard," Comus says,

My mother *Circe* with the Sirens three,
Amidst the flow'ry-kirl'd *Naiades*,
Culling their Potent herbs and baleful drugs,
Who as they sung, would take the prison'd soul,
And lap it in *Elysium*; *Scylla* wept,
And chid her barking waves into attention,
And fell *Charybdis* murmur'd soft applause:
Yet they in pleasing slumber lull'd the sense,
And in sweet madness robb'd it of itself,
But such a sacred and home-felt delight,
Such sober certainty of waking bliss,
I never heard till now.   (252–64)

As Martz remarks, "Circe and her crew put on an operatic performance
all their own" in these lines.[39] Still, however pleasant, that performance
enervates those who hear it. Not so with the Lady's song. In a subtle
chiasmus, Milton allows the "waking bliss" (263) that she inspires to undo
the "pleasing slumber" (260) caused by Circe. Here, at least, one could
reverse the identification of the Lady with order, Comus with energy.
Beneath their debate over nature, Milton allows these opponents, then,
some surprising poetic affinities and exchanges. In this respect the two
debaters resemble L'Allegro and Il Penseroso more than the Christ and
Satan of *Paradise Lost*.

To recognize such moments of paradox in the development of *A Mask* prepares us to interpret the epiphany of Sabrina near its close. A reading of that concluding episode, in turn, may show how one may discern Milton's poetic apprehension of nature.

As Christopher Hill has said, Sabrina is "a necessary piece of machinery" in Milton's drama.[40] She is required to undo the magic of Comus, enabling the children and their parents to be reunited, an outcome celebrated in the closing dances. Her undoing of Comus' charms suggests, at first, an antithesis between them. Just as the Lady proves able to unlock her lips and oppose Comus in debate, so, in magic, Sabrina "can unlock / The clasping charm and thaw the numbing spell" (852–53). She herself calls attention to the antithetical nature of her task as she frees the Lady:

> this marble venom'd seat
> Smear'd with gums of glutinous heat
> I touch with chaste palms moist and cold.
> Now the spell hath lost his hold.   (916–19)

Such passages can support the view, expressed fully in A. S. P. Woodhouse's famous articles on *A Mask*, that Sabrina represents the mechanism of divine grace and that her undoing of Comus' charms also expunges from the text his interpretation of nature's abundant self-generation.[41]

Nevertheless, Sabrina's contribution to the masque may be understood in another way. Her function is synthetic as well as mechanical, for she brings together in one capacious being distinctive features of almost all the other important masquers. Most obviously, of course, she resembles the Lady.[42] She, too, was the daughter of a British ruler. She, too, "a Virgin pure" (826) but endangered, "Commended her fair innocence to the flood" (831), just as the Lady entrusts herself perforce to Comus, hoped trustworthy. Likewise, as Terry Kidner Kohn has noted in "Landscape in the Transcendent Masque," Sabrina also anticipates the Lady's longed-for transformation "from body back to spirit."[43] In this respect, of course, Sabrina's experience also resembles and yet reverses those of Comus' followers, also transformed and also content to remain what they have become.

As befits her mythological status, however, Sabrina has affiliations with more numinous beings. She shares some traits with the Attendant Spirit, for example. Like him she is "swift / To aid a Virgin" (855–56). She, too, passes between earth and a purer element, rising from the luminous stream as the Spirit descends from the liquid air. If Kohn is correct, Sabrina also resembles Neptune in such mediations, for "her landscape is an intermediate one between earth and the realms beyond."[44] Among the gods, Pan is also an analogue. Like him Sabrina receives bucolic and perhaps unseemly worship. According to the Attendant Spirit,

> the Shepherds at their festivals
> Carol her goodness loud in rustic lays,
> And throw sweet garland wreaths into her stream
> Of pansies, pinks, and gaudy Daffodils.   (848–51)

Doubtless, these ceremonies would please the Lady better than the more wanton liturgies of Pan seem to do. But words like "loud" and "gaudy" in this passage hint that Sabrina accepts a worship differing only in degree, not kind.

Sabrina even bears a certain resemblance to Comus himself. She presides over the Severn as he does over the woodlands of the Welsh borders. They both offer something like a sacrament, her baptismal sprinklings correcting his mock-eucharistic cup. Thus, although her function in the plot is antithetical, Sabrina becomes an important synthetic symbol in A Mask. Her appearance gives body to the play of Milton's poetry so that, as Fletcher writes, "a transcendent unity may be achieved."[45]

One might object that such resemblances or even syntheses cannot undo the banishment of Comus from the final clarifications of A Mask, which Sabrina herself effects. But she is no mere dea ex machina, appearing on cue to ratify Christian humanism and refute the philosophy of generative nature. Rather, as Kohn points out, "her immortal power, if submerged (literally and figuratively), has been present throughout the action, controlling the surroundings and rendering them harmless and innocent."[46] Milton shows her to have been a generously attentive and synthesizing spirit. For this reason, one may understand Sabrina less as an unequivocal symbol of grace than as one of those supreme, if fictitious, presences in Renaissance literature: the "gentleman or noble person" fashioned "in vertuous and gentle discipline" by Spenser's Faerie Queene, or humanist Man himself, Pico's creature "of indeterminate nature" or Vives's "multiform Proteus."[47] Sabrina may not be as large as these other philosophic beings, of course. If we recognize her multiformity, however, then we should not expect that her mode of existence will validate exclusively either conception of nature expressed in the masque. Not choosing between order and energy, she instead shows both to be aspects of a single real substance or nature.

Certain traces of paradox in the final moments of A Mask may illuminate this interpretation. (From the start, we learn that like Comus she dwells among paradoxes.) One arises in the first statement made about Sabrina, even before the Attendant Spirit gives her name. "There is a gentle Nymph," he says, "not far from hence, / That with moist curb sways the smooth Severn stream" (824–25). The phrase "moist curb" combines the existential liquidity of Comus with the metaphysical clarity of the Spirit. The verb "sways" suits this oxymoronic union. It suggests, shimmering between transitive and intransitive meanings, both responsive movement and abiding control. Sabrina both holds sway over the river and sways with it.

Similar paradoxes recur in the song Sabrina rises from the river singing:

> By the rushy-fringed bank,
> Where grows the Willow and the Osier dank,
>   My sliding Chariot stays,
> Thick set with Agate and the azurn sheen
> Of Turquoise blue and Em'rald green
>   That in the channel strays,
> Whilst from off the waters fleet
> Thus I set my printless feet
> O'er the Cowslip's Velvet head,
>   That bends not as I tread;
> Gentle swain at thy request
>   I am here.   (890–901)

By unfolding in this song the paradox of her own "moist sway," Sabrina also echoes and includes other notes sounded earlier in *A Mask*. Her authority, though real, is "printless," ruling without treading underfoot. Likewise, her motion, though unchecked, also "stays," granting the Severn an identity beneath its perceptible flux. Because of this gentle power to recollect and govern paradoxical opposites, in turn, Sabrina is able to echo correctively both sides in the debate over nature. Thus, like the "airy shell" (231) of her counterpart Echo, Sabrina's liminal dwelling by "the rushy-fringed bank" (890) recalls and naturalizes the unearthly "starry threshold" with which the masque begins. Likewise, the gems she casually mentions — agate, turquoise, emerald — refract and soften the pale brilliance of Comus' "unsought diamonds" upon "the forehead of the Deep" (733), giving earth's colors to his dire philosophy of nature. Sabrina's epiphany, therefore, affords what Martz has called a "rich union."[48] When she says, "I am here," she comes close to pronouncing the imaginative motto of *A Mask*.[49]

Best to see how Sabrina's synthetic powers transform earlier ideas of nature, one must recognize the place for energy Milton allows her to clear amid the final order. Though Comus is gone from the scene, his style reappears in Milton's verse by means of certain effects Sabrina works on the Attendant Spirit's concluding songs. Invoking her to "Listen and save" (866), the Spirit's voice finds new rhythms. He slips into those incantatory rhyming couplets that only Comus has used previously: "Listen and appear to us / In name of great *Oceanus*" (867–68).[50] The thought of Sabrina thus quickens his speech. To strengthen his summons the Spirit adjures Sabrina in the name of one water deity after another, from Oceanus to "all the *Nymphs*" (869–84). Here, too, the expectation of Sabrina recovers another trace of Comus, who earlier promises "all . . . dues" to Cotytto, "none left out" (137). Furthermore, though the deities invoked may be lost in mythography, almost all the epithets applied to them here have something to do with motion, errant lines, or display — images previously associated with Comus. Triton's shell is "winding" (873), Nereus' look "wrinkled" (871). Tethys paces, and Neptune shakes the earth (869–70), while Thetis wears tinselled slippers and, seated upon rocks of diamond, Ligea preens with a golden comb (877, 880–82). Thus, like the nymphs he describes, the Spirit lets his verse "dance . . . with wily glance" (883–84). As the crucial epiphany of Sabrina approaches, he begins, though with a difference, to sound more like Comus.

That complex echo persists after Sabrina descends. Let to pronounce a blessing, the Spirit lets generative energy supply his matter as well as his manner. He returns to the powers of *natura naturans*, now reclaimed from Comus, as he thanks Sabrina for freeing the Lady:

> Virgin, daughter of *Locrine*
> Sprung of old *Anchises'* line,
> May thy brimmed waves for this
> Their full tribute never miss
> From a thousand petty rills,
> That tumble down the snowy hills:
> Summer drouth or singed air
> Never scorch thy tresses fair,
> Nor wet *October's* torrent flood
> Thy molten crystal fill with mud;
> May thy billows roll ashore
> The beryl and the golden ore,
> May thy lofty head be crown'd
> With many a tower and terrace round,
> And here and there thy banks upon
> With Groves and myrrh and cinnamon.   (922–37)

Some readers may find the natural energy and fecundity here described to be tame by comparison with Comus' earlier account of the self-generating world. Yet one may also see here a coloring vision much deeper than the Spirit offers at the beginning of *A Mask*.

Perhaps the final couplets of the blessing point toward the latter interpretation. This landscape is not the one Comus depicted, but it is a locus of eroticism, however spiritualized, and natural abundance. The Spirit bestows upon Sabrina the turreted crown of Cybele, the *Magna Mater*, and upon the children, whose mansion, Ludlow Castle, stands nearby, thresholds of fragrant experience like that in Solomon's song.[51] In the plot of *A Mask*, this language of abundance is motivated by what Sabrina has done, but a deeper influence can perhaps be felt to flow from what she is. Because her nature is synthetic, both *naturans* and *naturata*, Sabrina moves across the Spirit's language as a magnet moves across a bit of iron, imparting its own potencies. And because those potencies include those found by Comus in nature, Sabrina is able to pass on the "poetic fluency" of *natura naturans* to the staid rationality of *natura naturata*. Here for Milton, as in the "blissful bower" of Adam and Eve before they fell, generation coincides with obedience.

If one understands Sabrina's role in *A Mask* as, in part, to mediate between opposing thoughts about nature, it becomes difficult to agree with Demaray, among others, that the Lady and Comus are in their debate over nature "figures whose views are irreconcilably and inalterably opposed."[52] On the other hand, given the interpretation offered here, the readings of Tillyard, Watkins, Fletcher, Kohn, and others who find a reconciliation of opposites in Milton's masque become more convincing. Such reconciliation need not lessen the power of virtue. *A Mask* is so "obstreperously moral," as Watkins says, that Milton could safely let *natura naturans* remain in his scheme when Comus himself must depart.[53]

It may be felt that this interpretation ignores the ending of *A Mask*. After all, Milton leaves us there not with Circe's son, nor even with Sabrina, but only with the Attendant Spirit back where the action began. This much is undeniable. Yet we are not exactly where we started either, as any reading of the Spirit's opening and concluding speeches in quick succession will confirm. For in spite of its drive to transcend the merely natural world (a drive matching the Platonic condescension of the Spirit's prologue), the Spirit's last speech retains that new sensitivity to the greening earth that Sabrina's animal magnetism first elicited from him. His voice now responds to motion, generation, and fluidity in a newly flexible way. Though perhaps intended allegorically, the flesh, fruit, and tones in the Hesperian landscape he creates are especially warm, those "happy climes" and "Gardens fair" where "Revels the spruce and jocund

Spring" (977, 981, 985). In the "bounties" and "eternal Summer" (987–88) freely deployed amid the "odorous banks" or "Beds of *Hyacinth* and Roses" (993, 998) of this neo-Spenserian garden of Adonis, one may sense the natural energy of Comus' language as it, through the mediation of Sabrina, has colored the discourse of the Attendant Spirit.

True, perhaps here and certainly in the lines that follow, the Spirit is depicting a transcendent realm. His final measures move beyond "the green earth's end" (1014) and leave no doubt concerning the unmediated spirituality of Youth and Joy, those children of "Celestial *Cupid*" and his "dear *Psyche*" (1004–05). And yet the difference in tone between the Spirit's prologue and his epilogue remains and pleasantly vexes allegorical clarities. *A Mask* begins with astronomy and music, but it ends, almost, with an idealization of nature on the mere earth. That shift of dominant metaphor, and the concomitant growth in copiousness of the Spirit's style, marks out the accommodation in Milton of *natura naturans* with *natura naturata*. Such an accommodation, if it cannot reclaim the masque from the strict fold of morality, can nevertheless keep Milton's art open to more common natures.

Auburn University

NOTES

1. John Carey, *Milton* (London, 1969), pp. 50–52; John G. Demaray, *Milton and the Masque Tradition: The Early Poems, "Arcades," and "Comus"* (Cambridge, Mass., 1968), pp. 89–90.

2. Samuel Johnson, *Lives of the English Poets*, ed. George Birkbeck Hill (Oxford, 1905), I, pp. 168–69; E. M. W. Tillyard, *Studies in Milton* (London, 1951), p. 82.

3. Madsen's study appears in Richard B. Young et al., *Three Studies in the Renaissance: Sidney, Jonson, Milton*, Yale Studies in English, no. 138 (New Haven, 1958), pp. 181–283.

4. Philip Brockbank, "The Measure of 'Comus,'" *Essays and Studies*, XXI (1968), 46–61; Kathleen M. Swaim, "Allegorical Poetry in Milton's Ludlow *Mask*," in *Milton Studies*, XVI, ed. James D. Simmonds (Pittsburgh, 1982), pp. 174–77 (the quotation appears on p. 174).

5. The text of Milton's works cited throughout this study is Merritt Y. Hughes, ed., *John Milton: Complete Poems and Major Prose* (Indianapolis, 1957); hereafter called Hughes.

6. Louis Martz, *Poet of Exile: A Study of Milton's Poetry* (New Haven, 1980), p. 28.

7. W. C. Curry, *Shakespeare's Philosophical Patterns*, 2nd ed. (Baton Rouge, La., 1959), pp. 29–49.

8. Balachandra Rajan, *The Lofty Rhyme: A Study of Milton's Major Poetry* (London, 1970), p. 33.

9. Demaray, for example, asserts that the Lady, "though enchanted, forcefully refutes Comus' opinions on the subject of nature's bounty" (*Milton and the Masque Tradition*, p. 89). Barbara K. Lewalski adds that "an examination of her speech and of Comus' response to it reveals clearly enough that the victory is hers" ("Milton on Women—Yet Once More," in *Milton Studies*, VI, ed. James D. Simmonds [Pittsburgh, 1974], p. 16). Martz concludes that "the Lady proves to have a power of eloquence that defeats the sensual music of Comus" (*Poet of Exile*, p. 28).

10. Richard Hooker, *Of the Laws of Ecclesiastical Polity*, ed. Christopher Morris (London, 1907), I, p. 182.

11. In the Bridgewater version of the 1634 text, the Lady, in fact, does not take up Comus' minor premise but ends her speech where my quotation ends. See the text reproduced in John S. Diekhoff, ed., *"A Maske at Ludlow": Essays on Milton's "Comus"* (Cleveland, 1968), p. 232.

12. See Young et al., *Three Studies*, pp. 185–213.

13. A. S. P. Woodhouse and Douglas Bush, eds., *A Variorum Commentary on the Poems of John Milton*, gen. ed. Merritt Y. Hughes (New York, 1972), II, iii, 950.

14. "Allegorical Poetry," p. 177.

15. *Variorum Commentary*, II, iii, 951.

16. Richard McKeon, *The Philosophy of Spinoza: The Unity of His Thought* (New York, 1928), p. 69. That in 1650 Sir John Denham entitled a lyric "Natura Naturata" suggests the currency of these terms before Spinoza. See Theodore Howard Banks, Jr., ed., *The Poetical Works of Sir John Denham* (New Haven, 1928), pp. 106–07.

17. Baruch Spinoza, *"Ethics" and "On the Improvement of the Understanding,"* Hafner Library of Classics, no. 11 (New York, 1949), pp. 65–66.

18. Stuart Hampshire, *Spinoza* (1951; rpt. London, 1956), pp. 36–37.

19. See Young et al., *Three Studies*, p. 204.

20. Alfred North Whitehead, *Process and Reality: An Essay in Cosmology* (1929; rpt. New York, 1960), p. 143 (part II, chapter iii, section 3).

21. Ibid., p. 146.

22. For a full treatment of the distinction between stative and dynamic modes in grammar, see Randolph Quirk et al., *A Grammar of Contemporary English* (New York, 1972), pp. 39, 47–48, 93–97, 265. An exemplary application of these terms to literary texts is made by Marie Borroff, *Language and the Poet: Verbal Artistry in Frost, Stevens, and Moore* (Chicago, 1979), pp. 96–99.

23. Ovid, *Metamorphoses*, ed. and trans. Frank Justus Miller (London, 1926), II, p. 70. One should not distinguish too sharply between Orpheus and Jesus here, for it was also part of the classical and Renaissance tradition that Orpheus could hush the waves. See, for example, Horace, *Odes* I, xii, 9–10: *"arte materna rapidos morantem / fluminum lapsus celerisque ventos"* ("With his mother's art [Orpheus] checked the rapid currents of the streams and the rushing winds"); Latin quoted from *The Odes and Epodes*, ed. and trans. C. E. Bennett (London, 1914), p. 34. In *Ad Patrem* 52–53, Milton himself says that the *Orphea cantus* (Orphic song) held still (*tenuit*) the rivers. See Hughes, p. 84. The real distinction I wish to make here is that between the binding and the release of natural energy, whoever the agent.

24. *Poet of Exile*, p. 23.

25. John Hollander, *The Figure of Echo: A Mode of Literary Allusion in Milton and After* (Berkeley and Los Angeles, 1981), pp. 26–29.

26. Gale H. Carrithers, Jr., "Milton's Ludlow *Mask*: From Chaos to Community," *ELH*, XXXIII (1966), 27.

EPIGRAMS AND SONNETS:
MILTON IN THE MANNER OF JONSON

Judith Scherer Herz

M ILTON'S SONNETS seem both to belong to and stand apart from
the English sonnet tradition. Our sense of their distinctness from
that tradition has to do in part with that elusive quality we call Milton's
voice, the quality that we seem so readily to recognize (although we may
find it difficult to account for in any systematic way), no matter whether
it orates, prophesies, laments, denounces, or sings. It also must have
something to do with our tendency to read the sonnets as if they were
Paradise Lost "contracted into an inch . . . [that] was a span,"[1] a tendency that no doubt began with Milton himself, for whom all the earlier
works proleptically contained that vast epic which was to be their origi-
nator and culmination. And it has a great deal to do with the relationship between Milton's sonnets and the heroic sonnets of Bembo, della
Casa, and Tasso. This last point has long been recognized and recently
has been the subject of a fruitful study that places them in relation to
the high style of the Italian heroic sonnet on the one hand and to the
low and middle styles of the English sonnet tradition on the other, in order
to show how Milton developed the high or grand style in his sonnets "not
merely [as] a means of moving men to action [the traditional function
of the high style in Ciceronian terms] but also [as] a visionary medium."[2]

However, such an approach not only does not account for many
aspects of Milton's work in that form; by its very emphasis on heroic scale
it closes our ears to quite another range of tones and to quite a different
kind of vocabulary. In our attempt to honor the intention of the conceit —
the colossus carved on the cherry stone — we have too often pursued the
colossal, forgetful of the constraints of what was by its nature a miniatur-
izing form, based on the principles of brevity and diminution. For there
is another feature of the Miltonic sonnet which may account for that
double sense of like and unlike that I noted at the start, that is, its mark-
edly epigrammatic nature. It is this quality that puts it in direct relation
to the poetry of Jonson, for example, and at the same time marks it off
from the heroic poetry of della Casa and Tasso.

Thus without at all denying the heroic and visionary aspects of cer-

29

tain of these poems, I propose looking for a quite different context, one
that can account for those qualities that are not directly a part of the grand
style, but rather are found at the other end of the rhetorical scale. The
epigram, in its flexible tonal range that moves from the aphoristic, witty,
and satiric to the meditative, complimentary, and self-reflective, can provide such a context. And in this light the epigrams of Jonson are especially significant as they, unlike many contemporary English epigrams,
were themselves, in their serious moral purpose and frequently lofty tone,
occasionally touched by the high style. Before examining the possible links
between these epigrams and Milton's sonnets, however, it will be necessary to consider both the generic and formal affinities between epigram
and sonnet as well as to establish a context where Milton's reading of Jonson can be made to bear directly on his experiments in a genre in which
Jonson showed little interest.

It has been clearly demonstrated, most notably by Rosalie Colie in
her chapter, "Problems in Sonnet Theory," in *Shakespeare's Living Art*,
that the epigram and sonnet are generically very close and were so perceived in the sixteenth and seventeenth centuries.[3] Colletet's definitions in
his *Traité du sonnet* (1658) point to this: "Le sonnet approche le plus près
de l'epigramme"; and, he continues, the sonnet may even be considered
an extended and bounded epigram.[4] Indeed the distinction was often
blurred. Scaliger called Petrarch's sonnets "Epigrammata Amatoria," and
insofar as Petrarch was considered the Italian equivalent of Martial (for
his sonnets, like della Casa's and Tasso's, touched on political and philosophical as well as amatory themes), the sonnet was viewed as a form
of epigram in the common language (a point the dictionaries cited by
Colletet also make). The last sonnet of Du Bellay's *Les Regrets*, for example, was used again in a Latin version as the first of his *Epigrammata*.

What distinctions there were had to do with subject matter. Sebillet,
in *L'Art poétique françoys* (1548), argues that whereas the epigram can
accommodate all sorts of subjects, sonnets tend more to gravity: "la matiére de l'epigramme et la matiére du Sonnet sont toutes unes, fors que la
matiére facécieuse est repugnante à la gravité du sonnet." For Sebillet,
moreover, the sonnet "n'est autre chose que le parfait epigramme de
l'Italien, comme le dizain du François."[5]

Certainly the epigram and sonnet were among the most popular
forms of late sixteenth and early seventeenth century poetry, the epigram
taking over at the end of the period of the sonnet sequence's popularity.
There were, for example, about fifty collections of epigrams published
between 1598 and 1620.[6] Most of these epigrams, however, were direct
descendants of medieval allegory and type-satire. Jonson's collection, on

the other hand, although it comes toward the end of this period, does not so much sum it up as point in a quite different direction. Thus he was not exaggerating when, in contrast to contemporary practice, he claimed both classical precedent and originality for his more inclusive mode: "To thee my way in epigrammes seems new, / When both it is the old way and the true."[7] Indeed Jonson's way was even more inclusive than Martial's, his avowed source, for into the theater of his epigrams, Jonson claims in his preface to Pembroke, "Cato, if he liv'd, might enter without scandal." Martial, in his prefatory letter to the reader, had warned Cato off.

In formal terms, too, the sonnet and the epigram bear interesting resemblances. For both, self-containment, self-exhaustion, and absolute closure are crucial. Barbara Herrnstein Smith, for example, points to the epigram's "suicidal impulse," the form's tendency to exhaust itself, leaving nothing more to say.[8] This tendency is perhaps more visible in the satiric epigrams, for epigrams of praise do not always demand conclusion in this self-consuming fashion. Part of their stance is the implied assumption that the poet has isolated only one hyperbole among many and has enacted only one of the several possible relationships between poet and subject. In the satiric epigram the subject *is* the trait; there is no space left for meditation, certainly none for revision. The expectation that the poem will fix and frame is built into the genre from its origins in epitaph and inscription; in the sonnet these expectations are more a function of form.

If these are self-consuming forms, however, they are so in a peculiarly phoenixlike fashion. For out of the ashes of one sonnet springs another and another. The sonnet is dead, long live the sonnet. Much the same sort of statement can be made about the epigram, for it too draws upon a clearly identifiable vocabulary, set of gestures, voices, and stances. Even in terms of formal expectations, one could argue that wit and brevity impose something of the same sort of structural constraint upon the epigram as volta and couplet do upon the sonnet. With the close of both sonnet and epigram the only way to go on is to begin all over again.

It is, of course, that beginning all over again that allows for the sonnet sequence, but it is also the quality that makes it very difficult to determine if a cluster of sonnets does indeed constitute a sequence, or, as in the case of Jonson, a cluster of epigrams. I am going to work with the assumption generally supported by most recent writing on the subject, that at least after the fact, the poems, which were in many instances obviously occasional, were drawn together so as to make pattern visible.[9] For Jonson this occurred when he arranged the epigrams for publication in the 1616 Folio; for Milton the process seems to have begun in the Trinity manuscript and to have been continued in the 1645 and 1673 editions. Mary Ann Radzinowicz's subtle accounting for this notion of sequence after the fact certainly can be made to apply to Jonson's epigrams as well.[10]

In the remainder of this essay I want to explore how Milton's sonnets, both individually and taken together, constitute Milton's most Jonsonian writing. There Milton compliments and condemns, invokes the past, rebukes the present, invites his friends, scorns his enemies, takes the measure of the reader, and both judges and justifies himself. The connections between Jonson and the early Milton have long been observed. What I am interested in, however, is not Milton's appropriation of a clarified Spenserian vocabulary and certain aspects of what we not altogether accurately call Jonson's plain style, but his response to Jonson's "book" — the 1616 Folio, recognizing in *The Epigrammes* an ordered grouping of poems whose concerns touched directly on those he was elaborating in his sonnets. Thus, given what we know of Milton's reading of Jonson from ". . . a Fair Infant" onward, and given the generic affinities, especially as these were understood in the seventeenth century, between the epigram and the sonnet, it should be useful to consider the ways in which Jonson's epigrams could have served as one of Milton's models.

This is not to say that Milton had to look outside the sonnet tradition for a source, for as Anna Nardo carefully argues, Milton "as sonneteer . . . fell heir to a single-sonnet tradition rich in humorous, occasional, satiric, heroic, friendly and elegiac sonnets, and to a sequence tradition which had broadened its content to include the ideals of civilization."[11] But both traditions, as the earlier discussion set out to demonstrate, were linked to the epigram. Moreover, the single sonnet tradition she refers to was not an English one, and those sequences that idealized civilization in the figure of the Virgin Queen were, as Nardo admits, not much more than panegyrics written on command. Neither tradition provides an adequate context for viewing Milton's achievement in this form. Going back behind them, to Martial and to Horace, turns out to be a journey on a circular roadway that brings one around to Jonson, whose remaking of these very sources was "aimed at the creation of language itself," as John Hollander argues in his superb account of Jonson's accomplishment. Hollander's description of Jonson's enterprise clearly has resonance for this argument, for his claim that what Jonson was doing in his poetry — "creating discourse in an ideal community" — is very close to Nardo's argument for Milton, suggested even in the title of her book.[12]

A good starting point for examining the link between Milton's sonnets and Jonson's epigrams occurs in sonnet 8 for it is, in a literal sense, a self-enacting epigram. Although the copyist's title — "on his dore when ye Citty expected an assault" — was deleted by Milton, who then entitled it *When the assault was intended to ye citty*, the sonnet still retains the quality of an inscription.[13] It is a sonnet-epigram committed to an obviously Jonsonian notion of the past, although it is at once more playful and more elegiac than Jonson's usual manner. Nonetheless it is most Jonsonian as it sets up resonances with the immediate past of Spenserian romance ("knight at arms," "muses bower," "deed of honour") and the further past of classical poetry. The poet not only can confer fame upon the doer of a gentle deed, poetry itself can change history as "the great Ermathian conqueror bid spare the house of Pindarus." If the song of Euripides had "the power to save th'Athenian walls from ruine bare," then this poem makes a like claim by inscribing on those walls, now modestly become the poet's door, its own evidence. That royalist ethos of good wine, fine talk, staunch men, and poetry that Jonson bequeathed to his sons became for them an escape during the "hard season" of Cromwell's winter. For Milton, no son, though possibly cousin, it may also have been a refuge, even if he would have associated Cromwell with the sun and not the cold and gloom.[14] The poem's present moment, nonetheless, is of "ruin bare," its tone one of rueful melancholy as he muses on the small space left for a "deed of honour," withdrawing as a result to some Athens of the imagination where his poetry can take its place with Pindar's and Euripides'.

I cite sonnet 8, however, not because it is like some particular poem of Jonson's, but because it is close to the epigram in its manner and matter. Sonnet 10, however, is also at base an epigram, but much closer in its practice to many of Jonson's. The essential conceit of sonnet 10 is that Margaret is her father's epigram in much the same way as Pembroke "is an epigramme on all man-kind" (epig. 102). Not only is she the image of her father's virtues, the means by which they are felt in this diminished present day — "yet by you / Madame, methinks I see him living yet" — but she literally epitomizes them, "so well your words his noble vertues praise" (this presumably referring to her written account of his life in which she had related these same virtues "true").

Like many of Jonson's epigrams, this sonnet depends structurally upon the circle, a figure most movingly elaborated in epigram 128 on Sir William Roe's circular voyage. There the circular structure demands the act of rereading, a process that Ilona Bell claims is built into the poem as a requirement of its first reading, as poet and reader and subject undertake a circling, whereby one "can reassess the beginning in terms of the ending."[15] Milton's circlings clearly send one back to the beginning as well, but to confirm and complete, rather than to rediscover. The subject moves from type (daughter) to named individual ("Honour'd Margaret"), all the while absorbing into her role those qualities she has dedicated her life to enacting, preserving, making known. Milton uses this sonnet (perhaps even intended, like many of Jonson's poems, to appear in the published version of her father's life) to inscribe these two lives, one the palimpsest of the other, in a single epigram.

There is also a nice structural decorum at work here. The father's part of the poem is the octave. Grammatically it is presided over by the daughter (as she presided over his house), but it is his space and it is ample in its range of reference — Isocrates, Chaeronea — to his full and unstained life, a life made all the more admirable given the backdrop of private corruption and public violence. The speaker enters only in the sestet, a smaller space he shares with the daughter who now takes her place, beginning in line nine, as the rightful subject (and metaphor) of the poem. It is a much more intimate space, a result of the poet's friendship with the daughter. Unlike 8, this poem does not keep opening up ever larger vistas, but circles to enclosure: the poet judges the daughter judging the father, to whose career as judge the poem testifies epigrammatically in the daughter's name.

The handling of names, both syntactically and metaphorically, constitutes another link between Jonson's practice and Milton's. The name often occupies the first foot (as it does in many of Tasso's sonnets), setting up, as a result, a counterweight to the rest of the poem, which, by the conventions of compliment, becomes to some degree beside the point (all one need write is Bedford's name). Metonymic and talismanic values are similar, too; indeed the act of naming is a constant of Milton's style, particularly noticeable in the prose where he is most directly engaged in vilifying and praising. The sonnets, however, reveal this quality the more clearly, for there these devices do not serve some larger rhetorical purpose. The name stands for the person, becomes the person, and then, enlarged by that person, becomes the type of virtue.[16] The subjects of these poems must validate the virtues the poet claims for them. They take the measure and are themselves the measure; they are both mirror and reflection. But they ought not to regard these reflections too complacently, for both poets mistrust to some degree those figures their poetry enshrines. Both Jonson and Milton speak in a public voice in a poetry that is normative but that is also, in its inwardness, idiosyncratic, personal, and wary of public statements as well as of public postures.

The reader's relationship to the text provides another area of simi-

larity, for both poets make our participation in the double ritual of ex-
coriation and celebration that occurs in their epigrams and sonnets a
privileged one. The reader clearly must earn his entry into Jonson's fictive world: "Pray thee, take care, that tak'st my book in hand, / To reade
it well: that is, to understand" (epig. 1).[17] Here the admonitory voice
("take care") mingles with the gravely beseeching ("pray thee"). The
physical gesture, "tak'st . . . in hand," punningly suggests a notion of
metaphoric control over the text (take the text in hand). But what the
author demands cannot be so readily granted, for the act of reading is
ultimately outside his control. Thus as "take in hand" moves to "understand," it must also refer back to the admonitory "take care," which thus
comes to mean not only read carefully but interpret rightly. And who
are these readers to be? Certainly those identified in epigram 9 will find
their scattered names in his book and those referred to in 10 will find
their natures. But the reader of epigram 1, who is not among those suggested in 9, will make it his business not to be the type of vice denounced
in 10. He will thus take in hand with considerable care and understanding. For it is not just in this first epigram that Jonson makes his designs
on his readers clear. Epigrams 2, 3, 9, 18, 36, 49 are also programmatic,
and many others, by way of explaining the nature of the praise or blame
dispensed, set out the guiding assumptions of the collection as a whole.

In Milton's sequence, the line that makes a like demand upon the
reader occurs in *I did but prompt the age*, where the barbarous readers
are taught the true meaning of their crying for liberty and we are admonished that "who loves that must first be wise and good." The claim
is identical with the one Milton makes upon himself when in *The Apology
for Smectymnuus* he argues that the true poet must himself be a true poem.
And that concern is the primary preoccupation of the poet of the
sonnets — to test each life as it exemplifies "the strictest measure even" of
the yet unwritten (although from another perspective, eternally and finally composed) poem.

If we are admonished, so too are the subjects of these poems. (Radzinowicz makes this point nicely in relation to Milton, "for every grain
of panegyric there will be a gram of advice.")[18] However, admonition
in Jonson's epigrams is, for the most part, implicit rather than explicit.
The warning is the praise itself; the caveat, our awareness that the subject may not be able to live up to the praise. There is also the added
complication that while the flattery is never merely servile, it may be
self-serving. To the rhetorical question that opens *To Robert Earle of
Salisburie* "What need hast thou of me? or of my muse?" (epig. 43), an
ironic answer is provided in line 8 when Jonson acknowledges that he

will reap the greater benefit by receiving the patronage of so great a statesman. And *To Esme Lord Aubigny* (epig. 127), while it has as background a much closer personal relationship than *To Salisburie*, sets the transactional relation of poem to patronage in sharp relief: "I know no abler way / To thanke thy benefits: which is, to pay." But even a flattery so practically based has a larger purpose. As Ira Clark has demonstrated in his discussion of *To King James* (epig. 4), "Risking possible flattery by honoring James in order to urge him to greatness, the epigram also borders on satirizing him if he fails to live up to the eulogy."[19] This sense of risk-taking runs through the epigrams; it gives them much of their edge and complicates what from another point of view could be interpreted as fulsomeness. What prevents this is not only the complex voice within the epigram but the context created by the surrounding poems, both satiric and encomiastic. The poet does not place his portraits according to rank and lineage (he is, we recall, no herald). Rather the ordering principles seem at once aesthetic, moral, and political. The epigrams taken together thus constitute a total society; they both make and remake reality.[20]

Although the strategy is similar in Milton's sonnets to Fairfax and Cromwell, judgment, by contrast, is more difficult. The praise is more inclusive, but so are the misgivings. Praise of Fairfax, for example, is never turned against him, but it is qualified by the recognition that the fame he has acquired may be in vain "while avarice and rapine share the land." And·Fairfax is curiously absent from his poem; the name seems somewhat less than the man. To be sure the name is a word that amazes all Europe, but it seems not quite sufficient here at "home . . . [where] new rebellions raise / thir Hydra heads." The poem begins with the past, those deeds that Fairfax's "firm, unshak'n virtue" had accomplished, and ends with the present, a time of violence, fraud, avarice, and rapine. It points to a future of truth, right, and public faith, but that time is outside the poem and will occur only if Fairfax can accomplish this still awaiting "nobler task." The sestet is a litany of abstractions; there seems little place for Fairfax, who has essentially departed the poem at line 9, leaving behind the question whether he is the man who can end what seems an endless cycle: "For what can War, but endless warr still breed." Indeed his absence from the sestet curiously foreshadows the event that will give to those lines the special pathos of retrospect. For perhaps it was precisely that fear, that war can only breed war, that caused Fairfax to resign his appointment as commander-in-chief in 1650, between the Irish and the Scottish campaigns. Moreover, one realizes by the poem's end that a double, Horatian voice has been there from the start. The shift occurs most noticeably at the volta, where admonition takes the place of praise, but it has been prepared for in the very language used to praise: "jealous monarchs," "rumours loud."

One hears that voice even more clearly in sonnet 16, to Cromwell, where the ambivalence that qualifies the praise is a function even of the ennobling imagery. For we are asked to see Cromwell as if he were the presiding figure on Ruben's Whitehall ceiling of the apotheosis of James I, a benign and mighty ruler, appearing through a cloud, overcoming detractions and rebellions, guided by faith and fortitude, moving to peace and truth.[21] It is an imagery that the ceiling perpetually depicts and that the masques intended for presentation below it, enacted more fleetingly but also more urgently. However, the verb, "plough'd," that ends that clause, "who through a cloud . . . thy glorious way hast plough'd," jolts us back to the bloody present, as does the image that follows, "And on the neck of crowned Fortune proud / Hast rear'd Gods trophies," a violent restatement of Marvell's central conceit in *The Horatian Ode*. Thus even before the clearly admonitory sestet, we are given a double view of Cromwell that prevents our total acquiescence in Milton's presentation of him as our "chief of men."

In the sestet, the oxymoron of peace's victories as the remaining conquest is the trope by which Milton would urge Cromwell to his task, but it is a task, we are made to feel, that Cromwell might be unable to accomplish. In the *Second Defense*, Milton will extend even further his sense of uneasiness with Cromwell, particularly the possibility that Cromwell might be tempted to accept the crown or might listen to some of those close to him who, unlike Milton, may be urging him to be less rather than more. For there he argues that by refusing the crown Cromwell would make himself morally more by making himself symbolically less. Perhaps the first four lines of sonnet 16 speak to that same uneasiness as it was felt two years earlier.[22] For there is only one line describing Cromwell in unequivocal terms: "Guided by faith and matchless fortitude." It becomes part of the tense irony of the poem that even virtue and all those victories testifying to his strength and valor may not be enough to "save free conscience from the paw / Of hireling wolves." The poem's structure confirms this reading. It is linear rather than circular; one waits for that extraordinarily postponed predicate. Finally when it does occur (literally a cry for "helpe"), it is in the one wholly separable syntactic unit, the couplet close, itself the epigram's epigram in epitome.

The last of the three Horatian sonnets to public figures, sonnet 17 to Vane, has no trace of ambivalence in the relationship it depicts between poet and subject. In that sense it is close to such epigrams as 14 (to William Camden) or 91 (to Sir Horace Vere), poems that honor friends and public figures where the implicit admonition is directed toward the country to deserve such friends. It is, for example, to Camden that Jonson claims "my countrey owes / The great renowne, and name wherewith she goes."

In the octave of sonnet 17, Vane is constituted from a series of oppositions, a structural pattern that mimes the poem's argument. The pairs — youth/age, time/wisdom, Rome/Carthage, war/peace, iron/gold — simultaneously characterize Vane and give a special urgency to his chief mission, which the sestet elaborates: to keep distinct the boundaries between the "spirituall powre and civill." By his accomplishment, Vane both admonishes those who would blur that critical boundary (Milton's poem is as much warning to such as they as celebration of Vane), and achieves the triumph of being at once the perfect statesman and religion's "eldest son."

If Milton's epideictic manner shares traits with Jonson's, so does his satiric and denunciatory. He certainly did not learn this voice from Jonson. Indeed it must have been second nature to him, as so much of the prose and even parts of *Paradise Lost* suggest. But it functions within the sonnets in much the same way as it does in the epigrams. Epigram 3 (*To My Bookseller*) invites comparison with sonnet 12 ("A book was writ . . .") in its similarly expressed contempt for those who in Jonson's words "scarse can spell th'hard names," or who in Milton's even more vivid cartoon "in file / Stand spelling fals." For both poets the spectacle of ignorance is comically unmasked, although a not so comic anger rumbles beneath. Neither plays to the "world's loose laughter, or vaine gaze" (epig. 2). For both, the satiric context gives an added urgency to the virtues praised, makes the praises awarded in the surrounding poems seem the harder won.

Similarly the sonnets praising friendship, good talk, wine, the pleasures that may be won from the hard season, recall Jonson's *Inviting a Friend to Supper* (epig. 101), or the epigrams to William Roe or Henrie Cary. Milton's sonnet to Lawes recalls Jonson on Ferrabosco; the sonnet on his wife recalls Jonson on his son. But it is not necessary to establish a likeness poem for poem; rather one is looking for a more general context, more in touch with the shape and sound of Milton's sonnets than that provided by either the Elizabethan sonnet sequence or the Italian heroic sonnet. Jonson's *Epigrammes* seems just that, a collection of poems whose subjects and concerns approximate those Milton handles in his sonnets, and that speak with a voice startlingly like Milton's own.

In Milton's sonnets there is no hidden narrative, no love interest, no meditation on transiency, although there is everywhere the felt urgency of time. There is, moreover, a poet speaking out to his readers, urging them "to measure life," to learn "what may be won / From the hard season gaining," to "bate [not] a jot of heart or hope," and inveighing against those "who bawle for freedom in their senceless mood." Milton's voice in the sonnets thus has a tonal range much like Jonson's beseeching his readers to "take care," "to understand," applauding the man with weight and authority in his speech, but scorning the false spellers, those covetous of "self-fame," and those who "call'st me poet as a term of shame."

Did Milton learn this voice from Jonson? The question is finally unanswerable and probably beside the point. However, that Milton saw in Jonson a poet not so much like himself (there is nothing epic in Jonson's range, no indignation on the scale of *The Late Massacre*) as like one version of himself — the poet-legislator, remaker of society through a re-created language — is a proposition we can readily entertain. It is chiefly in *The Epigrammes* that Milton observed this poet, and it is in the sonnets that we have the best record of that encounter.

Concordia University

NOTES

1. John Donne, *The First Anniversary: An Anatomy of the World* 136, in *The Epithalamions, Anniversaries and Epicedes of John Donne*, ed. W. Milgate (Oxford, 1978).

2. William B. Stull, "Sacred Sonnets in Three Styles," *SP*, LXXIX (1982), 78–99; and see F. T. Prince, *The Italian Element in Milton's Verse* (Oxford, 1954).

3. Rosalie Colie, *Shakespeare's Living Art* (Princeton, 1974), pp. 68–134; see also the discussion in her *The Resources of Kind: Genre Theory in the Renaissance*, ed. Barbara K. Lewalski (Berkeley and Los Angeles, 1973), p. 68. Herford and Simpson also point out the close relationship between epigram and sonnet, describing Davies's epigrams as "easy variations upon the sonnet form," and suggesting that the "sonnet had always been an epigram *in posse*," a statement that is probably more accurate in its reverse form (*Ben Jonson*, vol. II, *The Man and His Work*, ed. C. H. Herford and Percy Simpson [Oxford, 1925], p. 346).

4. "The sonnet comes closest to the epigram." Guillaume Colletet, "Discours du Sonnet," *Traité du sonnet*, ed. P. A. Janini (Geneva, 1965), p. 124.

5. Thomas Sebillet, *L'Art poétique françoys*, ed. Félix Gaiffe (Paris, 1932): "The matter of the epigram and the matter of the sonnet are all one, except that facetious matter is repugnant to the dignity of the sonnet" (p. 116); "The sonnet is nothing but the perfect epigram of the Italian style as the dizain is of the French" (p. 114).

6. See Bruce R. Smith, "Ben Jonson's *Epigrammes*: Portrait Gallery, Theatre, Commonwealth," *SEL*, XIV (1974), 93.

7. Epigram 18, *Ben Jonson*, vol. VIII, *The Poems and the Prose Works*, ed. C. H. Herford, Percy Simpson, and Evelyn Simpson (Oxford, 1947). Henceforth all references will be made in the text.

8. Barbara Herrnstein Smith, *Poetic Closure: A Study of How Poems End* (Chicago, 1968), p. 198.

9. All recent studies of Jonson make this assumption. For Milton see William McCarthy, "The Continuity of Milton's Sonnets," *PMLA*, XCII (1977), 96–109; Mary Ann Radzinowicz, *Toward "Samson Agonistes"* (Princeton, 1978), pp. 128–44; Anna K. Nardo, *Milton's Sonnets and the Ideal Community* (Lincoln, Neb., 1979). E. A. J. Honigmann suggested a "serial interest" and established many of the important verbal and thematic links in *Milton's Sonnets* (London, 1966), pp. 59–75. In a study with a rather different focus, Carol Thomas Neely, "The Structure of English Renaissance Sonnet Sequences," *ELH*, XLV (1978), 359–89, argues that Milton's sonnets resemble the Elizabethan sequences insofar as they constitute an expandable structure allowing for ongoing revision and addition. However, Milton's sonnets can only be included with those of Sidney, Spenser, Shakespeare, Watson, Barnes, Drayton by a reading which puts disproportionate emphasis on 1–6 as a love sequence and considers 7–22 as "excursions into political concerns."

10. Radzinowicz, *Toward "Samson,"* pp. 128–29.

11. Nardo, *Milton's Sonnets*, p. 17.

12. John Hollander, "Ben Jonson and the Modality of Verse," in *Vision and Resonance* (New York, 1975), pp. 183, 184. The recent study of Richard S. Peterson, *Imitation and Praise in the Poems of Ben Jonson* (New Haven, 1981), demonstrates in extraordinary detail this process of appropriating and re-creating.

13. I follow E. A. J. Honigmann's edition, *Milton's Sonnets*. Henceforth cited in the text.

14. A wonderfully subtle and allusive reading of Milton as Son of Ben can be found in Robert Hinman's "'A Kind of a *Christmas* Ingine': Jonson, Milton, and the Sons of Ben in the Hard Season," in *Classic and Cavalier: Essays on Jonson and the Sons of Ben*, ed. Claude J. Summers and Ted-Larry Pebworth (Pittsburgh, 1982), pp. 255–78.

15. Ilona Bell, "Circular Strategies and Structures in Jonson and Herbert," in Summers and Pebworth, *Classic and Cavalier*, p. 164.

16. There have been several studies exploring this idea: W. H. Herendeen, "Like in a Circle Bounded in Itself: Jonson, Camden and the Strategies of Praise," *The Journal of Medieval and Renaissance Studies*, XI (1981), 137–67; David Wykes, "Ben Jonson's 'Chaste Book' — *The Epigrammes*," *Renaissance and Modern Studies*, XIII (1969), 76–87; Edward Partridge, "Jonson's *Epigrammes*: The Named and the Nameless," *Ben Jonson Quadricentennial Essays* in *Studies in the Literary Imagination*, VI (1973), 153–98; Don E. Wayne, "Poetry and Power in Ben Jonson's *Epigrammes*: The Naming of 'Facts' or the Figuring of Social Relations," *Renaissance and Modern Studies*, XXIII (1979), 79–103.

17. I am very much indebted to Ilona Bell's reading of this epigram in "Circular Strategies," pp. 160–61.

18. Radzinowicz, *Toward "Samson,"* p. 135.

19. Ira Clarke, "Ben Jonson's Imitation," *Criticism*, XX (1978), 123.

20. See Wayne, for example, who argues that Jonson "in order to legitimate the 'new aristocray'" . . . [had to] draw their portraits in an environment that . . . [had] the appearance of being real" ("Poetry and Power," p. 88).

21. The imagery of the central apotheosis oval emphasizes the peace and plenty of James's reign. In the end panel, "The Benefits of the Government of James I," Wisdom defends the throne against War while Peace is about to begin her reign. In the side ovals,

Bounty stands over the bound figure of Avarice, and Reason holds a bridle over Discord. Per Palme's description of the significance of the imagery helps us to see more clearly how Milton appropriated a royalist iconography for Cromwell: "The crowning glory of King James's reign is conceived as a state of conflict and excitement turned to triumph, a scene of light and goodness victoriously fighting the dark powers of evil" (*The Triumph of Peace: A Study of the Whitehall Banqueting House* [Stockholm, 1956], p. 241). It should be noted that once the Rubens paintings were in place, the Banqueting House was no longer used for the presentation of masques.

22. Milton's relationship to Marvell moves in a two-way direction here: from Marvell's *Horatian Ode* to Milton's sonnet, then to the *Second Defense* and back to Marvell's *The First Anniversary of the Government under His Highness the Lord Protector*. See my "Milton and Marvell: The Poet as Fit Reader," *MLQ*, XXXIX (1978), 241; and Annabel Patterson, "Against Polarization: Literature and Politics in Marvell's Cromwell Poems," *ELR*, V (1975), 265–66.

MILTON AND THE
ICASTIC IMAGINATION

Paul Stevens

F OR SOME time now Milton criticism has labored under the suspicion that the poet ultimately disapproved of poetry. Implicit throughout Stanley Fish's *Surprised by Sin* is the notion that *Paradise Lost* as a poem is a "self-consuming artifact" — that is, a work which "succeeds at its own expense,"[1] a poem which, like Wittgenstein's ladder, leads the reader to the point where the poem and, more important, poetry itself are no longer necessary. According to Fish, the reader is measured by his response to the deliberately unpoetic style of the poem's closing books, "the relentless drone" which returns us "to the expository rhetoric of God's speeches and to the flinty clarity of his illusionless vision." The fit reader will not regret the passing of the poetry, but having learnt to suspect verbal virtuosity, having experienced a world in which the Devil speaks like a poet and God like a logician, he will be "able to greet the 'bodiless' style of XI and XII as Adam does, with joy."[2] When Milton dismisses the self-parodying Grand Style with which the kingdoms of the earth are displayed (XI, 385–411), when his abrupt check, "but to nobler sights," "flicks out contemptuously (like the verb 'fell' at I.586) to mock the pomp and decadence of false earthly paradises, and to dismiss along with them the 'swelling epithets' of literary styles," for the fit reader there is no surprise — "he has long ago put away these childish things."[3] This conception of the poem as a "self-consuming artifact" crystallizes the tendency in modern criticism to explain Milton's attitude toward poetry as one of covert disapproval. According to Peter Berek, "suspicion of poetry and rhetoric, with their power to deny truths or conceal falsehoods, is a powerful force in both [of Milton's] epics," while Christopher Grose claims it as "an undeniable and paradoxical fact" that *Paradise Lost* "is a poem that ultimately abjures poetry." "It may be said," Berek continues, "that it is very strange for a great poet, one of the greatest of all poets, to make the skill he had in such abundance the object of such suspicion. There is no answer; to do this is strange."[4]

It would indeed be strange if it were true; but Berek's formulation is inaccurate. Milton is not suspicious of poetry; he is suspicious of that kind of poetry which like Circe's narcotic songs only lulls the sense. Against this must be set that kind of poetry which like the Lady's song in the *Mask* offers such sober certainty of waking bliss. The tendency to see Milton as a poet educating his readers out of poetry rests on a fundamental misunderstanding of Milton's attitude toward the mental faculty chiefly responsible for poetry, the imagination. And it is against the derogation of imagination implicit in this misunderstanding that the present essay is directed.

For Milton, imagination at its highest potential is not simply a necessary evil — the means by which those of soft and delicious temper may be brought to look upon truth.[5] It is a God-given faculty which has a specific purpose in assisting man toward knowledge of his Maker. It is certainly true that imagination divorced from judgment, fancy uninformed by reason, leads to delusion.[6] But the *educated* imagination is the peculiar instrument of grace. It provides the psychological mechanism by which we come to see and believe the evidence of things not seen; it provides the psychological mechanism by which we come to faith. Bacon explains it thus:

For we see that in matters of faith and religion our imagination raises itself above our reason; not that divine illumination resides in the imagination; its seat being rather in the very citadel of the mind and understanding; but that the divine grace uses the motions of the imagination as an instrument of illumination, just as it uses the motions of the will as an instrument of virtue; which is the reason why religion ever sought access to the mind by similitudes, types, parables, visions, dreams.[7]

Imagination at its highest potential, imagination as the instrument of illumination, the vehicle of faith, operates like a mirror, not the mirror of the eighteenth-century "mechanical philosophy" faithfully reflecting the visible world,[8] but rather like the mirror of Plato's later dialogues[9] or St. Paul's glass darkly reflecting the invisible. During the Renaissance this elevated operation of the imagination came to be called *icastic*, and perhaps the best-known instance of the term in English occurs in Sidney's defense of poetry.

I. The Icastic Imagination in Poetry

For I will not deny but that man's wit may make Poesy, which should be *eikastike*, which some learned have defined, "figuring forth good things," to be *phantastike*, which doth contrariwise infect the fancy with unworthy objects; as the painter, that should give the eye either some excellent perspective, or some fine picture, fit for building or fortification, or containing in it some notable example, as Abraham sacrificing his son Isaac, Judith killing Holofernes, David fighting with Goliath, may leave those, and please an ill-pleased eye with wanton shows of better hidden matters.[10]

Sidney distinguishes between two kinds of poetry — *phantastike* and *eikastike*. What he means by *phantastike* — "the nurse of abuse, infecting us with many pestilent desires, with a siren's sweetness drawing the mind to the serpent's tale of sinful fancy" (p. 123) — clearly suggests poetry as the verbal manifestation of fancy ungoverned by reason. What he means by *eikastike* — "figuring forth good things" — is a little more vague. Though at first it seems to suggest poetry as the verbal manifestation of fancy creating or inventing the good, it becomes increasingly apparent that it actually means poetry as a product of fancy procreating or reflecting the good.

The intensely empirical representation of imagination in, for instance, Shakespeare's *Tempest* (fancy as the creator of the good, the inventor of new realities, brave new worlds), appears to receive a sanction in Sidney's theory of the poet as the maker of a second nature:

Only the poet, disdaining to be tied to any such subjection, lifted up with the vigour of his own invention, doth grow in effect into another nature, in making things either better than Nature bringeth forth, or, quite anew, forms such as never were in Nature. . . .
[Nature's] world is brazen, the poets only deliver a golden. (P. 100)

However, Prospero claims that poetic invention, the creations of fancy, are images of nothing but themselves, insubstantial and baseless:

> These our actors,
> As I foretold you, were all spirits and
> Are melted into air, into thin air;
> And, like the baseless fabric of this vision,
> The cloud-capped tow'rs, the gorgeous palaces,
> The solemn temples, the great globe itself,
> Yea, all which it inherit, shall dissolve,
> And, like this insubstantial pageant faded,
> Leave not a rack behind.[11]

Sidney, on the other hand, indicates two ways in which poetic invention is anything but baseless: it is both a cause and a consequence of something substantial. The first way, poetic invention as a cause, is already implicit in *The Tempest* itself. The play stands as an assurance of things hoped for. The substance of the play's vision, the rack it does leave behind, is the very idea of fancy's creativity and the model of a new nature, the brave new world that fancy can create. The possibility of a new society, the "Fair encounter / Of two most rare affections" (III, i, 74–75), is engineered by Prospero's art, by spirits "call'd to enact / My present fancies" (IV, i, 121–22). Sidney explains it in these terms: the golden world that the poet delivers "is not wholly imaginative [that is, imaginary], as we are wont to say by them that build castles in the air; but so far substantially it worketh, not only to make a Cyrus, which had been but a particular excellency as Nature might have done, but to bestow a Cyrus upon the world to make many Cyruses, if they will learn aright why and how that maker made him" (p. 101).

The second way, poetic invention as a consequence, makes it clear that Sidney's understanding of *eikastike* is not fancy creative or innovative, but fancy procreative or reflective. It is here that Sidney and Shakespeare part company. For the nature that fancy creates, according to Sidney, is not really new, but the re-creation of an original nature, now lost: the images that fancy creates are in fact reflections of Ideas. When fancy is *eikastike*, when it figures forth good things, its inventions are the consequence or imprint of Ideas. Fancy's new actuality is an imitation not of the sensible world, but the ideal: consider, says Sidney, whether or not nature has brought forth

so true a lover as Theagenes, so constant a friend as Pylades, so valiant a man as Orlando, so right a prince as Xenophon's Cyrus, so excellent a man in every way as Virgil's Aeneas. Neither let this be jestingly conceived, because the works of the one be essential, the other in imitation or fiction; for any understanding knoweth the skill of the artificer standeth in that *Idea* or fore-conceit of the work, and not in the work itself. And that the poet hath that *Idea* is manifest. (Pp. 100–01)[12]

Frequently, Sidney suggests a purely innovative fancy, as when he says that the most excellent poets "most properly do imitate to teach and delight, and to imitate borrow nothing of what is, hath been, or shall be"; but he then so qualifies it as to render it reflective — these poets "range, only reined with learned discretion, into the divine consideration of what may be and should be" (p. 102). Thus, whereas Bacon's reason bows and buckles the mind to the actual nature of things,[13] Sidney's fancy bows and buckles the mind to the ideal nature of things. For Sidney purely creative fancy is in fact reflective, and it is for this reason, not because they lose themselves in a divine madness, that poets are prophets: "These be they that, as the first and most noble sort may justly be termed *vates*" (p. 102). For Shakespeare the substance of fancy's inventions is in their effect; for Sidney, the substance is also in their effect, but much more in their cause, in the ideas they shadow or reflect.

The origin of Sidney's term for the reflective process of fancy, *eikastike*, is not difficult to find. The immediate source is Italy and the literary criticism to which Milton refers as the "*Italian* commentaries of *Castelvetro, Tasso, Mazzoni* and others."[14] There, in Tasso in particular, imagination as the sensible reflection of ideas is identified with the icastic imagination or likeness-making that Plato in the *Sophist* opposes to phantastic imagination or semblance-making.[15] Using analogies drawn from the visual arts to explain image-making in speech, Plato says that likeness-making means producing an exact copy, "a copy which is executed according to the proportions of the original, similar in length and breadth and depth, each thing receiving also its appropriate colour," while semblance-making means producing an image that as a result of deliberate illusion, such as perspective, only seems to resemble the original.[16] For Plato, as Panofsky puts it, the distinction is "between objectively correct and *trompe l'oeil* imitation." But for the Renaissance, in a writer such as Comanini, the distinction had come to mean "the contrast between the representation of actually existing objects and the representation of actually nonexisting objects."[17] In Tasso's *Discourses on the Heroic Poem* (1594), the distinction is developed a stage further.[18] Since the only truly existing things are intelligible, not visible, icastic imagination comes to mean the faithful copy not of the actual but of the ideal: "But if [the poet's] images are of existing things, this imitation belongs to the icastic imitator. But what shall we say exists, the intelligible or the visible? Surely the intelligible, in the opinion of Plato too, who put visible things in the genus of non-being and only the intelligible in the genus of being" (p. 32). In the light of this, William Kerrigan's dismissal of icastic in Sidney as "historical and quotidien" seems a little hasty.[19] As examples of what he means by icastic images, Tasso offers "the images of the angels that Dionysius describes . . . the winged lion, the eagle, ox, and angel, which are the images of the evangelists" (p. 32). Though these images may appear to be fantastic, they are in fact icastic. Mazzoni, commenting on the "beautiful poetic phantasies" of the Song of Solomon, explains how

the purely phantastic poem, which by its nature looks on the false in the way that has been explained, was not known to the Hebrews, and the poem of the Song of Solomon is not of that kind, but is one of those which under the husk of the literal sense conceals pure and complete truth. Hence it can be called phantastic with respect to the literal sense, but icastic with respect to the allegorical sense.[20]

Because icastic images are reflections of the intelligible, Tasso speculates on the existence of two kinds of fancy. Besides the fancy that resides in the sensible part of the soul, there may be another, higher kind of fancy in the intellectual part: icastic images "do not belong principally to phantasy and are not its proper object, since phantasy is [a faculty] in the divisible part of the mind, not the indivisible, which is the intellect pure and simple, unless besides the phantasy which is a faculty of the sensitive soul there were another which is a faculty of the intellective" (p. 32). He goes on to identify this "intellectual imagination" with Dante's *alta fantasia*, the imaginative power that allows the poet access to a vision of God: of intellectual phantasy he writes:

> although both our theologians and the Platonic philosophers postulate this faculty, Aristotle neither knew of nor admitted it. Nor did Plato in the *Sophist*; otherwise he would not have distinguished icastic from phantastic imitation, since the icastic too would belong to the intellectual imagination. Perhaps this is what Dante was referring to when he said:
>
> > Here power failed the high phantasy
> > [*Par.* xxxiii, 142]
>
> and elsewhere:
>
> > Then rained down within the high fantasy
> > One crucified, scornful and fierce.
> > [*Purg.* xvii, 25–26]   (P. 33)

Whether, however, *alta fantasia* implies two different faculties or one faculty operating in two different ways, it seems fairly clear that Tasso's icastic fancy and Dante's *alta fantasia* both refer to the same reflective operation of the imagination,[21] as the lines preceding Tasso's quotation from the *Purgatorio* confirm:

> O imaginativa che ne rube
> > talvolta sì di fuor, ch'om non s'accorge
> > perché dintorno suonin mille tube,
> chi move te, si 'l senso non ti porge?
> > Moveti lume che nel ciel s'informa,
> > per sé o per voler che giù lo scorge.
> De l'empiezza di lei che mutò forma
> > ne l'uccel ch'a cantar più si diletta,
> > ne l'imagine mia apparve l'orma;
> e qui fu la mia mente sì ristretta
> > dentro da sé, che di fuor non venìa
> > cosa che fosse allor da lei ricetta.
> Poi piovve dentro a l'alta fantasia
> > un crucifisso, dispettoso e fero
> > ne la sua vista, e cotal si moria.

[O imagination, that do sometimes so snatch us from outward things that we give no heed, though a thousand trumpets sound around us, who moves you if the sense affords you naught? A light moves you which takes form in heaven, of itself, or by a will that downward guides it.

Of her impious deed who changed her form into the bird that most delights to sing, the impress appeared in my imagination, and at this my mind was so restrained within itself, that from outside came naught that was then received by it. Then rained down within the high fantasy one crucified, scornful and fierce in his mien, and so was he dying.][22]

Although the impress that forms in the imagination has a sensible appearance, its substance is intelligible, that is, it originates in heaven, in the mind of God. *Alta fantasia* is the imagination when it is moved by God, when he imprints the sensible images of ideas in it, and it seems likely that *alta fantasia* is what Milton means by "our high-rais'd phantasie" and the "Poet soaring in the high region of his fancies."

Underlying the conception of the reflective operation of the imagination is the conviction that for man in "the dark lanthorn of the body"[23] knowledge, especially knowledge of God, is impossible without images. This conviction is apparent in the fundamental association of knowledge with seeing: "How does knowing differ from opining and believing? . . . The true answer to this question can be given in three words, 'By being vision.'"[24] When knowledge is of things not in the visible world, it remains vision through its dependence on sensible symbols held in the imagination. In the *Convivio*, when Dante explains the failure of *alta fantasia* to apprehend the divine fully, he indicates the dependence of understanding on fancy:

Our intellect, by defect of that power whence it draws whatsoever it contemplates (which is an organic power, to wit the fantasy), may not rise to certain things, because the fantasy may not aid it, for it hath not wherewithal. Such are the substances sejunct from matter, which, even though a certain consideration of them be possible, we may not understand nor comprehend perfectly.[25]

The same sense of the impossibility of knowing without picturing is apparent in Aristotle:

Now for the thinking soul images take the place of direct perceptions. . . . Hence the soul never thinks without a mental image;[26]

in Aquinas:

It is impossible for our intellect, in its present state of being joined to a body capable of receiving impressions, actually to understand anything without turning to sense images. . . .

. . . The proper object of the human intellect, on the other hand, since it is joined to a body, is a nature or 'whatness' found in corporeal matter — the intellect, in fact, rises to the limited knowledge it has of invisible things by way of the nature of visible things;[27]

and in Milton:

our understanding cannot in this body found it selfe but on sensible things, nor arrive so cleerly to the knowledge of God and things invisible, as by orderly conning over the visible and inferior creature.[28]

As Raphael points out, even for unfallen man, it is from "Fansie and understanding" that "the Soule / Reason receives, and reason is her being" (*PL* V, 486–87). Reason here may mean both the absolute and the faculty that allows us to apprehend it, but the process of apprehension still depends upon fancy and its sensible images.

Because knowledge of God is not available through imageless reasoning, when Milton looks to heaven, the icastic imagination is very much in evidence.

In the early poetry, the desire that his fancy might "figure forth good things," reflect images of the ideal or the divine, is especially intense. Just as the vision of God is presented to Dante's *alta fantasia*, so Milton prays that the vision of divine poetry, "That undisturbed Song of pure concent, / Ay sung before the saphire-color'd throne" may be presented "to our high-rais'd phantasie" (*At a Solemn Musick*, 6–7, 5).[29] The image of the poet "soaring in the high region of his fancies with his garland and his singing robes about him" (*Reason of Church-Government*, YP I, p. 808) leads us back to the aspirations of the early poetry. In *At a Vacation Exercise*, the poet appears searching for the appropriate language, the "richest Robes, and gay'st attire" with which to clothe "some naked thoughts" (21–23). Chief among these thoughts is the desire itself for such a language, such robes "as may make thee search thy coffers round" (31), a language that he might use in the service of "some graver subject" (30) — to "cloath my fancy in fit sound" (32). When he gives an example of what that graver subject might be, we know he is referring to the sensible reflection of Ideas: such service

> where the deep transported mind may soare
> Above the wheeling poles, and at Heav'ns dore
> Look'in, and see each blissful Deitie
> How he before the thunderous throne doth lie.   (33–36)

As Irene Samuel points out, this image is an allusion to the festival of the gods which "in *Phaedrus* is the grand occasion for sight of the Ideas."[30]

There Plato writes as both philosopher and "fabulator maximus" (as Milton refers to him in *De Idea Platonica* 38). He uses both figure and abstraction, lively images and bare words. The figure is the festival to which Milton alludes:

Zeus, the mighty lord, holding the reins of a winged chariot, leads the way in heaven, ordering all and taking care of all; and there follows him the array of gods and demi-gods. . . . They see many blessed sights in the inner heaven, and there are many ways to and fro, along which the blessed gods are passing, every one doing his own work. . . . But when they go to the banquet and festival, then they move up the steep vault of heaven. (246e–47b)

At the outset Plato explains that the gods themselves are figurative, only sensible images of the divine: "fancy, not having seen nor surely known the nature of God, may imagine a mortal creature having both a body and also a soul which are united throughout all time" (246c–d). And when the figure approaches its climax, the sight of the Ideas, Plato abandons his singing robes and adopts the language of a philosopher:

But of the heaven which is above the heavens, what earthly poet ever did or ever will sing worthily? It is such as I will describe; for I must dare to speak the truth, when truth is my theme. There abides the very being with which true knowledge is concerned; the colourless, formless, intangible essence, visible only to mind, the pilot of the soul . . . justice, and temperance, and knowledge absolute, not that to which becoming belongs, nor that which is found, in varying forms, in one or other of those regions which we men call *real*, but real knowledge really present where being is. (247c–e)

Plato's careful distinction between figure and abstraction is not apparent in Milton. First, when Milton arrives at the same climactic point in the *Vacation Exercise*, he turns away from the abstract description of the Ideas and descends through a series of sensational images that are meant to represent practical knowledge of the sensible world:[31]

> Then passing through the Spheres of watchful fire,
> And mistie Regions of wide air next under,
> And hills of Snow and lofts of piled Thunder,
> May tell at length how green-ey'd *Neptune* raves.   (40–43)

Second, when he does deal with the Ideas in a poem of the same period, they appear almost as personifications, fully integrated into the figure:

> And Joy shall overtake us in a flood,
> When every thing that is sincerely good
> And perfectly divine,
> With Truth, and Peace, and Love shall ever shine

About the supreme Throne
Of him, t'whose happy-making sight alone,
When once our heav'nly-guided soul shall clime,
Then all this Earthy grosness quit,
Attir'd with Stars, we shall for ever sit,
    Triumphing over Death, and Chance, and thee O Time.

(*On Time* 13–22)

The ultimate source of this integration is perhaps St. Augustine's assimilation of the abstract Ideas of Plato into the mind of the personal God of Christianity.[32] It is in Milton's turning away from pure abstraction that he and Plato part. Despite the concessions made to imagination in the later dialogues, truth for Plato, if not mathematical, is a matter of dialectic, reasoning, or logic that owes nothing to imagination, and the good is apprehended through a state of mind called "*intelligence or rational intuition* (noesis) *and knowledge* (episteme . . .) *in the full sense.*"[33] By rational intuition or intuitive reason, Plato means discursive reason writ large: "Then by the second section of the intelligible world you may understand me to mean all that unaided reasoning apprehends by the power of dialectic . . . never making use of any sensible object, but only of Forms, moving through Forms from one to another, and ending with Forms" (*Republic* 511). By intuitive reason, Milton means something different. Raphael certainly agrees with Plato that, for unfallen man at least, the difference between intuitive and discursive reason is only a matter of degree. But then, as we have seen, reason at any level, according to Raphael, does not discard fancy but depends upon it, and cognition without imagination, according to the *Reason of Church-Government*, is not possible in this life: "For Truth, I know not how, hath this unhappinesse fatall to her, ere she can come to the triall and inspection of the Understanding, being to passe through many little wards and limits of the severall Affections and Desires, she cannot shift it, but must put on such colours and attire, as those Pathetick handmaids of the soul please to lead her in to their Queen" (YP I, p. 830). It is precisely appropriate colors and attire that Milton is searching for in the *Vacation Exercise* — to "cloath my fancy" — and it is precisely the possibility of this coloring of truth that Plato rejects in the *Phaedrus:* "For sight is the most piercing of our bodily senses; though not by that is wisdom seen; her lovelines would have been transporting if there had been a visible image of her, and the other ideas, if they had visible counterparts, would be equally lovely" (250d). But Sidney reverses Plato's point, emphasizing that visible images of the ideal constitute the peculiar glory of poetry: "if the saying of Plato and Tully be true, that who could see virtue would be wonderfully ravished with love of her beauty — this man [the poet] sets her out to make her more lovely in her holiday apparel, to the eye of any that will deign not to disdain until they understand" (p. 119). As the closing phrase suggests, underlying Sidney's reversal of Plato is Christianity's reversal of Platonic rationalism: "Unless you believe, you shall not understand" (Isa. vii, 9). The precedence of belief over comprehension sanctions the poet's desire to elevate imagination over ratiocination.

In *At a Solemn Musick* high-raised fancy is again implicitly elevated over discourse as an integral part of intuitive reason. For there the vital operation of poetry, Orpheus' art — "Dead things with inbreath'd sense able to pierce" (4) — coincides with the life-giving operation of Scripture in that both bypass discourse and appeal directly to the eye of the soul: "But let them chaunt while they will of prerogatives, we shall tell them of Scripture; of custom, we of Scripture; of Acts and Statutes, stil of Scripture, til the quick and pearcing word enter to the dividing of their soules, & the mighty weaknes of the Gospel throw down the weak mightines of mans reasoning" (YP I, p. 827).

The belief in icastic imagination evident in the early poetry leads to a yearning for the "Prophetic strain" and, as we shall see, the icastic imagination that moves poetry at its highest potential also moves prophecy.

II. THE ICASTIC IMAGINATION IN PROPHECY

[Prophecy] is the highest degree of man and the ultimate term of perfection that can exist for his species; and this state is the ultimate term of perfection for the imaginative faculty. This is something that cannot by any means exist in every man. And it is not something that may be attained solely through perfection in the speculative sciences and through improvement of moral habits, even if all of them have become as fine and good as can be. There still is needed in addition the highest possible degree of perfection of the imaginative faculty in respect of its original natural disposition.[34]

John Smith's discourse *Of Prophecy* (1660) provides the most comprehensive contemporary account of the function of imagination in prophecy. By prophecy Smith does not mean just the prophetic books, but the whole of Scripture — for prophecy is *"the way whereby revealed truth is dispensed and conveyed to us."*[35] Following the rabbinical tradition of Maimonides and his commentator, Joseph Albo, Smith distinguishes four degrees of prophecy "according to the relative proportion of rational understanding to imaginative sensation."[36] The highest degree, the *gradus mosaicus*, occurs when there is a direct illumination of the understanding without the aid of imagination. The second degree, the prophetic grade proper, occurs in dreams and visions, usually mediated by an angel, when there is an indirect illumination of the understanding through imagination controlled by reason — "when the rational power is most predominant; in which case . . . the mind of the prophet is able to strip those things, that are represented to it in the glass of fancy, of all their materiality and sensible nature, and apprehend them more distinctly in their own naked essence" (p. 183). The third grade, the hagiographical, says Smith quoting Albo, occurs in "words of wisdom, or song, or divine praise, in pure and elegant language" (p. 238) when there is an indirect illumination of the understanding through the joint operation of imagination and reason — "when the strength of the imaginative and rational powers equally balance each other" (p. 183). The lowest degree occurs "when the imaginative power is most predominant, so that the impressions made upon it are too busy, and the scene becomes too turbulent for the rational faculty to discern the true mystical and anagogical sense of them clearly" (p. 181). With this kind of prophecy, illumination is possible only on rational analysis after the event and then "with much obscurity still attending it" (p. 182). There is another degree which Smith rather confusingly refers to as the lowest degree, the *filia vocis*. This was a voice heard descending from heaven directing affairs, but not a part of true prophecy.

Basil Willey used Smith's discourse as evidence for the "dissociation of sensibility" in his scholarly substantiation of T. S. Eliot's theory, *The Seventeenth-Century Background*.[37] Willey used the discourse to show among other things the growing intellectual aversion to imagination in the seventeenth century. This aversion, he feels, is epitomized in the juxtaposition of the lowest and highest degrees of prophecy: "The inferiority of mere 'imagination' to 'Reason' could not be more emphatically stated: 'The Pseudo-Prophetical Spirit is seated onely in the Imaginative Powers and Faculties inferior to Reason'; whereas in the *gradus mosaicus* 'all imagination ceaseth, and the Representation of Truth descends not so low as the Imaginative part; but is made in the highest stage of Reason and Understanding'" (p. 136). Willey's emphasis here, however, and his "impression" that Smith when handling imagination is "dealing with comparatively uncongenial material" (p. 137), amount to a considerable distortion of the text.

First, the inferiority of mere "imagination" to "Reason" is hardly a notion that arose in the seventeenth century. Indeed, it is difficult to imagine anyone before the Romantic period defending imagination against reason when imagination separate from or in opposition to reason was by definition considered delusory—"begot of nothing but vain fantasy." Second, the identification of the lowest degree of prophecy with false prophecy or the pseudo-prophetical spirit—"This last group, then, includes all the pseudo-prophets" (p. 136)—is a misrepresentation. Smith carefully distinguishes between the pseudo-prophetical spirit, which"is seated only in the imaginative powers" (p. 193), and the lowest degree of prophecy, where the imaginative power is not alone but only "most predominant" (p. 181). If Willey's identification were true, then the prophecies of this lowest degree—Zachariah, Ezekiel, and Daniel—would be false. Third, the juxtaposition of highest and lowest degrees obscures the fact that most of the discourse is devoted to those degrees, especially the second, the prophetic grade proper, where the role of imagination is essential. Though it is certainly true that Smith's transcendental temper draws him to the prospect of a mode of cognition that is imageless,[38] it is equally true that when he is thinking of prophecy in general, he is thinking primarily of those degrees that most fruitfully involve imagination. This is especially clear, for instance, when Smith announces that his prime interest is in the psychology of prophecy: "But the main thing that we shall observe in this description is, that faculty or power of the soul upon which these extraordinary impressions of divine light or influence are made; which, in all proper prophecy, is both the rational and imaginative power" (p. 180). Or when he turns aside to deal with false prophecy and touches on the familiar Janus-faced nature of imagination: fancy ungoverned by reason leads to illusion, while fancy governed by reason leads to illumination: false prophecy is "seated only in the imaginative power, from whence the first occasion of this delusion ariseth," but "that power is also the seat of all [true] prophetical vision" (p. 194).

When Smith actually describes how the imagination works in prophecy, his description corresponds exactly to the reflective operation of fancy that the literary critics refer to as icastic. Although he refers to the *locus classicus* of reflective imagination in the *Timaeus* (70d–72b) only in terms of disapproval (pp. 192, 197), as he proceeds through the various degrees of prophecy the basic idea of fancy as a mirror reflecting sensible images of the intelligible back to the mind remains constant. Analyzing the dreams and visions of prophecy proper, he describes the reflective operation thus:

Now to these ecstatical impressions, whereby the imagination and the mind of the prophet was thus ravished from itself, and was made subject wholly to some agent intellectual informing it and shining upon it, I suppose St. Paul had respect. "Now we see . . . by a glass, in riddles or parables;" for so he seems to

compare the highest illuminations which we have here, with that constant irradia-
tion of the Divinity upon the souls of men in the life to come: and this glassing
of divine things by hieroglyphics and emblems in the fancy which he speaks of,
was the proper way of prophetical inspiration. (P. 185)

In conflating the mirror images of the *Timaeus* and I Corinthians xiii,
12, Smith makes imagination the glass, not as he says earlier (in the discourse on *Divine Knowledge*) a blemish on the glass, "a gross dew on the
pure glass of our understandings" (p. 22). Here imagination is operating
as an integral part of a cognitive process. Plato's suspicion of reflective
imagination is reversed: revelation is not made as in the *Timaeus* to the
foolishness of men but to their wisdom, to understanding through imagination, to those whose faculties are rationally ordered: "A troubled fancy
could no more receive these ideas of divine truth to be impressed upon
it, and clearly reflect them to the understanding, than a cracked glass,
or troubled water, can reflect sincerely any image to be made upon them"
(p. 253). The fact that imagination is operating reflectively, however,
does not mean that the cognitive process is passive, but, like Drayton's
account of the poet's mind, it "by inspiration conceaveth / What heaven
to her by divination breatheth":[39]

It may be considered that God made not use of idiots or fools by whom to reveal
His will, but such whose intellects were entire and perfect; and that He imprinted
such a clear copy of His truth upon them; as that it became their own sense, being
digested fully into their understandings; so as they were able to deliver and represent it to others, as truly as any can paint forth his own thoughts. (P. 284)

Thus, apart from the mosaic grade, prophecy for Smith was largely
the creation of the icastic imagination. Despite his reliance on rabbinical
sources, Smith's discourse is, as Kerrigan has pointed out, well within
the mainstream of traditional Christian thought on the psychology of
prophecy: "Smith rarely cited Thomas Aquinas, although he arrived at
a theory of degrees of inspiration which recapitulates Aquinas almost perfectly."[40] Aquinas describes the process of prophetic revelation using the
same key metaphor of the mirror:

It is these similitudes [the figurative language of prophecy], made light by the
divine light, which deserve the name of mirror for [*sic*] more than the divine
essence. For in a mirror images are formed from other realities, and this cannot
be said of God. Yet the enlightening of the mind in a prophetical mode can be
called a mirroring, in so far as is reflected in it an image of the truth of the divine
foreknowledge.[41]

However, by identifying the mirror of prophetic imagination with the
glass of St. Paul, Smith not only emphasizes the function of imagination

in knowing God, but, most important, he identifies this psychology of prophetic revelation as it appears in the Old Testament with every Christian's way of knowing God in the New. Although the ultimate goal, a goal not attainable in this life, is, as it was for St. Augustine and Aquinas, intellectual vision, a knowledge of God that transcends the sensible, the way to that goal is through the sensible—through imagination. As Donne puts it, the Christian comes to know God "by reflexion" in a glass of "darke similitude and comparison."[42]

Although Smith never uses the term *icastic*, other contemporary commentators on prophecy do. Henry More, for instance, in his *Synopsis Prophetica* refers to his catalogue of figurative devices used in prophecy as "the chief *Icastick* terms that occur in the Prophetick style," and these icastic figures that occur in visions and dreams are "divinatory Impresses."[43] Literary critics like Mazzoni, of course, saw prophecy as the model of icastic imagination: "the ancient Hebrews did not know the kind of poetry that deals with the false, but only that which deals with the true, and by Plato is called icastic."[44]

It becomes increasingly apparent that poetry at its highest potential and prophecy, "the way whereby revealed truth is dispensed and conveyed to us," are produced by the same psychological process. As the poet is an icastic imitator so he is a prophet, and as the prophet is an icastic imitator so he is a poet. Both parts of the equation, poet as prophet and vice versa, are apparent in Sidney:

And may not I presume a little further, to show the reasonableness of this word *vates*, and say that the holy David's psalms are a divine poem? . . . For what else is the awakening his musical instruments, the often and free changing of persons, his notable *prosopopeias*, when he maketh you, as it were, see God coming in his majesty, his telling of beasts' joyfulness, and hills leaping, but a heavenly poesy, wherein almost he showeth himself a passionate lover of that unspeakable and everlasting beauty to be seen by the eyes of the mind, only cleared by faith. (P. 99)

And though he denies the first part of the equation, poets as prophets, Smith implicitly accepts the second part, prophets as poets, when he transforms the mirror metaphor into that of a stage: "*the prophetical scene or stage upon which all apparitions were made to the prophet, was his imagination;* and that there all those things which God would have revealed unto him were acted over *symbolically, as in a masque*" (p. 229).

The equation is also implicit in the introduction to the second book of the *Reason of Church-Government*.[45] There in the context of his role as the Jeremiah-like prophet denouncing error in "the cool element of

by the mighty weakness of revelation. The tone of revelation is poetic:[47] "On a green shadie Bank profuse of flours / Pensive I sate me down" (VIII, 286–87) recalls the poetic activities of the Attendant Spirit, the agent of revelation in the *Mask:*

> I sate me down to watch upon a bank
> With Ivy canopied, and interwove
> With flaunting Hony-suckle, and began
> Wrapt in a pleasing fit of melancholy
> To meditate upon my rural minstrelsie,
> Till fancy had her fill.   (VIII, 542–47)

These lines are themselves a reversal of the negative operation of fancy perpetrated by Oberon in A *Midsummer Night's Dream:*

> I know a bank where the wild thyme blows,
> Where oxlips and the nodding violet grows,
> Quite over-canopied with luscious woodbine,
> With sweet musk-roses, and with eglantine;
> There sleeps Titania sometime of the night,
> Lulled in these flowers with dances and delight;
>   . . . .
> And with the juice of this I'll streak her eyes,
> And make her full of hateful fantasies. (II, i, 249–54, 257–58)

The actual process of revelation corresponds to the second, Isaiah-like degree of prophecy as described by Smith. Adam's invocation to the sensible world, "Tell me, how I may know him, how adore" (VIII, 280), is answered by the sensible world only inasmuch as divine knowledge is reflected to the understanding as sensible images in the fancy:

> When suddenly stood at my Head a dream,
> Whose inward apparition gently mov'd
> My fancy to believe I yet had being,
> And livd: One came, methought, of shape Divine.
>   (VIII, 292–95)

Revelation is not, as Hunter maintains, to the imagination alone, but through imagination to intuitive reason.[48] The harmony of imagination and reason is manifest in the harmony between what is seen and what is heard: the visual sensations of the dream are informed by the verbal explanation of the shape divine:

> thy mansion wants thee, *Adam*, rise,
> First Man, of Men innumerable ordain'd
> First Father, call'd by thee I come thy Guide
> To the Garden of bliss, thy seat prepar'd.   (VIII, 296–99)

Adam has a complete and accurate understanding of what is happening as it is happening, and the accuracy of what his imagination perceives is confirmed when the dream turns out to be literally true: "whereat I wak'd, and found / Before mine Eyes all real, as the dream / Had lively shadowd" (VIII, 309–11). The lively reflection of Eden turns out to be real and what is more important so does that of the shape divine:

> hee who was my Guide
> Up hither, from among the Trees appeer'd
> Presence Divine. Rejoycing, but with aw
> In adoration at his feet I fell
> Submiss: he rear'd me, and Whom thou soughtst I am,
> Said mildely.
>
> (VIII, 312–17)

The significance of this realization of the dream is complex. As far as prophetic revelation is concerned, the awakening imitates the progression from the second to the mosaic grade. Instead of lively shadows, or sensible images, Adam sees the divine face to face. But what he sees is no different from the simulacrum of the dream: the image turns out to have been icastic in the most prosaic Platonic sense of an exact copy. This may be meant to emphasize both the unfallen state of Adam and the fallen state of the reader: that before the fall Adam never has to see through a glass darkly — he always sees *in speculo lucido*, whereas after the fall the reader can only see what Adam saw through the dark glass of sensible images. Of course, Milton is only representing God as he represents himself in Genesis — but by prefixing a prophetic dream of that representation he underlines a favorite theme of his monism — that invisible and visible realities may be more alike than we suppose. As he points out in the *Christian Doctrine*, "After all, if *God is said to have created man in his own image, after his own likeness*, Gen. i.26, and not only his mind but also his external appearance . . . and if God attributes to himself again and again a human shape and form why should we be afraid of assigning to him something he assigns to himself?" (YP VI, pp. 135–36). This sentiment is echoed in Raphael's references to Adam — "Inward and outward both, his image faire" (VIII, 221) — and to Eve — "In outward also her resembling less / His image who made both" (VIII, 543–44). It is also related to the angel's famous conjecture — "though what if Earth / Be but the shaddow of Heav'n, and things therein / Each to other like, more than on earth is thought?" (V, 574–76). It all indicates a turning away from the prospect of the imageless reality "imagined" by Smith and the Platonic tradition.

More important than this, however, the realization of the dream is the substantiation of faith. For Adam's dreams not only imitate the process of icastic imagination in both poetry and prophecy, they imitate the process of faith. Like the Lady's song — an act of fancy that effects "Such sober certainty of waking bliss" (*Mask* 262) — the imagination of the good in Adam's dream is a persuasion to believe — "a dream, / Whose inward apparition gently mov'd / My fancy to believe." The garden of bliss created in his imagination is the idealization of nature — compared to Eden "what I saw / Of Earth before scarce pleasant seemd" (VIII, 305–06) — common to both poetry and faith. "Only the poet," says Sidney, "doth grow in effect into another nature, in making things either better than Nature bringeth forth, or, quite anew, forms such as never were in Nature" (p. 100). While "the wonderful power of saving faith," says William Perkins, is that it "makes things which are not in nature, to have in some sort a being and subsistence."[49] On awakening, Adam's belief in things not seen gives way to sight: for just as faith, according to St. Augustine, "is to believe that which you do not yet see, the reward of that faith is to see that which you believe."[50] It is certainly true that imagination raises and erects the mind by submitting the shows of things to the desires of the mind, but when those desires are for the good and are inspired by heaven, then imagination is the instrument of faith.[51] In Adam's dreams, through the operation of icastic or reflective imagination, poetry, prophecy, and faith all come together.

Adam's experience on coming to consciousness, his account of "how human Life began" (VIII, 250), reveals a pattern of cognition that recurs throughout Milton's poetry. The pattern describes how the frustrated striving of the "eye" is arrested and superseded by revelation to the "ear." The symbolic antithesis between eye and ear, so apparent in the *Mask*, is ultimately explained by the traditional Christian antithesis between sight and faith: Milton's reference in the *Reason of Church-Government* to those that live "by sight and visibility, rather then by faith" (YP I, p. 778) is an allusion to the *locus classicus* of the tradition in St. Paul: "We walk by faith not by sight" (II Cor. v, 7). By "sight" is meant discursive knowledge of the actual world — as R. G. Collingwood puts it, "the perception by which we apprehend the particular finite things in the world of sense." By faith is meant the intuitive knowledge of the ideal world, and, since St. Augustine placed the Platonic Ideas in the divine mind, it means intuitive knowledge of the divine, the perception "by which we apprehend the infinite and wholly spiritual nature of God."[52] Both "sight" and faith are then perceptions or kinds of seeing: whereas "sight" means seeing in the sense of understanding the visible world, faith means seeing in the sense of understanding the invisible; whereas the object or medium of "sight" is nature, the book of God's works, the medium of faith is Scripture, the book of God's words. Because the medium of "sight" is visible, God's works, the physical sense that symbolizes its mode of apprehension is the eye. Thus, in the process of Adam's apprehension of the actual world the activity of the eye is stressed: "my wondring Eyes I turnd, / And gaz'd . . . about me round I saw . . . / My self I then perus'd, and Limb by Limb / Survey'd" (VIII, 257–68). Because the medium of faith is invisible, God's words, the physical sense that symbolizes its mode of apprehension is the ear — "Is it the Eye alone that wee live by?" asks Vaughan, "We live also by the eare and by that Inlet wee receive the glad tydings of Salvation."[53] Thus, the kind of knowledge not available to the eye or the "weak mightines of mans reasoning" is revealed, not indirectly through Scripture, but in Adam's case immediately to his mind in God's words. The power of "sight" so evident in Adam's ability to name "What e're I saw" (VIII, 273) cannot provide knowledge of the ideal or divine—that is a matter for faith.

Now, the process of faith is persuasion: it is, according to Milton, a "FIRM PERSUASION IMPLANTED IN US BY THE GIFT OF GOD, BY VIRTUE OF WHICH WE BELIEVE, ON THE AUTHORITY OF GOD'S PROMISE, THAT ALL THOSE THINGS WHICH GOD HAS PROMISED US IN CHRIST ARE OURS, AND ESPECIALLY THE GRACE OF ETERNAL LIFE" (*CD* I, xx; YP VI, p. 471). Just as Adam's dream, a prophetic revelation to his fancy, persuades him to believe, so the realization of that dream, a poetic revelation to the reader's fancy, is meant to persuade us to believe. Like the realization of the desires of Ferdinand and Miranda in *The Tempest*, it is an assurance of things hoped for. In *The Certainty of Faith*, Henry More emphasizes the naturalness of this process of persuasion: "Faith and Belief, though they be usually appropriated to Matters of Religion, yet those Words in themselves signifie nothing else but, *A Perswasion touching the Truth of a thing arising from some ground or other*."[54] The point is, however, precisely this—what ground? The radical difference between natural and supernatural knowledge is the different ground or evidence for persuasion: "sight" or natural knowledge is the evidence of things seen, faith is the evidence of things not seen; the object which "sight" contemplates is the visible world, the object which faith contemplates is the invisible world of Scripture—"For God's mysteries," says Calvin, "pertaining to our salvation are of the sort that cannot in themselves and by their own nature (as is said) be discerned; but we gaze upon them only in his Word."[55] The Word is made available to the understanding through the imagination of the biblical writers to the imagination of the reader.[56] The only way that the gap between visible and invisible realities may be leapt is through imagination, not imagination as pure invention (*phantastike*), but imagination as the visible reflection of the invisible (*eikastike*), the kind of seeing that comes by means of the ear. In this sense imagination provides the ground or evidence of faith.

It is because of the incompetence of discursive reason, a form of reason whose proper object is the visible world, to deal with the invisible world that Bacon admits that "in matters of Faith and Religion, we raise our Imagination above our Reason; which is the cause why Religion sought ever access to the mind by similitudes, types, parables, visions, dreams."[57] Bacon's point is acceptable if by "imagination" we undertand fancy educated by conscience, and by "reason" we understand discursive knowledge of the sensible world. In the translation of his *De Augmentis*, as we saw above, Bacon goes on to provide a classic account of the function of the imagination in the process of faith:

For we see that in matters of faith and religion our imagination raises itself above our reason; not that divine illumination resides in the imagination; its seat being rather in the very citadel of the mind and understanding; but that the divine grace uses the motions of the imagination as an instrument of illumination, just as it uses the motions of the will as an instrument of virtue; which is the reason why religion ever sought access to the mind by similitudes, types, parables, visions, dreams.[58]

The theory outlined by Bacon explains the experience described by William Perkins — faith is implicitly grounded in an act of imagination:

this saving faith hath this power and property, to take that thing in it selfe invisible, and never yet seene, and so lively to represent it to the heart of the beleever, and to the eie of the minde, as that after a sort he presently seeth and enjoyeth that invisible thing, and rejoyceth in that sight, and enjoying of it: and so judgement is not onely convinced, that such a thing shall come to passe, though it be yet to come; but the mind (as farre as Gods word hath reuealed, and as it is able) conceiues of that thing, as beeing really present to the view of it.[59]

Though Perkins never mentions the word *imagination*, in Bishop Reynolds' *Treatise of the Passions and Faculties of the Soule of Man* the importance of imagination in the process of persuasion becomes explicit. Dealing with the office of imagination in this process, Reynolds points out: "And therefore, in that great worke of mens *conversion* unto God, he is said to *allure* them, and to speak *comfortably* to them, to *beseech*, and to *perswade* them; to set forth Christ to the Soule, as *altogether lovely*, as the *fairest of ten thousand*, as the *desire of the Nations*, as the *Riches of the World*, that men might be inflamed to love the beauty of Holinesse" (pp. 19–20). Reynolds then goes on to make the connection between poetry and prophecy in the reformation of the will, the persuasion of faith:

And this was done by those Musicall, Poeticall, and Mythologicall perswasions; whereby men in their discourses, did as it were paint Vertues and Vices; giving unto spirituall things Bodies and Beauties, such as might best affect the Imagination: Yea, God himselfe hath been pleased to honour this way of setting out higher Notions, in that wee finde some roome in the holy Scripture for Mythologies . . . for Parables, Similitudes and Poeticall numbers and Raptures, whereby heavenly Doctrines are shadowed forth, and doe condiscend unto humane frailties. (P. 21)[60]

Thus, just as God revealed himself through the imagination of the prophets, so the success of that revelation depends upon the reciprocal operation of the imagination in the reader: "There must be a double light. So there must be a Spirit in me, as there is a Spirit in Scripture before I can see any thing."[61] When the reader's imagination operates icastically, as a glass faithfully reflecting sensible images of the divine, he too becomes a kind of prophet: Scripture, says Milton, "must not be interpreted by the intellect of a particular individual, that is to say, not by his merely human intellect, but with the help of the Holy Spirit, promised to each individual believer. Hence the gift of prophecy, I Cor. xiv" (*CD* I, xxx; YP VI, pp. 579–80). The revelation of Scripture, if it is to effect the persuasion of faith, needs to be answered by the imaginative re-creation of the Word in the mind of the reader: "Having prophecy," says Perkins, "let us prophecy [*sic*] according to the proportion of faith."[62] In order to know Christ you must picture him — you must "behold him often, not in the wooden crucifix after the Popish manner, but in the preaching of the word, and in the Sacraments, in which thou shalt see *him crucified* before thine eies, Gal. 3.1. Desire not here upon earth to behold him with the bodily eie but looke upon him with the eie of truth and lively faith."[63] It is the answering operation of "lively faith" or the icastic imagination, the spirit of prophecy in the reader re-creating the revelation of prophecy in Scripture, that is the mark of the indwelling Christ, the interior teacher. The internal manner of Christ's teaching is paralleled by the external: "our Saviour Christ's manner of teaching," says Richard Sibbes, "was by a lively representation to men's fancies, to teach them heavenly truths in an earthly, sensible manner."[64] Now when this re-creation of revelation is directed toward other men, we have the "prophecy" of preaching and, more important, what Milton calls "another persuasive method,"[65] the "prophecy" of poetry. *Paradise Lost* is the response in Milton of the spirit of prophecy to Scripture, but directed toward eliciting a similar response in others — fit though few. It is in this way that Milton hopes by justifying the ways of God to men to justify himself.

The clearest evidence for the icastic imagination as the ground of faith is in the invocations to *Paradise Lost.* The invocation to Book III, for instance, has certain obvious similarities to the apostrophe to *alta fantasia* in *Purgatorio* xvii, 13–27. In Dante the images formed in the fancy originate not in the sensible world but in heavenly light:

> O imaginativa . . .
> chi move te, se 'l senso non ti porge?
>   Moveti lume che nel ciel s'informa,
>   per sé o per voler che giù lo scorge.
> De l'empiezza di lei che mutò forma
>   ne l'uccel ch'a cantar più si diletta,
>   ne l'imagine mia apparve l'orma;
> e qui fu la mia mente sì ristretta
>   dentro da sé, che di fuor non venia
>   cosa che fosse allor da lei recetta.

[O imagination . . . who moves you if the sense affords you naught? A light moves you which takes form in heaven, of itself, or by a will that downward guides it.

Of her impious deed who changed her form into the bird that most delights to sing, the impress appeared in my imagination, and at this my mind was so restrained within itself, that from outside came naught that was then received by it.]

In Milton the sensible images of poetry cannot originate in the sensible world because for him in his blindness the "Book of knowledg fair" is "expung'd and ras'd" (III, 47, 49). At first poetry appears to originate in other poetry (III, 26–40). Despite his blindness, Milton continues to read poetry; despite the universal blank that is now nature's works, he continues to wander through imagined landscapes: "Yet not the more / Cease I to wander where the Muses haunt" (III, 26–27). Reading over the creations of imagination precipitates a reciprocal imaginative response. This is evident implicitly from the metaphoric quality of the description of his reading, and explicitly from

> Then feed on thoughts, that voluntarie move
> Harmonious numbers; as the wakeful Bird
> Sings darkling, and in shadiest Covert hid
> Tunes her nocturnal Note.   (III, 37–40)

The "as" is both temporal and modal: Milton writes both at the same time and in the same manner as the nightingale sings. As the final lines of the invocation suggest, however, the response of icastic imagination to the Bible and the classics depends upon the operation of the spirit within, the spirit which itself originates in heavenly light. Before Milton can see the sensible images of the divine council, images which owe so much to Sion and blind Maeonides, before he can re-create them, "thou Celestial light" must "Shine inward":

> So much the rather thou Celestial light
> Shine inward, and the mind through all her powers
> Irradiate, there plant eyes, all mist from thence
> Purge and disperse, that I may see and tell
> Of things invisible to mortal sight.
>   Now had the Almighty Father from above. . . .   (III, 51–56)

These lines, of course, not only refer to the sensible reflection of the divine, the icastic operation of imagination, but to the heavenly grace of faith: in Scripture "the grace of Holy Spirit is compared to light."[66] Milton is consistent in his use of his own blindness as a metaphor for the transition from "sight" to faith. A good example is sonnet 19 which turns on the familiar pattern of the frustrated striving of the eye being arrested and superseded by revelation through the ear. The first part of the poem is cast as a question.

> When I consider how my light is spent,
>   Ere half my days, in this dark world and wide,
>   And that one Talent which is death to hide,
>   Lodg'd with me useless, though my soul more bent
> To serve therewith my Maker, and present
>   My true account, least he returning chide,
>   Doth God exact day-labour, light deny'd,
>   I fondly ask.

In these lines Milton simulates the working of "sight," the attempt of discursive reason to unravel unaided the moral consequences of a physical problem. The irony consists in the nature of the problem, the loss of sight itself. Thus, the loss of physical sight is imitated by the failure of figurative "sight" — discursive reasoning. The growing anxiety of the labyrinth of conditional clauses — "When I consider . . . though my soul more bent / To serve . . . least he returning chide" — only yields a foolish question: "Doth God exact day-labour, light deny'd." Consolation, however, is implicit in such failure, for "sight" must give way to faith. And so the answer is a moment of faith:

> But patience to prevent
> That murmur, soon replies, God doth not need

> Either man's work or his own gifts, who best
> Bear his milde yoak, they serve him best, his State
> Is Kingly. Thousands at his bidding speed
> And post o're Land and Ocean without rest:
> They also serve who only stand and waite.

What the eye cannot see, the ear hears: foolish discourse is arrested and superseded by words whispered in the ear. But this whispering, the reply of patience personified, is an act of imagination, and this act (the imagined voice and the vision of God's glory that its words unfold) operates as a persuasion to believe — hence the conviction of the closing statement: "They also serve who only stand and waite."

So in the invocation, the meditation on his blindness becomes the occasion of a prayer for faith. "So much the rather thou Celestial light / Shine inward" depends for its full significance on the switch from the literal to the figurative meaning of the loss of sight in the preceding lines. Hence the preparatory emphasis on the sensible world as "the Book of knowledg fair," the "ground" or object of discursive knowledge — a book now closed "And wisdom at one entrance quite shut out" (III, 50). The pivotal "So much the rather" indicates the superiority of the new wisdom. The new seeing, the eyes with which Milton hopes to see "things invisible to mortal sight" are planted ("there plant eyes"), just as faith itself is "A FIRM PERSUASION IMPLANTED," or fame in *Lycidas* is "no plant that grows in mortal soil" (78). True fame ("eternal life, which will never allow the memory of the good deeds we performed on earth to perish")[67] is the fruit of faith; it "lives and spreds aloft by those pure eyes, / And perfet witness of all-judging *Jove*" (81–82); that is, true fame lives by "pure-ey'd Faith" (*Mask* 212). Thus, "things invisible to mortal sight" refers to both what the imagination reflects and what faith sees — what is reflected in the imagination is what faith sees. The persuasion that is faith turns on what the imagination reflects: the icastic imagination thus provides the ground or evidence of faith, or, as Bacon puts it, grace uses the motions of the imagination as an instrument of illumination.

In the invocation to Book I there is, as we shall see, something similar. Faith, the new seeing, is apprehended through the ear: so in *Lycidas*, after the poet exhausted foolish discourse, Phoebus "touch'd my trembling ears" (77) and whispered the revelation of faith. In *Paradise Lost*, the seeds of the new seeing are also planted through the ear. In the prologue to Book IX, the heavenly muse brings the substance of things seen "nightly to my Ear" (IX, 47). She is able to do this because Milton reads the Scriptures nightly:

> Yet not the more
> Cease I to wander where the Muses haunt
> Cleer spring, or shadie Grove, or Sunnie Hill,
> Smit with the love of sacred Song; but chief
> Thee *Sion* and the flowerie Brooks beneath
> That wash thy hallowed feet, and warbling flow,
> Nightly I visit.
>
> (III, 26–32)

The heavenly muse is the Holy Spirit,[68] that is, the indwelling spirit of prophecy in Milton imaginatively re-creating the prophecy of revelation as he nightly broods over the Scriptures,[69] just as the Holy Spirit itself "that dost prefer / Before all Temples th'upright heart and pure . . . satst brooding on the vast Abyss / And mad'st it pregnant" (I, 17–18, 21–22).

The references to Sion and its flowery brooks explains why in the invocation to Book I, "*Sion* Hill . . . and *Siloa*'s Brook that flow'd / Fast by the Oracle of God" (I, 10–12) might "Delight" the heavenly muse more than the revelation to Moses on Oreb and Sinai. Though the sequence of biblical place-names certainly "summarizes the progressive revelation of God to His people,"[70] Kerrigan's observation does not really explain either the emphasis on "Delight" or the opposition between the two pairs of place-names. Sion Hill and its brooks, as their context in Book III amplifies, are associated with the most poetical or imaginative parts of prophecy — the Psalms, Isaiah — while the word "delight" has obvious associations with poetry and the imagination: ever since Horace the end of poetry has been "to teach and delight." "Delight thee more" thus suggests the poetic or the imaginative as the instrument of illumination. In the *Purgatorio* (xxviii, 80–81), Matilda explains the effect of Sion's songs: "ma luce rende il salmo *Delectasti*, / che prote disnebbiar vostro intelletto" ("but the psalm *Delectasti* gives light that may dispel the cloud from your minds"). This states in microcosm the process described by Milton in Book III. Reading the Scriptures — the delight of Sion hill and its flowery brooks — gives the light that moves imagination, which in turn moves faith: "there plant eyes, all mist from thence / Purge and disperse." It also explains what Sidney means by "the eyes of the mind, only cleared by faith" when he talks of the "heavenly poesy" of the Psalmist "wherein almost he showeth himself a passionate lover of the unspeakable and everlasting beauty to be seen by the eyes of the mind, only cleared by faith" (p. 99). Poetry at its highest potential is the ground of faith: the pictures imagined by the Psalmist are conceived as part of the process of faith clearing the eyes of the mind, a process which will finally result in the sight of that unspeakable and everlasting beauty.

The final and most important opposition between Sinai and Sion is of course the opposition between the law and the gospel — or as Vaughan puts it, "thy *Gospel,* and thy *Law* . . . *Faith,* and *Awe.*"[71] Sion is associated with the gospel because through Christ we "are come unto Mount Sion" (Hebrews xii, 22) — "but now since we to Sion came, / And through thy cloud thy glory see."[72] The gospel delights Milton's muse more because it is poetic, poetic in the very precise sense that the gospel fulfils and replaces the law with faith, and faith requires the activity of the icastic imagination. Siloa's brook is not only the place where Christ gave new sight to the faithful (John ix), but one of Sion's flowery brooks.

University of Richmond

NOTES

1. Stanley E. Fish, *Self-Consuming Artifacts* (Berkeley and Los Angeles, 1972), p. 3.

2. Stanley E. Fish, *Surprised by Sin* (New York, 1967), p. 307.

3. Ibid., p. 302.

4. Peter Berek, "'Plain' and 'Ornate' Styles and the Structure of *Paradise Lost,*" *PMLA,* LXXXV (1970), 246; Christopher Grose, *Milton's Epic Process* (New Haven, 1973), p. 7.

5. See Fish, *Surprised by Sin,* pp. 69–70.

6. Milton, like most of his contemporaries, uses *fancy* and *imagination* interchangeably. Cf. Pierre de la Primaudaye, *Suite de l'Académie Françoise* (Paris, 1580; rpt. Geneva, 1972), p. 61: "il n'y aura point de danger, si nous usons de ces noms [l'imagination et la fantasie] indifféremment"; or Sir Thomas Browne, *Religio Medici* i, 47, in "*Religio Medici" and Other Works,* ed. L. C. Martin (Oxford, 1964), p. 45: "in my retired and solitary imaginations, to detaine me from the foulenesse of vice, [I] have fancyed to my selfe the presence of my deare and worthiest friends."

The framework of Milton's psychology is the traditional Aristotelian psychology of the Renaissance. Cf. for instance, Adam's explanation of Eve's dream (*PL* V, 100–13) with such standard contemporary accounts as Gianfrancesco Pico della Mirandola, *On the Imagination* [1501], trans. Harry Caplan (1930; rpt. Westport, Ct., 1971); la Primaudaye, *Suite de l'Académie Françoise;* Thomas Wright, *The Passions of the Minde* (London, 1601; rpt. Hildesheim, 1973); Peter Charron, *Of Wisdome,* trans. Samson Lennard (London, n.d. [before 1612]; rpt. Amsterdam, 1971); Robert Burton, *The Anatomy of Melancholy* [1620], ed. Floyd Dell and Paul Jordan-Smith (London, 1931); or Edward Reynolds, *A Treatise of the Passions and Faculties of the Soule of Man* (London, 1640; rpt. Gainesville, Fla., 1971).

For modern treatments of the subject, see Murray W. Bundy, *The Theory of Imagination in Classical and Medieval Thought* (Urbana, 1927); Lawrence Babb, *The Elizabethan Malady* (East Lansing, Mich., 1951); J. B. Bamborough, *The Little World of Man*

(London, 1952); Kester Svendsen, *Milton and Science* (Cambridge, Mass., 1956); and E. Ruth Harvey, *The Inward Wits* (London, 1975).

7. *De Augmentis* V, i, quoted from *The Works of Francis Bacon*, ed. James Spedding et al., 5 vols. (London, 1858–61; rpt. Stuttgart, 1963), IV, p. 406.

8. See M. H. Abrams, *The Mirror and the Lamp* (New York, 1958), esp. pp. 160–63.

9. See *Timaeus* 70d–72b and the discussion of it in Bundy, *Theory of Imagination*, pp. 51–54.

10. Sir Philip Sidney, *An Apology for Poetry*, ed. Geoffrey Shepherd (London, 1965), p. 125. Hereafter cited in the text.

11. IV, i, 148–56. Shakespeare is quoted from *William Shakespeare: The Complete Works*, gen. ed. Alfred Harbage, rev. ed., The Pelican Shakespeare (London, 1969).

12. Cf. S. K. Heninger, Jr., "Sidney and Milton: The Poet as Maker," in *Milton and the Line of Vision*, ed. Joseph Anthony Wittreich, Jr. (Madison, 1975), esp. pp. 66–69.

13. See *Advancement of Learning* II (*Works* III, pp. 343–44).

14. *Of Education*, quoted from *Complete Prose Works of John Milton*, ed. Don M. Wolfe et al. (New Haven, 1953–82), II, p. 404. Milton's poetry is quoted from *The Works of John Milton*, ed. Frank Allen Patterson et al. (New York, 1931–38). Hereafter cited as YP and CM.

15. On Tasso see Baxter Hathaway, *The Age of Criticism* (Ithaca, N.Y., 1962), esp. pp. 394–96; and Bernard Weinberg, *A History of Literary Criticism in the Italian Renaissance*, 2 vols. (Chicago, 1962), esp. I, pp. 339–41. See also Erwin Panofsky, *Idea*, trans. Joseph J. S. Peake (Columbia, S. C., 1968), pp. 165, 212–15n, 242n; Shepherd, in Sidney, *Apology*, pp. 202–03n; Introduction, in Tasso, *Discourses on the Heroic Poem*, ed. Mariella Cavalchini and Irene Samuel (Oxford, 1973), p. xxvii (hereafter cited in the text); James Nohrnberg, *The Analogy of the Faerie Queene* (Princeton, 1976), pp. 102–10; Isabel G. MacCaffrey, *Spenser's Allegory* (Princeton, 1975), pp. 3–10.

16. 235d–e. Plato is quoted from *The Dialogues of Plato*, trans. B. Jowett, 4th ed., 4 vols. (Oxford, 1953).

17. *Idea*, p. 215n.

18. "The *Discorsi del poema heroica* was not published until 1594, but it was probably written between 1575 and 1580" (Weinberg, *History of Literary Criticism*, I, p. 340). See also Introduction, in Tasso, *Discourses*, pp. xi–xii.

19. *The Prophetic Milton* (Charlottesville, Va., 1974), p. 56.

20. *On the Defense of the Comedy of Dante* III, vi, quoted from *Literary Criticism: Plato to Dryden*, ed. Allan H. Gilbert (New York, 1940), p. 390.

21. See Bundy, *Theory of Imagination*, pp. 225–56; and Hathaway, *Age of Criticism*, p. 379n.

22. *Purg.* xvii, 12–37. The text and translation are quoted from Dante Alighieri, *The Divine Comedy*, trans. Charles S. Singleton, 3 vols. (Princeton, 1970–75).

23. Nathanael Culverwell, *Spiritual Opticks* (London, 1652), p. 178.

24. A. E. Taylor, quoted in John Hick, *Faith and Knowledge*, 2nd ed. (Ithaca, N.Y., 1966), p. 200.

25. *Convivio* III, iv, 9, quoted in *Divine Comedy* III, pt. 2, p. 586.

26. *De Anima* III, vii, quoted from Aristotle, *On the Soul, Parva Naturalia, On Breath*, trans. W. S. Hett, rev. ed., Loeb Classical Library (London, 1957), p. 177.

27. *Summa Theologiae* I, 84, 7, quoted from St. Thomas Aquinas, *Summa Theologiae*, gen. ed. Thomas Gilby, O.P., 60 vols. (New York, 1968), XII, p. 41.

28. *Of Education* (YP II, pp. 368–69).

29. Cf. Rosemond Tuve, *Images and Themes in Five Poems by Milton* (Cambridge, Mass., 1957), p. 59, on *phantasia*, the "sole faculty by which man can be rapt beyond man's mortal limits to see the perfection he can no longer see plain." Cf. also Sharon Cumberland and Lynn Veach Sadler, "Phantasia: A Pattern in Milton's Early Poems," *MQ*, VIII (1974), esp. p. 55.

30. Irene Samuel, *Plato and Milton* (Ithaca, N.Y., 1947), p. 137.

31. Cf. Prolusion III (YP I, pp. 246–47).

32. See *City of God* XI, 10, in *The Works of . . . Augustine*, ed. Marcus Dods, vol. I (Edinburgh, 1872), pp. 447–50.

33. *The Republic of Plato*, F. M. Cornford ed. (1941; rpt. Oxford, 1966), pp. 218–19. This edition cited in the text.

34. Moses Maimonides, *The Guide of the Perplexed*, trans. Shlomo Pines, introd. Leo Strauss (Chicago, 1963), p. 369.

35. John Smith, *Select Discourses*, ed. H. G. Williams, 4th ed. (Cambridge, 1859), p. 171. Hereafter cited in the text. Smith's treatise is discussed in relation to Milton by Basil Willey, *The Seventeenth-Century Background* (1934; rpt. Harmondsworth, 1964), pp. 134–41; William B. Hunter, Jr., "Prophetic Dreams and Visions in *Paradise Lost*," *MLQ*, IX (1948), 277–85; and Kerrigan, *Prophetic Milton*, pp. 108–12. See also John Spencer Hill, *John Milton: Poet, Priest, and Prophet* (Totowa, N.J., 1979), esp. pp. 77–113.

36. Kerrigan, *Prophetic Milton*, p. 111.

37. The influence of Eliot's theory, which is implicit throughout Willey's book, becomes explicit at pp. 44–45, 83–84.

38. Cf., for instance, his attitude to mathematics: "*mathemata*, or mathematical contemplations, whereby the souls of men might farther shake off their dependence upon sense, and learn to go as it were alone, without the crutch of any sensible or material thing to support them" (*The True Way or Method of Attaining Divine Knowledge*, in *Select Discourses*, p. 11).

39. *Endimion and Phoebe* 521–22, quoted from *The Works of Michael Drayton*, ed. J. W. Hebel et al., 5 vols. (1941; rpt. Oxford, 1961). Cf. MacCaffrey, *Spenser's Allegory*, p. 13.

40. Kerrigen, *Prophetic Milton*, p. 108.

41. *Summa Theologiae* II–II, 173–1 (Gilby, ed., XLV, p. 53).

42. *The Sermons of John Donne*, ed. Evelyn M. Simpson and George R. Potter (Berkeley, 1962), VIII, 220, 225.

43. *Synopsis Prophetica; The Second Part of the Enquiry into the Mystery of Iniquity*, quoted from *The Theological Works of . . . Henry More* (London, 1708), p. 557.

44. *Defense of the Comedy of Dante* III, vi (Gilbert, *Literary Criticism*, p. 390).

45. Cf. John F. Huntley, "The Images of Poet and Poetry in Milton's *The Reason of Church-Government*," in *Achievements of the Left Hand*, ed. Michael Leib and John T. Shawcross (Amherst, Mass., 1974), pp. 83–120. For a slightly different view, see Hill, *John Milton*, pp. 105–06.

46. See Hunter, "Prophetic Dreams."

47. The tone is so poetic that, for Keats, Adam's dream became a symbol of the poetic imagination: "The Imagination may be compared to Adam's dream — he awoke and found it truth. . . . Adam's dream will do here, and seems to be conviction that Imagination and its empyreal reflexion is the same as human life and its spiritual repetition" (letter to Benjamin Bailey, 1817, quoted in D. G. James, *Scepticism and Poetry* [London, 1937], p. 188).

48. Hunter, "Prophetic Dreams," p. 283.

49. *A Clowd of Faithfull Witnesses,* in *The Workes of . . . Mr. W. Perkins,* 3 vols. (Cambridge, 1608–37), III, p. 9.

50. Sermon 43, quoted from *Introduction to the Philosophy of Saint Augustine,* ed. John A. Mourant (University Park, Pa., 1964), p. 39.

51. Cf. Pico, *On the Imagination,* p. 89: "The Light of Faith, . . . making perspicuous the verities of Holy Writ that are impervious to the light of nature, is of greatest service to either type of imagination [that is, the imagination moved by either simple physical desires or more complex mental ones]. It supports and conducts each by the hand, sweeping each up, so to speak, and elevating it above its own nature."

52. *Faith and Reason,* ed. Lionel Rubinoff (Chicago, 1968), p. 110.

53. *The World Contemned,* quoted from *The Works of Henry Vaughan,* ed. L. C. Martin, 2nd ed. (Oxford, 1957), p. 326. Vaughan's poetry is also quoted from this edition.

54. *A Brief Discourse of the True Grounds of the Certainty of Faith in Points of Religion* (*Works,* p. 765).

55. *Institution of the Christian Religion [Basel, 1536],* trans. Ford Lewis Battles (Atlanta, 1975), p. 59.

56. The writers of the New Testament are inspired in the same way as the prophets of the Old. As Peter explains after the descent of the Holy Spirit at Pentecost, Christian witness means the restoration of the prophetical spirit: "For these are not drunken, as ye suppose. . . . But this is that which was spoken by the prophet Joel. . . . I will pour out in those days of my Spirit; and they shall prophesy" (Acts ii, 15–18). Cf. Smith, *Of Prophecy* (*Select Discourses,* pp. 278–83).

57. *Advancement of Learning* II (*Works* III, p. 382).

58. V.i (*Works* IV, p. 406).

59. *A Clowd of Faithfull Witnesses* (*Workes* III, p. 2).

60. Cf. Richard Sibbes, *The Soules Conflict with it selfe* (London, 1635), pp. 258–59: "Whilest the soule is joyned with the body, it hath not only a necessary but a *holy* use of *imagination,* and of *sensible* things whereupon our imagination worketh; what is the use of the *Sacraments* but to help our *soules* by our *senses,* and our *faith* by *imagination;* as the soule receives much *hurt* from imagination, so it may have much good thereby." Sibbes, however, goes on to make it clear that imagination only helps confirm an existing faith; it is not instrumental in the creation of faith.

61. Sibbes, quoted in Geoffrey F. Nuttall, *The Holy Spirit in Puritan Faith and Experience,* 2nd ed. (Oxford, 1947), p. 23.

62. *The Art of Prophecying* (*Workes* II, p. 649).

63. *A Declaration of the True Manner of Knowing Christ Crucified* (*Workes* I, p. 625).

64. *The Soules Conflict,* p. 256.

65. *Reason of Church-Government* II, Introduction (YP I, p. 819).

66. *The Enchiridion of Erasmus,* trans. and ed. Raymond Himelick (Bloomington, Ind. 1963), p. 102.

67. Prolusion VII (YP I, p. 302).

68. For a different view, cf. Hill, *John Milton,* pp. 110–11.

69. Not forgetting the classics, because, as Nohrnberg points out, "all good words are an analogy for this Word" (*Analogy,* p. 105).

70. Kerrigan, *Prophetic Milton,* p. 126.

71. "The Law, and the Gospel" 27–28. Cf. James Hoyle, "'If Sion Hill Delight Thee More': The Muse's Choice in *Paradise Lost,*" *ELN,* XII (1974), 20–26.

72. "The Law, and the Gospel," 11–12.

MILTON AND THE MEANING OF GLORY

John Peter Rumrich

C USTOMARILY, WE hear the word *glory* in the formulae of religious language and, customarily, we ignore it or rest content in
our familiar distance from it. Even that most knowledgeable scholar and
evangelist, C. S. Lewis, admitted his perplexity regarding the idea of
glory: "this idea is very prominent in the New Testament and in the early
Christian writings . . . but it makes no immediate appeal to me at all,
and in that respect I fancy I am a typical modern."[1] Lewis here limits
his discussion to early Christianity, but those familiar with the literature
of renaissance England also have encountered glory regularly. In *Paradise Lost*, for example, glory and its cognates occur more frequently than,
and in as crucial locations as, the often-noticed *fruit*. Glory appears so
prominently in Milton's creation epic because, as C. A. Patrides reports,
Christianity "has traditionally asserted that 'the principal end of our Creation' is the glory of God."[2] To understand Milton's justification of God's
ways, therefore, we must, in Merritt Hughes's words, "see the historical
process from the world's creation to its end as begun for the glory of God
and ending in the glory of both men and God."[3]

Scholars have generally concluded that for Milton glory is a worldly
temptation to achieve fame or preeminence, a temptation which lures
noble minds in particular to forsake God's will. In *Paradise Regain'd*
Christ certainly construes Satan's temptation to glory in this way (III,
47f.). But this assessment does not mean that either Christ or Milton consider Satan's definition of glory adequate. The meaning of glory in Milton's works goes beyond its secular manifestation as fame, beyond even
its heavenly manifestation as fame in God's eyes. Indeed, I hope to show
that the idea of glory pervades Milton's thought and that we cannot
understand the relationship Milton draws between God and his creation
until we understand the meaning of glory.

Milton's renditions of various psalms suggest that he understood
glory to be a split concept. Consider, for example, his relatively literal
translation of Psalm vii:

> Let the enemy persecute
> my soul and take it;

> yea, let him tread down
> my life upon the earth
> and lay mine honor
> in the dust.   (AV vii, 5)

> Let th' enemy pursue my soul
> And overtake it, let him tread
> My life down to the earth and roll
> In the dust my glory dead,
> In the dust and there outspread
> Lodge it with dishonor foul.   (13–18)[4]

The Authorized Version distinguishes between a man's life and his honor (which here translates the Hebrew *kabod*, usually translated as glory). Milton's addition of line sixteen, however, allows a certain ambiguity in the meaning of glory: "glory" in "my glory dead" can be taken either as a poetic restatement of "life" from the preceding line, or it can be construed with the following lines as a reference to the dead man's reputation. In his departure from a literal translation of these particular lines, Milton nonetheless holds true to the meaning of *kabod* as it occurs throughout the Psalms. As a brief examination of the etymology of glory will reveal, *kabod* can indicate either reputation or the very being of a man.

The meaning of *kabod* begins in the idea of weight.[5] Genesis describes the wealthy Abram as heavy (*kabod*) "in cattle, in silver, and in gold" (xiii, 2). Moses uses *kabod* when he complains that his heavy speech will hinder him as God's spokesman (Ex. iv, 10). The intensity of a severe famine or plague could also be marked by *kabod* (Gen. xii, 10; Ex. ix, 3). When St. Paul contrasts the early Christians' "slight momentary affliction" with their ultimate reward, "an eternal weight of glory," he may be punning on the Hebrew sense of the word (II Cor. iv, 17). Hence, whether it refers to the abundance of mass in a tangible object or to the profundity of an intangible state of being, *kabod* signals the substantiality and magnitude of what it characterizes. True glory thus concerns something almost tangible, something weighty, sober, grave. Modern, secular equivalents of *kabod* might include "guts," "intestinal fortitude," or even "the right stuff." Milton describes as "grave" the "sober Race of Men" in Book XI of *Paradise Lost*, who eventually "yield up all thir virtue, all thir fame" (XI, 585, 621, 623). The women who seduce them he describes as devoid of glory, in other words, "empty of all good wherein consists / Woman's domestic honor and chief praise" (XI, 616–17). Satan typifies the loss of glory in this as in other respects. Despite his regal appearance, which dilates as the occasion warrants, God's scales reveal him "how light, how weak" (IV, 1012).

Men and especially women of *kabod* are particularly distinguished by their success as parents. While gravity denotes the *kabod* of the biblical male, gravidity marks that of the female. Sarah and Abraham become the standard of biblical *kabod* because of the abundance of their progeny. If one tends automatically to show respect to certain men simply because of their grave bearing, certainly one also defers automatically to a woman who will bear children. Raphael thus greets Eve according to the unexpressed *kabod* which nonetheless resides within her: "Hail Mother of Mankind, whose fruitful Womb / Shall fill the World more numerous with thy Sons / Than with these various fruits the Trees of God / Have heap'd this Table" (V, 388–91). Procreative monstrosities such as Satan authors, on the other hand, signal a corresponding perversion and diminishment of *kabod*.

The generations which follow the misalliance of the Sons of God with the daughters of Cain, "prodigious Births of body or mind, / . . . Giants, men of high renown," eventually pervert the very standards by which men will recognize glory:

> To overcome in Battle, and subdue
> Nations, and bring home spoils with infinite
> Man-slaughter, shall be held the highest pitch
> Of human Glory, and for Glory done
> Of triumph, to be styl'd great Conquerors,
> Patrons of Mankind, Gods, and Sons of Gods,
> Destroyers rightlier call'd, and Plagues of men.
> Thus Fame shall be achiev'd, renown on Earth,
> And what most merits fame in silence hid.
>
> (XI, 687–88, 691–99)

Wisdom, not military prowess, is the most infallible mark of glory, but in the ferocious world envisioned by Michael, men like Enoch, "eminent / In wise deport," suffer at the hands of tyrants unless God protects them (XI, 665–66; cf. *PR* III, 68–99). Satan's crew, of course, sets the pattern for the pursuit of glory through military strife (VI, 377–85).

Biblically, wisdom signals *kabod* in a man because wisdom consists in knowledge and praise of his creator. Here, as we will soon see, *kabod* suggests the Greek word *doxa*, which New Testament authors use to mean glory and which translates *kabod* in the Septuagint. The failure to show respect or to render praise—*kabod* as fame—to a man of *kabod* or to God as the source of *kabod* is the mark of a fool and thus an indication of the negligent one's own lack of glory. This secondary use of *kabod*, as the fame or respect owed to a substantial person, makes it an effective antithesis for disgrace or shame, even as the wise man of *kabod* is an effective antithesis for the barren fool: "the wise shall inherit glory [*kabod*]: but shame shall be the promotion of fools" (Prov. iii, 35). The use of "inherit" tells us that the wise man or woman does not merely enjoy fame or progeny, but that he stands entitled to it — it belongs to him. All modern prudence aside, a woman of wisdom, such as Sarah or the mother of Christ, will bear children.

As applied to man in the Psalms, *kabod* generally concerns the relations between man and God and does not much concern the reputation of a man among men. The Psalmist glorifies God with his very being (his own glory): "I will sing and give praise, even with my glory [*kabod*]; awake psaltry and harp: I myself will awake early" (Ps. cviii, 1–2; cf. lvii, 8). "I myself" joins the psaltry and harp as an instrument for the praise of God. The Psalmist also says that God blesses him "to the end that my glory [*kabod*] may sing praise. . . . O Lord my God I will give thanks to thee for ever" (Ps. xxx, 12). Here *kabod* directly parallels the "I" in the verse. In recognizing his dependence on God, he recognizes the complementary nature of his own *kabod* and praises him as he is blessed.

We witness a similar moment in *Paradist Lost* when Adam and Eve retire to their "shady Lodge" and turn with "adoration pure / Which God likes best" to sing their evening praises. Everything that exists, and even that which will exist, reminds them of their maker:

> Thou also mad'st the Night,
> Maker Omnipotent, and thou the Day,
> Which we in our appointed work imploy'd
> Have finisht happy in our mutual help
> And mutual love, the Crown of all our bliss
> Ordain'd by thee, and this delicious place
> For us too large, where thy abundance wants
> Partakers, and uncropt falls to the ground.
> But thou hast promis'd from us two a Race
> To fill the Earth, who shall with us extol
> Thy goodness infinite.   (IV, 724–34)

In their psalmic recognition and praise of their creator's glory, Adam and Eve wisely recognize not only the plenitude of God but also their own complementary fertility.

When *kabod* refers to God himself, as opposed to the glory creatures give God, we can once again distinguish two chief meanings. First, as

Joseph Mead writes, "glory . . . often signifies the *Divine Presence*"; another meaning of glory noted by Mead also falls into the first category — "the high and glorious *Supereminency* or *Majesty of God.*"[6] In either case glory refers mainly to sensible manifestations of God. The Old Testament associates the presence of God with unbearable light, thunder, the sound of a trumpet, lightning, fire, and with moments of imminent wrath or favor (Ex. xvi, 17, xxx, 18–19; Levit. ix, 6, 23; Num. xx, 6, xiv, 10, xvi, 19, 42). The brilliant lustre of Moses' face as he leaves the mount reflects the splendor of God's *kabod* (Ex. xxxiv, 29–35). In *Paradise Lost* Milton relies heavily on the Exodus narrative where "the glory [*kabod*] of the Lord appeared in the cloud" (vi, 10). The second chief meaning concerns God himself or the person of God; as Mead again writes, "in the Scripture, and among the Hebrews, *His Glory*, or the *Glory of the Lord*, is used to note the *Divine Essence* or *Deity* itself."[7]

It should not surprise us that the meaning of *kabod* includes or sets the foundation for everything Milton means by glory. At this point then, it will help generally to summarize the various meanings of *kabod* which Milton applies to glory: (1) the essence or substance of God or man — what one might call "the thing itself"; (2) weight, gravity, sober deportment; (3) potency or fertility of body or mind; (4) praise or reputation; (5) lustre and other sensible manifestations of presence. Overall, we will find that Milton uses glory to indicate something about the relationship between creature and creator. In order to focus more closely on this relationship, we must turn now to the Greek version of glory.

The Greek word for glory, *doxa*, reverses the Old Testament emphasis on what is internal and invisible. The Greeks may have assumed that a man of weight and power deserves the admiration of his fellows, but they never denoted both virtue and the response which virtue evokes with the same word. Where the Hebrew located the real man in that which gives him impact, the Greek, despite his emphasis on the development of human potential, most valued the impression which the great man leaves behind, the impact itself. As C. M. Bowra says of the happy Greek who won a great reputation, "the man so remembered was the true man, the essential self, who by his exertions had found his full range and passed outside the changing pattern of his development into his ultimate reality."[8]

Doxa derives from *dokeo*, which means "I think" or "I suppose" and by extension, "I have an opinion." Perhaps the Greek translator of the Hebrew bible used *doxa* to render *kabod* simply because it stressed the side of *kabod* which he recognized as primary — the opinion of others and not some intangible dimension of the internal man. Naturally, we can only guess whether or not the Greek translator was stressing opinion and reputation by using *doxa* for *kabod*. But Milton would have remembered *doxa* as originally meaning opinion from his reading of Plato. For Plato, the faculty of opinion acts as an epistemological daemon which has as its object the world "between that which purely and absolutely is and that which wholly is not," in other words, the world of becoming in which man leads his daily life.[9] Gerhard Kittel well explains the problem in having a word for opinion translate glory: "When the translator of the Old Testament first thought of using *doxa* for *kabod*, he initiated a linguistic change of far-reaching significance, giving to the Greek term a distinctiveness of sense which could hardly be surpassed. Taking a word for opinion, which implies all the subjectivity and therefore all the vacillation of human views and conjectures, he made it express something absolutely objective, i.e., the reality of God."[10] The use of *doxa* to translate *kabod* thus underlines the possibility of a semantic split in the idea of glory — a split between the objective fact of glory and subjective recognition of it.

In Book III of *Paradise Lost* Milton dramatizes the split between objective glory — "the thing itself" — and subjective recognition of it. The invocation demands a revelation of glory at its brilliant source; Milton in fact offers himself as a suitable shrine for the Divine Presence after the Old Testament model: "cloud . . . and ever-during dark / Surrounds me" (III, 45–46). Like Moses, Milton wants to be with God inside the dark clouds that radiate his presence. While Milton witnesses the absolute clarity of God's council in heavenly paradise, Satan alights in the Paradise of Fools, a region described with imagery that recalls the meaning of *doxa* as changeable, airy opinion. A "windy Sea of Land" awaits those who would build "thir fond hopes of Glory or lasting fame" on vain pursuits, "naught seeking but the praise of men" (III, 440, 449, 453). The inhabitants' perversion of true glory appears in their false or unnatural births: "unaccomplisht . . . / Abortive, monstrous, or unkindly mixt" — "embryos and Idiots" (III, 455–56, 474). Here we see a climate characterized by clouds without the mercy of light, "Dark, waste, and wild, under the frown of Night / Starless expos'd, and ever-threat'ning storms / Of *Chaos*, blust'ring round, inclement sky" (III, 424–26). This realm's vaporous citizens dissolve into the "devious Air," fly "up . . . like Aereal vapors," to a world filled with "things transitory and vain," where those who pursue false glory "find / Fit retribution, empty as their deeds" (III, 489, 445, 446, 453–54).

After the Fall, opinion obviously gets sidetracked fairly easily from the pursuit of real glory in order to pursue worldly fame or some other version of false glory, some other idol. Nevertheless, man's definitive task in a world of growth and change is to approach the objective glory of God through his subjective recognition of it. Man must in fact understand the growth and change which shapes the world of opinion as a dimension of that objective glory. Learning and inquiry directed toward this end, as Milton explains in Prolusion VII, become almost a devotional duty:

> The great Artificer of this mighty fabric established it for His own glory. The more deeply we delve into the wondrous wisdom, the marvellous skill, and the astounding variety of its creation (which we cannot do without the aid of learning), the greater grows the wonder and awe we feel for its Creator and the louder the praises we offer Him, which we believe and are fully persuaded that He delights to accept. Can we indeed believe, my hearers, that the vast spaces of boundless air are illuminated and adorned with everlasting lights, that these are endowed with such rapidity of motion and pass through such intricate revolutions, merely to serve as a lantern for base and slothful men, and to light the path of the idle and the sluggard here below? . . . By our unresponsiveness and grudging spirit He is deprived of much of the glory which is His due, and of the reverence which His mighty power exacts. If then Learning is our guide and leader in the search after happiness, if it is ordained and approved by almighty God, and most comfortable to His glory, surely it cannot but bring the greatest blessings upon those who follow after it.[11]

Milton sings the praises of learning in this passage, but only as the means to a nobler end—a more accurate opinion of God's power and majesty in accordance with man's duty to glorify the creator. The congruity suggested by the term "conformable" again emphasizes Milton's characteristic depiction of human glory as a reverent, epistemological progress toward a being who desires and requires that reverence and that progress.

Consequently, whenever we find mention of the pursuit of knowledge in *Paradise Lost*, we also find mention of the glorification of God as the end of that pursuit:

> thy desire which tends to know
> The works of God, thereby to glorify
> The great Work-master, leads to no excess
> That reaches blame, but rather merits praise.   (III, 694–97)

> wee, not to explore the secrets ask
> Of his Eternal Empire, but the more
> To magnify his works, the more we know.   (VII, 95–97)

> what thou canst attain, which best may serve
> To glorify the Maker and infer
> Thee also happier, shall not be withheld.   (VII, 115–17)

> what recompense
> Equal have I to render thee, Divine
> Historian, who thus largely has allay'd
> The thirst I had of knowledge, and voutsaf'd
> This friendly condescension to relate
> Things else by me unsearchable, now heard
> With wonder, but delight, and, as is due,
> With glory attributed to the high
> Creator?   (VIII, 5–13)

Raphael's narration of the War in Heaven makes it clear that the rebels' loss of right opinion and subsequent failure to glorify God as creator triggers the rebellion: "We know no time when we were not as now," says the erring Satan, "know none before us, self-begot, self-rais'd" (V, 859–60).

The relations between God and creation, in which glory consists, parallel the relations between *doxa* and *kabod*. As I summarized them earlier, the various senses of *kabod* stress God as the weighty source of glory. The philosophical connotations of *doxa*, concerning the pursuit of knowledge and the nature of the good life, elaborate and revise *kabod*, conceived of as reverent, awe-filled praise elicited by the source of creation. The dynamic Greek version of glory complements the static Hebrew version. We will similarly find that *doxa* also complements *kabod* in its related meaning of potency or fertility. Whereas the meaning of *kabod* focuses on the creativity of God or of parents, *doxa* concerns the attitude of the child.

In representing Satan's contention that he created himself, Milton may have remembered Philo's assertion that God instituted circumcision among the Hebrews to portray the "putting away of the impious conceit [*doxa*] under which the mind supposed that it was capable of begetting by its own power."[12] Milton understood early that right opinion rests on one's awareness of one's own genesis. In *Ad Patrem*, for example, he explains, "no requital equal to your desert and no deeds equal to your gifts are within my power; let it suffice that with a grateful mind I remember and tell over your constant kindnesses and lay them up in a loyal heart" (111–114). Satan similarly recalls the debt he owed, but failed to acknowledge:

> I sdeign'd subjection, and thought one step higher
> Would set me highest, and in a moment quit
> The debt immense of endless gratitude,
> So burdensome, still paying, still to owe;
> Forgetful what from him I still receiv'd,

> And understood not that a grateful mind
> By owing owes not, but still pays, at once
> Indebted and discharg'd; what burden then?   (IV, 50–57)

As I already mentioned, the ancient Hebrew would not view the failure to recognize *kabod* in another man as a simple matter of mistaken opinion; he would consider it a robbery of rightful possession. Satan, in rejecting his creator, steals the recognition that he, simply by existing, owes God. Milton continually describes Satan as criminal — a "perfidious fraud" (V, 880; cf. I, 401; III, 152; IV, 555, 794; IX, 55, 84, 285–87, 643, 904, 1150), a pretender (V, 768), a counterfeiter (V, 771). Having refused to acknowledge his own debt to the Creator, Satan now proceeds to steal the right opinion of others — "as a Thief bent to unhoard the cash / Of some rich Burgher" (IV, 188–89).[13] As a consequence of his success, "the greatest part / Of Mankind . . . forsake[s] / God thir Creator, and th' invisible / Glory of him that made them" (I, 367–370).

The complementary relationship between *doxa* and *kabod* appears also in the visible glory of creatures who maintain right opinion. Like Moses in Exodus, the unfallen reflect the lustre of the creator. Those who forsake true belief, however, also suffer a visible loss of glory:

> If thou beest hee; But O how fall'n! how chang'd
> From him, who in the happy Realms of Light
> Cloth'd with transcendent brightness didst outshine
> Myriads though bright.   (I, 84–87)

Beelzebub does not endure this change "in outward luster" alone (I, 97). Satan, too, has seen his "Glory wither'd" and suffers embarrassment when Zephon later fails to recognize him (I, 612). "Not to know mee argues yourselves unknown," Satan declares to the angelic guard, but then realizes that he no longer possesses the distinctive glory he once enjoyed (IV, 830):

> Think not, revolted Spirit, thy shape the same,
> Or undiminisht brightness, to be known
> As when thou stood'st in Heav'n upright and pure;
> That Glory then, when thou no more wast good,
> Departed from thee, and thou resembl'st now
> Thy sin and place of doom obscure and foul.   (IV, 835–40)

Satan recognizes with shame that other creatures perceive "his lustre visibly impair'd" (IV, 850).

Milton conceives of unfallen creatures' lustre as a kind of God-given clothing that declares a creature's proper epistemological relationship with

God — its identity, if you will. Joseph Mead helps us to understand Milton's figure: "in a well-governed Commonwealth every sort and condition of men is known by some different habit, agreeable to his quality and so it seems it should be in God's great Commonwealth."[14] We need only consider Milton's elaborate description of various angels to see how he has realized Mead's dictum (e.g., III, 624–28, 636–44; V, 277–85; XI, 239–48). Just as the apparel proclaims the angel, so also in men "the image of thir glorious Maker shone: Truth, Wisdom, Sanctitude severe and pure" (IV, 292–93). Eve appears "in naked beauty more adorn'd, / More lovely than *Pandora*," and Adam requires none of the trappings and suits of royalty because "in himself was all his state" (IV, 713–14, V, 353). Even Eve's hair, hanging "as a veil down to the slender waist," testifies to her identity as Adam's glory: "in wanton ringlets wav'd / As the Vine curls her tendrils, which impli'd / Subjection, but requir'd with gentle sway" (IV, 305–08). We do not consider Adam and Eve naked, therefore, in the sense of being vulnerable or deprived, prior to the Fall. Rather, their covering provides a natural rather than accidental distinctiveness, as in the plumage of birds. After the Fall, however, Adam and Even lose "that first naked glory" (IX, 1115).[15]

If good creatures enjoy a covering of light and beauty which signals their right opinion, evil ones take refuge under a false cover that literally suggests their travesties of truth. Satan, though in despair, pretends to the height of glory and, having seduced Man from truth, enters Hell after God's own fashion, "invisible" until "at last as from a Cloud his fulgent head / And shape Star-bright appear'd, or brighter, clad / With what permissive glory since his fall / Was left him, or false glitter" (X, 449–52). Expecting to hear his praises sung with "universal shout and high applause," he instead hears "from innumerable tongues / A dismal universal hiss, the sound / Of public scorn" (X, 505, 507–09). Milton similarly satirizes the pretensions of "Eremites and Friars / White, Black, and Gray with all their trumpery" (III, 474–75). As with Satan before them, these holy frauds are reduced to their disguises: a strong wind blows "Cowls, Hoods, and Habits with thir wearers tost / And flutter'd into Rags" (III, 490–91). In either case of false glory — ambition for fame or superstitious posturing — evil, for Milton, reduces to mere evasion of responsibility to God as the source and end of being. Milton unfailingly represents this desertion as worthy not of admiration nor even of regret, but only of unsympathetic derision.

In this essay I have argued that for Milton glory indicates the relationship between creature and creator. More specifically, glory means the presentation of God *through* and *to* his creatures. All creation is an investiture with glory "as with a mantle," an investiture that transforms Chaos into creatures capable of response (III, 11). The entire cosmos imagined in *Paradise Lost* exemplifies this responsiveness, from the rarefied intelligences of highest heaven to the "humid Flow'rs" sending up "silent praise" (IX, 193, 195). In lines which allude to literary relationships as well as to Moses' contact with God, Adam vows to search for God and to "behold though but his utmost skirts / Of glory, and far off his steps adore" (XI, 332–33). Michael comforts Adam by emphasizing God's omnipresence and fatherly love: "still following thee, still compassing thee round / With goodness and paternal Love, his Face / Express, and of his steps the track Divine" (XI, 352–354). All of salvation history after the Fall will represent God to men, bringing the eternal into a temporal context, even as the multiplicity of creation proclaims an otherwise unintelligible unity—"through all numbers absolute, though One"—which underlies and transcends that multiplicity (VIII, 421). In such signs as Michael refers to, men may see God's face "express"—images of him literally pressed out of the omnipresence that "fills / Land, Sea, and Air, and every kind that lives" (XI, 337). Otherwise, revelation depends on men of interpretive wisdom inspired by God, men who provide a sacred history of the relationship between God and his people, a literary rendition of glory.

University of Texas, Austin

NOTES

1. C. S. Lewis, *The Weight of Glory* (New York, 1949), p. 8.
2. C. A. Patrides, *Milton and the Christian Tradition* (Oxford, 1966), pp. 38–39.
3. Merritt Y. Hughes, "Milton and the Sense of Glory," *PQ*, XXVIII (1949), 119.
4. The edition of Milton's poetry cited throughout is *Complete Poems and Major Prose*, ed. Merritt Y. Hughes (Indianapolis, 1957).
5. I use a number of sources in developing the etymology of glory. There is general agreement regarding the central points included in my presentation. Nevertheless, the word is a controversial one. For further study, see Gerhard Kittel, ed., and G. W. Bromiley, trans., *Theological Dictionary of the New Testament*, 10 vols. (Grand Rapids, Mich., 1964), II, pp. 223–55; L. H. Brockington, "The Greek Translator of Isaiah and His Interest in Doxa," *Vetus Testamentum*, I (1951), pp. 27–31; Everett Falconer Harrison, "The Use of Doxa in Greek Literature with Special Reference to the New Testament" (Ph.D. diss., University of Pennsylvania, 1950); Theodor Klauser, ed., "Gloria," *Gleicheit-Gnade: Reallexikon fur Antike und Christentum*, fascicle 82 (Stuttgart, 1979), pp. 196–225. I am indebted to the late Guenther G. Rumrich for his translation of the last source.

6. Joseph Mead, *The Complete Works*, ed. John Worthington (London, 1677), p. 92.

7. Ibid.

8. C. M. Bowra, *The Greek Experience* (Cleveland, 1957), pp. 200–01.

9. *Republic* V, 478d. All quotations are from *The Collected Dialogues*, ed. Edith Hamilton and Huntington Cairns (Princeton, 1961).

10. Kittel and Bromiley, *Theological Dictionary*, p. 238.

11. I, pp. 291–92. References to Milton's prose are by volume and page from *The Complete Prose Works of John Milton*, ed. Don M. Wolfe et al. (New Haven, 1953–82).

12. Philo, "The Migration of Abraham," *Philo* IV, ed. E. H. Warminton, The Loeb Classical Library (Cambridge, Mass., 1968), p. 185.

13. Raphael takes great pains to make Adam and Eve realize that although they possess right opinion, it can be lost, as Plato suggests, through theft, enchantment, or force (*Republic* III, 413b).

14. Mead, *Works* 224.

15. Mead and Milton agree again on the outward effects of the Fall: "the despoiling of the nature of Man . . . is insinuated by his outward *nakedness;* that is, the obscuration of that glorious and celestial beauty which he had before his sin: the difference whereof was so great, that he could not endure afterwards to behold himself any more, but sought for a covering, even to *hide* himself from himself" (*Works* 233). Compare Milton's contention that the first stage of death after the Fall is "the loss of divine protection and favor, which results in the lessening of the majesty of the human countenance, and the degradation of the mind" (VI, 394). Adam and Eve thus seek any "vain Covering" to hide "thir guilt and dreaded shame" (IX, 1114). The only adequate cover for man will be that provided by the Messiah (see X, 211–23). "Cover" translates the Hebrew word for sacrifice.

FRANCIS HAYMAN AND THE DRAMATIC
INTERPRETATION OF *PARADISE LOST*

Mary D. Ravenhall

I N 1 7 4 9 Jacob Tonson III and his brother Richard published a two-volume quarto edition of *Paradise Lost* with annotations by the Reverend Thomas Newton and twelve plates designed by the English artist Francis Hayman (1708–1776).[1] Although he is best known for his decorative paintings at Vauxhall and for his oils depicting a variety of subjects produced during the decade 1745–1755, Hayman was also employed extensively as an illustrator, his earliest known designs, for Samuel Richardson's *Pamela*, being published in 1742. These illustrations were undertaken in collaboration with the French engraver and draughtsman Hubert Gravelot (1699–1773) and were immediately followed by a second collaborative series of thirty-six plates for Sir Thomas Hanmer's edition of Shakespeare, published in 1743–1744.[2] It was presumably his success as an illustrator of Shakespeare which led to the Milton commission. A letter to Hayman from the actor David Garrick, dated October 1745, indicates that the artist and editor Newton were already at work on the project at that time.

Hayman's plates offer a marked contrast to those designed by Dr. Henry Aldrich, Sir John Baptist Medina, and Bernard Lens for the first illustrated edition of *Paradise Lost* published by Jacob Tonson, Sr., in 1688, only fourteen years after Milton's death.[3] These early illustrations show us how Milton's contemporaries interpreted his epic poem and reveal their appreciation for his Christian subject matter, his use of allegory, and his complex literary allusions. In the years between 1712 and 1745 a growing body of criticism, dominated by the *Spectator* essays of Joseph Addison, tended to redefine *Paradise Lost* as a tragic or dramatic poem rather than an epic, and to praise Milton for his delineation of character rather than for his theological exposition.[4] As editor, Newton attempted to reproduce the bulk of this critical commentary in the form of extensive footnotes. He was thus in a position to convey the essence of a generation of Milton criticism to illustrator Hayman. The shift of critical emphasis from the theological to the dramatic aspects of *Paradise Lost* appears to have had a direct influence on Hayman's choice of subjects for illustration and on his mode of interpreting those subjects which were retained from the Aldrich-Medina-Lens series.

Hayman's illustration for Book I (fig. 1) essentially repeats the subject introduced by Aldrich in 1688, "Satan Arousing His Legions from the Lake of Fire," but whereas Aldrich's illustration (fig. 2) conflates a number of descriptions and episodes including the Council in Pandaemonium, Hayman has represented a specific dramatic moment when Satan, with ponderous shield and mastlike spear, stands on the beach of Hell and issues the command, "Awake, arise, or be forever fallen."[5] Beside him stands Beelzebub, making his first appearance in Miltonic illustration. Hayman seems to have drawn his characterization of Beelzebub not from the brief mention in Book I, but from the fuller description in Book II. At the Council in Pandaemonium, Beelzebub, second only to Satan in eminence, rises with grave aspect:

> and in his rising seem'd
> A Pillar of State; deep on his Front engraven
> Deliberation sat and public care;
> And Princely counsel in his face yet shone,
> Majestic through in ruin.   (II, 301–05)

Newton may have suggested the inclusion of Beelzebub to Hayman because of the praise Addison bestowed upon this passage. Certainly it is an innovation in the illustration of *Paradise Lost*, and one that remained popular throughout the century. Hayman is unique, however, in having captured the deliberative character of Beelzebub stressed by Milton and praised by Addison. The gesture he gives to Beelzebub, who stands frowning, hand to mouth, is that described by John Bulwer, author of *Chirologia: or The Naturall Language of the Hand* (London, 1644), as *Inventione labora*. According to Bulwer: "The finger in the mouth gnawn and suckt, is a gesture of serious and deep meditation, repentance, envy, anger, and threatened revenge."[6] Beelzebub, as the angel who seconds and elaborates upon Satan's suggestion for seeking revenge by working the destruction of God's new creation, is thus fitly depicted by Hayman as one who meditates inventively.

Hayman is not only the first artist to include Beelzebub, he is also the first to give the figures of the fallen angels completely human, or angelic, form. The horns, pointed ears, snaky locks, and batlike wings found in Aldrich's illustrations have been eliminated; instead the evil nature of Satan is now indicated by his scowling expression and upright hair. While this expression cannot be related precisely to any single emotion described by the French painter Charles Le Brun in his famous *Conférence*, it re-

Figure 2. Satan arousing his legions, after Aldrich.

Figure 1. Satan arousing his legions, after Hayman.

sembles somewhat that of Rage as well as that of Extreme Despair (fig. 3). The brows drawn down, the open mouth with exposed teeth, and the hair upon on end are all indications of violent emotion.[7] In representing Beelzebub and Satan as fully human figures Hayman was responding to criticism of Aldrich's illustration which appeared as early as 1695 in the commentary of Patrick Hume.[8] The English painter Jonathan Richardson likewise objected to representing Milton's devils with "horns, saucer eyes, ugly faces, tayls, and cloven feet." According to Richardson, a ruined archangel must have masculine strength and beauty, but marred with "guile, envy, malice, rage, lust, grief [and] despair."[9] Richardson's catalogue of emotions appropriate to Satan may well have sent Hayman to Le Brun's essay. Like Beelzebub, Satan uses a traditional gesture which can be found in Bulwer's treatise (p. 162): the outstretched

Extreme Desespoir

Figure 3. Extreme Despair, after Charles Le Brun.

arm and pointed finger of command. For the single symbolic figure used by Aldrich, Hayman has substituted a pair of vengeful warriors shown in the opening action of a play.

The action moves forward in Hayman's illustration for Book II, showing Satan's departure through Chaos (fig. 4). Although both Aldrich and his successor Louis Cheron had depicted Satan, Sin, and Death at the Gates of Hell, neither of these earlier artists attempted to capture a specific dramatic moment. Aldrich's illustration (fig. 5) suggests the conflict between Satan and Death as well as the departure, while Cheron's static composition relies upon figures drawn from Ripa's *Iconologia*, seemingly unrelated to Milton's text.[10] Hayman's Satan spreads his "Sail-broad Vans" for flight, "and in the surging smoke / Uplifted spurns the ground" (II, 927–29). His pointing finger indicates the realm through which he intends to travel, while his backward glance toward Sin and Death reminds us of the confederacy rather than the momentary conflict of these characters.

The notion of the confederacy of Satan, Sin, and Death had been stressed by Addison, whose comments were quoted by Newton: "[The reader] will likewise observe how naturally the three Persons concerned in this Allegory are tempted by one common Interest to enter into a Confederacy together, and how properly Sin is made the Portress of Hell, and the only Being that can open the Gates to that World of Tortures."[11] It is noteworthy that Hayman expresses this sense of confederacy not only by the triangular composition of the figures and the understanding gaze exchanged by Satan and Sin, but also by Sin's posture, which indicates that she has just opened the Gates of Hell, making possible Satan's search for the new creation, and by the gesture of Death, who points toward his grinning mouth in sign of the hunger soon to be assuaged:

> and Death
> Grinn'd horrible a ghastly smile, to hear
> His famine should be fill'd.   (II, 845–47)

Hayman's figure of Death, which combines the emaciated human form used by Aldrich with the conventional skeleton found in Cheron's illustration, carries his deadly dart and is the first to wear the crown which critics since the time of Hume had found suitable to the "king of terrors." His conflict with Satan, which to Voltaire seemed meaningless, is not represented, but his menace to mankind is manifested by expression and gesture.[12]

Hayman is also the first artist to illustrate Sin as the portress of Hell. In her left hand she holds the massive key to Hell Gate, while with her right she lowers one of the iron bars which had held fast the door:

Figure 4. Satan's departure through Chaos, after Hayman.

Figure 5. Satan encounters Sin and Death, after Aldrich.

> Thus saying, from her side the fatal Key,
> Sad instrument of all our woe, she took;
> And towards the Gate rolling her bestial train,
> Forthwith the huge Portcullis high up drew,
>
> . . . .
>
> then in the key-hole turns
> Th' intricate wards, and every Bolt and Bar
> Of massy Iron or solid Rock with ease
> Unfast'ns.
>
> (II, 871–79)

Hayman does not attempt to depict the thrice three-fold gates described in lines 645–48, showing only one pair of massive doors, but his composition makes far clearer than those of his predecessors that the gates existed to keep the fallen angels in Hell, and that Satan encounters Sin and Death inside these gates, not outside on the verge of Chaos where Aldrich and Cheron place them. Hayman does seem to have derived from Aldrich, however, the idea of representing a broken door (that on the right hangs as if it were unhinged) as a means of indicating that once opened the doors of Hell may never again be closed.

Collins-Baker has noted that from the 1749 edition onward, "Sin became more human, more like Lady Hamilton, and more innocent. She was made as attractive as her serpent limbs would permit."[13] Certainly Hayman's Sin is a more feminine figure than the blindfolded masculine Sin of Cheron or the hybrid creature seated on a heap of writhing serpents depicted by Aldrich. Newton's notes on the lines which describe Sin indicate a continued scholarly awareness of the associations between Sin, Scylla, and Cerberus,[14] but Hayman eliminates any visual reference to this association in favor of a more literal adherence to the text. Sin is a fair woman to the waist, ending in many a scaly fold, the points of her limblike appendages intended to indicate her mortal sting. The cry of hellhounds about her waist renders Milton's monsters adequately. Voltaire had found Milton's description of Sin loathsome;[15] Hayman makes her beautiful without violating the letter of Milton's text. He exchanges the allegorical overtones and moral impact of the scene for an emphasis on the dramatic interaction of these characters.

In 1688 Medina chose to emphasize the theological content of Book III with a symbolic representation of the conflict between good and evil (fig. 6); the Son in Heaven confronts Satan, newly arrived on earth, in a manner indicative of Milton's meaning but not actually in accord with his narrative. In the background a tiny figure of Uriel in the Sun welcomes Satan, disguised as a stripling cherub. Hayman has elevated this background incident to the status of major theme (fig. 7); good and evil

Figure 7. Satan and Uriel, after Hayman.

Figure 6. The Son in Heaven, after Medina.

confront one another as in Medina's illustration, but now within the context of the deceptive encounter described by Milton himself. Addison, who considered the abstruse doctrines of predestination, freewill and grace, incarnation, and redemption which form the themes of Book III to be "dry in themselves to the generality of Readers" (III, p. 142), lavished praise upon this incident of Satan's encounter with Uriel. Addison's only stricture, his observation that Milton's remarks on hypocrisy constitute a digression in the poem, was answered by Newton, who found the digression necessary to explain Satan's ability to deceive Uriel (I, p. 219). Newton and Garrick seem to have been responsible for suggesting this subject to Hayman, since in the letter mentioned above the actor says, "your drawings for Milton will do you great service, I have promis'd the Doctor [Newton] to read the third book and give him my opinion for the Drawing, which I'll send you."[16]

To illustrate Book IV, Hayman chose an entirely new subject, "Satan Spying Upon Adam and Eve in Paradise" (fig. 8). In 1688 Bernard Lens included several tiny figures of Adam and Eve in his plate for this book, and showed Satan perched on a tree in the form of a cormorant. Lens's main emphasis, however, was on the angelic figure of Uriel, who descends on a cloud to confer with Gabriel and his guard. Hayman rightly uses his illustration to emphasize the characters identified by Addision as the Principal Actors in Milton's poem, Adam and Eve. Behind them Satan, as fallen angel rather than as cormorant, grimaces in envy of their happiness. A second letter from Garrick to Hayman, dated August 1746, suggests that once again the actor may have influenced Hayman's interpretation of a Miltonic scene. The expression Hayman gives to Satan in plate IV is not unlike that Garrick describes as suitable to Iago, "with his Eyes looking askance (as Milton terms it) on Othello."[17] In his letter Garrick offers to demonstrate the expression when he next sees the artist. The same expression, however, occurs in Le Brun's *Conférence* in the plate illustrating Jealousy or Hatred (fig. 9). Satan's gesture, elbow bent and fist clenched, also has a specific meaning which serves to reveal his inner emotions. Bulwer's treatise identifies this gesture as *Minor* and explains it as follows: "To shew and shake the bended fist at one, is their habit who are angry, threaten, would strike terror, menace, revenge . . . and offer injury" (p. 57). Although Satan conceals himself and his gesture from Adam and Eve, his intention to injure them is made clear in his soliloquy:

> One fatal Tree there stands of Knowledge call'd,
> Forbidden them to taste.
>
> .   .   .   .

Figure 8. Satan observes Adam and Eve.

> O fair foundation laid whereon to build
> Thir ruin!   (IV, 514–22)

Whether derived directly from treatises or absorbed from Garrick's dem-
onstrations, Hayman has selected the gesture and expression appropriate
to the emotions Milton attributes to Satan.

While it seems probable that Garrick influenced Hayman's use of
gesture and expression in this scene, it is even more likely that Addison's
criticism dictated the choice of subject. Addison praises the description
of Adam and Even given in Book IV and specifically relates it to Satan's
jealous response: "The Description of them as they first appear'd to *Satan*,
is exquisitely drawn, and sufficient to make the fallen Angel gaze upon
them with all the Astonishment, and those Emotions of Envy, in which

Figure 9. Jealousy or Hatred, after Charles Le Brun.

he is represented. . . . There is a fine Spirit of Poetry in the lines which follow, wherein they are describ'd as sitting in a Bed of Flowers by the side of a Fountain amidst a mixed Assembly of Animals, . . . The Devil turn'd away with Envy at the sight of so much Happiness" (III, p. 174–79). Hayman illustrates precisely the passage praised by Addison, complete with fountain (waterfall), animals, and envious Satan. No longer shown as a symbolic cormorant, Satan now participates like a human character in the tragedy of the Fall.

In Plate V, Hayman introduced yet another new subject, Adam admiring sleeping Eve. Adam and Eve asleep, Satan as a toad whispering in Eve's ear, had appeared as one of the minor episodes in Lens's illustration for Book IV, but Hayman chose the ensuing scene, in which Adam observes Eve's discomposure:

His wonder was to find unwak'n'd *Eve*
With Tresses discompos'd, and glowing Cheek,
As through unquiet rest: hee on his side
Leaning half rais'd, with looks of cordial Love
Hung over her enamor'd.   (V, 9–13)

Steele had praised this passage in the *Tatler* as early as 1709, and Addison quotes it at length, stressing the tenderness of its sentiment: "*Adam* upon his awaking finds *Eve* still asleep, with an unusual Discomposure in her looks. The Posture in which he regards her, is described with a wonderful Tenderness, as the Whisper with which he awakens her, is the softest that ever was convey'd to the Lover's Ear" (III, p. 197). Jonathan Richardson, who concludes his commentary on *Paradise Lost* with a list of forty-four "Pictures" to be found in the poem, omits this scene from his catalogue, yet in a note upon the lines describing Adam leaning half raised he exclaims, "What a picture!" (p. 195). Thus Hayman's choice of incident was responsive not only to a generalized approval of Adam and Eve as lovers but also to praise of this specific passage.[18]

Hayman's illustration owes little to the work of his predecessors. Both Medina and Cheron introduce the figure of Raphael into their illustrations for Book V and make reference to his discussion with Adam concerning the eating habits of angels. Hayman restricts his composition to the figures of the principal actors, Adam and Eve, and does not include Raphael until Book VII. By so doing he omits one of the digressions to which Addison had objected and also the visible warning which Raphael's presence in the garden conveys. The scene selected does, however, have its own overtones of impending disaster, for upon being awakened Eve tells Adam of her troublesome dream presaging the temptation. Addison comments on this feature of the scene (III, p. 199), and Richardson says of Eve's speech recounting her dream, "This is the Dawn of the Fall" (p. 196). To a reader familiar with the poem, Hayman's lovers in their idyllic setting are far from secure in their bliss.

To illustrate Book VI, Louis Cheron divided his representation of the War in Heaven into two parts, a headpiece depicting the first day's battle, which shows Michael trampling upon a nude Satan, and an endpiece illustrating the Son in his chariot, drawn by the symbolic beasts of Ezekiel and Isaiah. Hayman returns to the dramatic moment depicted by Medina, in which the Son is seen driving the rebel angels falling from Heaven (fig. 10). Hayman's angels are nude, like those of Cheron, rather than wearing the armor depicted by Medina and described by Milton, and Hayman seems to have derived from Cheron the notion of identify-

Figure 10. The Son defeats Satan, after Hayman.

ing Satan. There is nothing in Milton's text to justify this singling out of Satan, but clearly the figure who holds a spear and shakes his fist while glaring directly at the Son with an expression again resembling Le Brun's Extreme Despair is intended to represent the Arch Fiend. Hayman retains Satan as a major character in the drama of the Fall, although Milton has been careful to diminish his importance in this episode, concentrating instead on the victory of the Son.

Hayman has increased the dramatic impact of his design not only by identifying the figure of Satan but also by compressing the composition, enlarging the figure of the Son so that his gestures and expression are made far clearer than they are in the illustrations of Medina and Cheron, and bringing him into proximity with his enemies.[19] The composition is in fact based on an engraving after a drawing by Rubens showing St. Michael driving the rebel angels from Heaven; the Son's gesture and expression are both derived from this source, as is the foreground figure grasping a broken sword.[20]

The plates Hayman designed for Books VII and VIII closely resemble those illustrating Books IV and V, with their emphasis on the nude beauty of Adam and Eve and the lush foliage of Paradise. While the compositions themselves lack dramatic impact the subjects they represent (Raphael describing the Creation to Adam and Eve, Raphael departing from Paradise) continue the emphasis on a single group of three actors found in all of Hayman's illustrations excepting that for Book VI. Hayman does not attempt to depict the actual events of Creation, as Medina and Cheron had done, nor does he reveal the details of Adam's digressive story of his awakening in Paradise and meeting with Eve. Milton's retelling of Genesis is simply suggested by the discourse between man and angel found in plate VII. The departure of Raphael in plate VIII prepares the reader for the final act of Milton's tragedy.

Hayman's change of emphasis from the theological to the dramatic or psychological elements of *Paradise Lost* is nowhere more evident than in his plate for Book IX (fig. 11). Medina's original illustration depicted Milton's account of the Fall in a series of episodes showing the quarrel of Adam and Eve, their separation, Eve's temptation by the serpent, Adam's temptation by Eve, and their grief and fear upon realizing that they have sinned. The most important figure in Medina's illustration, however, is that of Satan, now grossly deformed, eyeing the unsuspecting serpent who will soon become his vehicle for the seduction of Eve. Medina stresses Satan's role in bringing about the Fall of Man. Hayman, on the other hand, eliminates the figure of Satan from his composition. He shows the precise moment when Eve, returning from her encounter with the serpent, offers the forbidden fruit to a horrified Adam:

> On th' other side, *Adam*, soon as he heard
> The fatal Trespass done by *Eve*, amaz'd,
> Astonied stood and Blank, while horror chill
> Ran through his veins, and all his joints relax'd;
> From his slack hand the Garland wreath'd for Eve
> Down dropp'd and all the faded Roses shed.   (IX, 888–93)

Hayman's Adam throws up his hands in a gesture of astonishment, while the dropped garland can still be seen in midair. Following Le Brun, Hayman gives Adam the round eyes and open mouth appropriate to his emo-

Figure 11. Adam astonished.

tional state; Eve is shown with her head inclined and her eyes moderately open, an expression of Simple Love. To Milton's succinct lines, "in her face excuse / Came prologue," Richardson added the commentary: "She put on those forc'd Smiles and Appearances of Love and Joy, which yet were intended as Silent Pleadings in Extenuation, or to cover a Consciousness of Guilt" (pp. 427–28). Hayman's illustration concentrates on this psychological interaction between husband and wife.

Newton himself, rather than Addison, must have served as Hayman's mentor in the selection of this scene. Addison merely mentions the incident as a pleasing preparation for the speech that follows. Newton, however, quotes the lines, "From his slack hand the Garland wreath'd for Eve / Down dropp'd," and comments upon them, "The beauty of the numbers, as well as the image here, must strike every reader" (II, p. 190). Newton also comments on the bough of fairest fruit which Hayman is careful to show.

In choosing to illustrate Book X by showing the judgment of Adam and Eve (fig. 12), Hayman was again rejecting the work of his predecessors in favor of an entirely new subject. The departing angels shown by both Medina and Cheron are omitted, as are the allegorical figures of Sin and Death. Addison had not approved of the inclusion of these figures in an epic poem, particularly in the active roles assigned them in Book X. He did, however, praise the judgment scene in a passage quoted by Newton, "The Guilt and Confusion of our first Parents standing naked before their Judge, is touch'd on with great Beauty" (Addison, III, p. 331).

Figure 12. The Son judges Adam and Eve.

Addison notes that the Son pronounces judgment upon the three offend-
ers, which perhaps explains why Hayman includes the serpent although
he is not described as being present at the scene in Milton's text. Newton
adds no new praise to Addison's, but his notes on the lines describing the
judgment stress how close the poem is to Scripture here. This closeness
to Scripture may have seemed to justify the use of elements drawn from
biblical paintings, although by doing this Hayman was forced to depart
at some points from the text of *Paradise Lost*.[21] He shows the Son arriving in Paradise accompanied by a cluster of supporting angels, while
Milton describes the attendant spirits as proceeding only as far as Heav-
en's gate (X, 88). Adam and Eve are not hidden among the trees (X,
100–01) but appear in full view of their approaching judge. Hayman does,
however, attempt to depict the Son as he is described by Milton, the mild
judge who tempers justice with mercy (X, 78, 96). Richardson devotes
a lengthy passage to the difficulties encountered by the artist who attempts
to represent the Son, as yet unincarnate, described by Milton:

Here must be a Picture Such as we have never known Aim'd at by any Master, . . .
Here 'tis Certain we must Avoid the Traditional Likeness of what he was on
Earth, or in Heaven Afterwards, we are alike to Avoid what is Usually given
to God when he is Represented by Painting, though 'tis said *the Son is the Express Image of his Person*, . . . There should be the Paternal Majesty shining in
the Filial Divinity; a Dignity and Beauty Different from the Angelic Characters,
Less Youthful and More Majestic; a Mediatorial Sweetness and Sublimity. . . .
what we are Speaking of is Vastly Beyond [Raphael's Transfiguration] and requires the Utmost Stretch of the Most Lively, Accurate, Judicious, and best In-
structed Imagination. (Pp. 100–01)

Hayman's Son is clearly more youthful than the traditional figure of God
the Father, though his bearded face imparts the necessary touch of paternal majesty. His mild expression attempts to convey the mediatorial sweetness described by Richardson, while the gesture he uses, forefinger bowed
down, indicates reproval (Bulwer, *Chirologia*, p. 170). The attendant
angels and rays of glory which surround the figure of the Son convey the
sublimity of his person. Hayman's use of readymade motifs has not pre-
vented him from adapting these in a manner which indicates his responsiveness to Milton's text. These borrowed motifs furthermore enable
Hayman to focus the reader's attention not only on Addison's Principal
Actors, but also on his choice for hero of *Paradise Lost*.

Michael revealing the future to Adam, the theme chosen by Hayman to illustrate Book XI, had been introduced as a background episode
by Medina and repeated by Cheron, who included a depiction of the war

among men in his headpiece. Hayman dramatized this traditional subject by placing large figures of Adam and Michael on a promontory in the foreground of his composition, while in the background he represents the first vision, the murder of Abel. Addision, who greatly admired Book XI and felt it had been unduly neglected by other critics, was generous in his praise of the episode of Cain and Abel, while Newton, after quoting Addison's remarks, added a long discussion of his own, concluding, "This is very properly made the first vision, and is so much inlarg'd upon, as it is of Adams immediate descendents" (II, p. 338–39). Thus in his reworking of a theme illustrated by his predecessors Hayman remained responsive to contemporary criticism. The vision of Abel's murder allowed him to depict the interaction of two characters rather than the diffuse masses found in the Flood or the Lazar House.

While the influence of Newton, Garrick, and Addison can be detected in many of Hayman's choices of subject, it is the critical commentary of Jonathan Richardson which corresponds most closely to the new interpretation Hayman gives to the Expulsion scene illustrating Book XII (fig. 13). Aldrich's composition (fig. 14), based on a design by Raphael for the Vatican Loggie, showed Michael driving Adam and Eve from Paradise with a fiery sword; Cheron's headpiece continued this biblical tradition. As early as 1695, however, Hume criticized Aldrich's plate as a misrepresentation of the more kindly description of the Expulsion given by Milton in lines 637–40:

> In either hand the hast'ning Angel caught
> Our ling'ring Parents, and to th'Eastern Gate
> Led them direct, and down the Cliff as fast
> To the subjected Plain.

According to Hume, Aldrich has represented the angel "shoving them out, as we say, by Head and Shoulders."[22] In 1712 Addision wrote at length on Michael's speech to Adam in Book XII, describing it as an attempt to offset the tragedy of the Fall by the promise of future Redemption and pointing out the parallel between Michael's leading of Adam and Eve and the story of Lot.[23] It was Richardson, however, who first extolled Milton's observance of the doctrine of *felix culpa*, or the Fortunate Fall. Richardson included "Adam and Eve Forsaking Paradise Led by the Angel" in his list of pictures to be found in *Paradise Lost* and described the pair as "Recompens'd with Comfort and Joy. . . . Now They and Wee Stand no longer on the Sandy Foundation of Our Own Righteousness but on God's Paternal Goodness . . . a Happier State Than that of Eden" (p. 535). Richardson further emphasized Milton's description of the Ex-

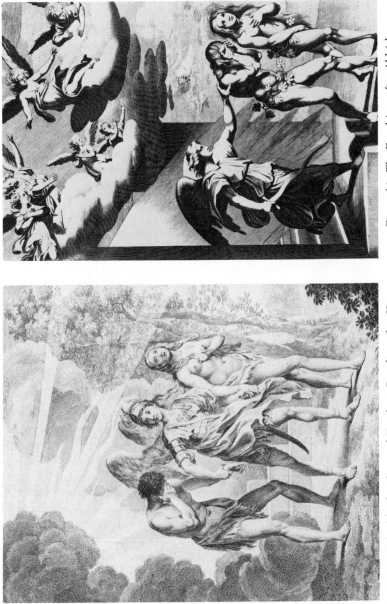

Figure 13. Michael leads Adam and Eve from Paradise, after Hayman.

Figure 14. The Expulsion, after Aldrich.

pulsion by quoting from Genesis the account of the removal of Lot from Sodom: "And while he Lingered the Men laid hold upon his Hand, and upon the hand of his Wife, and upon the Hand of his two Daughters, the Lord being merciful unto him: And they brought him forth" (Gen. xix, 16). Hayman is the first artist to show the archangel Michael leading Adam and Eve from Paradise rather than driving them forth with a fiery sword.[24] What makes Hayman's design more than a literal rendering of Milton's text, however, is the manner in which Michael grasps his charges by the hand. Bulwer calls this gesture *Admoneo* and relates it to the story of Lot:

To take hold gently of another's Hand, is a gesture used by those who admonish and perswade, . . . Such an intention of gesture, but with more vehemency of expression the Angels used to *Lot*, while he lingred in Sodome, laying hold upon his Hand, and upon the Hand of his wife, and upon the Hand of his two daughters, to admonish and perswade them to sudden departure from that accursed City. (Pp. 78–79)

Hayman's Michael uses precisely this gesture of admonition and persuasion, with additional vehemency of expression (shown by Michael's firm grasp upon Adam's wrist) which makes it appropriate to the parallel with Lot. The leading of Lot and his family was not an expulsion, however, but a salvation from an accursed city. By visually repeating the parallel between Milton's version of the Expulsion and Lot's rescue, Hayman reminds the viewer of the promise of salvation Michael brings to Adam and Eve along with God's order to remove them from Paradise.

In this discussion of Hayman's series of twelve plates for *Paradise Lost* I have attempted to demonstrate both the extent of his innovations and the interrelationship between these innovations and the critical assessments of Milton's poem published during the first half of the eighteenth century. Hayman's illustrations have been criticized for their theatricality and rococo prettiness. If Hayman's interpretation of *Paradise Lost* can be said to resemble a theatrical production, however, it is not because his scenes resemble stage sets or because his figures use gestures and expressions found as frequently in painting as in the theater, but because he depicts the poem as a series of specific dramatic actions: Satan calling his legions, Satan deceiving Uriel, Adam astonished by sinful Eve, and so on. Although this dramatized interpretation necessarily excludes the epic richness of the original, omitting the references to digressions, allegories, and literary allusions found in the work of earlier illustrators, it had a validity for Hayman's contemporaries that may be overlooked today. In Addison's words, "the Principal Actors in this poem are not only our Progenitors, but our Representatives. We have an Actual Interest in every Thing They do, and no less than our utmost Happiness is concerned, and lies at Stake in all their Behaviour" (II, p. 565). The figures of Adam and Eve, which so charmingly dominate Hayman's designs, held a universality for his viewers that must be recalled when appraising his dramatic mode of illustration.

University of Illinois at Urbana-Champaign

NOTES

1. Hayman's illustrations have been discussed briefly by C. H. Collins-Baker, "Some Illustrators of Milton's *Paradise Lost*," *The Library* 5th ser., III (1948), 1–21, 101–21; Leonard B. Kimbrell, "The Illustrations of *Paradise Lost* in England — 1688–1802," (Ph.D. diss., University of Iowa, 1965), pp. 157–207; and Marcia Pointon, *Milton and English Art* (Toronto, 1970), pp. 47–57. None of these scholars, however, has attempted a close examination of the designs in relation to the text, nor have they considered the connection between the subjects illustrated and contemporary criticism. This essay is an outgrowth of my doctoral dissertation, "Illustrations of *Paradise Lost* in England, 1688–1802," completed under the direction of Professor Jerrold Ziff at the University of Illinois at Urbana-Champaign in 1980. I wish to thank Professor Ziff for suggesting the dissertation topic and providing advice and encouragement during the preparation of several portions for publication.

2. For an account of the Shakespeare illustrations see W. M. Merchant, "Francis Hayman's Illustrations of Shakespeare," *Shakespeare Quarterly*, IX (1958), 141–47. Hayman's designs for *PL* were engraved by Simon François Ravenet (1706–1774) and Charles Grignion (1717–1810).

3. The 1688 illustrations are examined in the works cited in note 1; the complete set is reproduced in Pointon, *Milton and English Art*. Additional discussion may be found in Helen Gardner, "Milton's First Illustrator," *Essays and Studies*, n.s., IX (1956), 27–38; Suzanne Boorsch, "The 1688 *Paradise Lost* and Dr. Aldrich," *Metropolitan Museum Journal*, VI (1972), 133–50; and the author's "Sources and Meaning in Dr. Aldrich's 1688 Illustrations of *Paradise Lost*," *ELN*, XIX (1982), 208–18.

4. For a sampling of Milton criticism during this period see John T. Shawcross, *Milton: The Critical Heritage* (London, 1970), and *Milton, 1732–1801: The Critical Heritage* (London, 1972). Early eighteenth-century commentary on *Paradise Lost* is examined in more detail in the author's dissertation cited above, pp. 156–93 and 257–89.

5. I, 330. Quotations from *Paradise Lost* are from *John Milton: Complete Poems and Major Prose*, ed. Merritt Y. Hughes (Indianapolis, 1957).

6. Bulwer, *Chirologia*, p. 158. Most of the gestures described by Bulwer are illustrated in three plates and can be compared visually with the Hayman illustrations. Subsequent references in the text are to the 1644 edition. A facsimile edited by James W. Cleary (Carbondale, Ill., 1974) reproduces the illustrations.

7. Charles Le Brun, *Conférence sur l'expression générale et particulière des passions*, illus. B. Picart. 2nd ed. (Amsterdam, 1713) p. 27–29. Figures 3 and 9 are repro-

duced from this edition. First published in Paris in 1698, the *Conférence* appeared in English translation in 1701 and 1734 and included the Picart engravings.

8. Patrick Hume, *Annotations on Milton's "Paradise Lost"* (London, 1695), p. 39.

9. Jonathan Richardson, *Explanatory Notes and Remarks on Milton's "Paradise Lost"* (London, 1734), p. 37. Further citations will be given in the text.

10. In 1720 Jacob Tonson, Jr., published a two-volume edition of Milton's *Poetical Works* with headpieces, endpieces, and illustrated initials by Sir James Thornhill and Louis Cheron. Since the visual evidence suggests that Hayman was familiar with these designs, as well as those of Aldrich, Medina, and Lens, comparisons will be made where pertinent. Most of Cheron's illustrations have been reproduced in Pointon, *Milton and English Art*, pp. 17–26.

11. Joseph Addison, *The Spectator*, ed. D. F. Bond (Oxford, 1965), III, pp. 119–20. Subsequent references to Addison's essays on *Paradise Lost* will be given in the text.

12. Voltaire's remarks seem to have a direct bearing on Hayman's version of the scene: "I see with Admiration Sin, the Portress of Hell, opening the Gates of the Abiss, but unable to shut them again; that is really beautiful because tis true. But what signifies Satan and Death quarreling together, grinning at one another, and ready to fight?" *Voltaire's Essay on Epic Poetry*, ed. F. D. White (Albany, 1915), p. 140.

13. Collins-Baker, "Illustrators," p. 7.

14. John Milton, *Paradise Lost*, ed. Thomas Newton (London, 1749), I, pp. 128–29. Further citations of Newton's commentary in the text will refer to this edition.

15. "That Complication of Horrors, that mixture of Incest, that Heap of Monsters, that Loathsomeness so far fetch'd, cannot but shock a Reader of delicate Taste." Voltaire, *Essay*, p. 139.

16. K. A. Burnim, "The Significance of Garrick's Letters to Hayman," *Shakespeare Quarterly*, IX (1958), 150. The letter quoted is in the Folger Shakespeare Library, MSV a. 11.

17. Burnim, "Garrick's Letters," p. 151. The letter is in the Folger Shakespeare Library, Case II, folder b, 746.

18. Voltaire's comment (*Essay*, p. 133) is typical of early eighteenth-century response to Milton's lovers: "It is observable that in all other Poems Love is represented as a Vice, in Milton only 'tis a Virtue. The Pictures he draws of it, are naked as the Persons he speaks of, and as venerable. . . . There is Softness, Tenderness, and Warmth without Lasciviousness."

19. Pointon has described the Son as "perched on the edge of a column of cloud whilst below the rebel angels fall toward Hell" (*Milton and English Art*, p. 52). The figure of the Son as drawn by Hayman, however, is not perched upon a column of cloud but stands upon his chariot, immediately above the falling figures of Satan and the rebel angels. The column of cloud to which Pointon refers occurs only in later reworkings of Hayman's designs by the engraver J. S. Mueller, first published in 1750. Mueller reduced the size of Hayman's original plates from $8\frac{1}{2} \times 6\frac{3}{4}$ inches to $6 \times 3\frac{3}{4}$ inches, in most cases adding elements at the top and bottom of the composition to fill the new vertical space. In Plate VI, however, he extended the central cloud area, producing the effect noted by Pointon. A number of Pointon's remarks on the Hayman illustrations suffer from her apparent reliance on Mueller's reworkings of the artist's designs.

20. The engraving, made by Lucas Vorsterman in 1621, is discussed and illustrated in M. Rooses, *L'Oeuvre de P. P. Rubens* (Antwerp, 1886–89), I, pp. 94–95, pl. 22.

21. Hayman's composition for plate X is based on a combination of sources, engravings after two paintings by the seventeenth-century artists Antoine Coypel and Domenichino.

22. Hume, *Annotations*, p. 321.

23. Addison, III, 389. Addison's reference to this parallel is inaccurate; he mentions only a single angel while Richardson's quotation from Genesis reminds the reader that there were several angels.

24. Although Merritt Y. Hughes, "Some Illustrators of Milton: The Expulsion from Paradise," *JEGP*, LX (1961), 670–79, credits Blake with being the first artist to recognize the joyous aspect of the conclusion of *Paradise Lost*, a number of other scholars have observed Hayman's innovation in the illustration of this scene. See K. Svendsen, "John Martin and the Expulsion Scene of *Paradise Lost*," *SEL*, I (1961), 63–73; Collins-Baker, "Illustrators," p. 3; Pointon, *Milton and English Art*, p. 57; Kimbrell, "Illustrations of *PL*," p. 205.

MORTALS' CHIEFEST ENEMY

J. M. Evans

I N H I S useful study of education and literary taste in the seventeenth century John R. Mulder observes that "one of the most critical arguments in *Paradise Lost* finally turns upon an etymological pun."[1] The argument in question takes place shortly before the Fall in Book IX and concerns Eve's proposal that she and Adam should work in different parts of the garden. The pun is on the word "secure," which, according to Mulder, could mean either "safe, free from care" (*sine cura*) or "responsible for oneself, in one's own care" (*se cura*). Eve, he believes, has only the first of these senses in mind when she vigorously rejects any suggestion that the state of innocence might not be "secure to single or combin'd."[2] Adam, on the other hand, while admitting that "the word, so interpreted, indeed applies to their condition in paradise . . . goes on to say that it also implies that man must 'care for himself'":

> O Woman, best are all things as the will
> Of God ordain'd them, his creating hand
> Nothing imperfet or deficient left
> Of all that he Created, much less Man,
> Or aught that might his happie State secure,
> Secure from outward force; within himself
> The danger lies, yet lies within his power.   (IX, 343–49)

The progression from physical safety (*sine cura*) to personal responsibility (*se cura*) in lines 348–49 demonstrates, in Mulder's view, that "the two senses are interdependent: man in paradise is 'secure' or 'free from fear of external harm' *because* he is 'secure' or 'in his own care'" (pp. 87, 88).

This analysis, it seems to me, seriously underestimates the extent and wholly misinterprets the significance of Milton's pun. To begin with, the play on "secure" goes a good deal further than Mulder acknowledges, for, shortly after qualifying Eve's use of the word, Adam proceeds to use it in a third and very different sense. Fearing that his wife may actively seek out an opportunity to prove how "safe" she is "in her own care," he assures her that "trial will come unsought" (IX, 366). Then, as he ponders the implications of this prediction, he adds:

111

But if thou think, trial unsought may finde
Us both securer then thus warnd thou seemst,
Go; for thy stay, not free, absents thee more.   (IX, 370–72)[3]

If "secure" meant here what it meant less than twenty-five lines earlier,[4] Adam would be telling Eve that since it is safer to stay together and wait for temptation she should leave him and go off in search of it. Unless he has succumbed to the diversions of irony or the doom of nonsense (both, one would have thought, postlapsarian modes of discourse),[5] he must be telling her something else, as Richard Bentley was the first to remark. "Securer," he commented in his edition of Paradise Lost (1732), "is a word of ambiguous Meaning: it may signify Safer: or Carelesser, Negligenter; which Sense is here design'd."[6] Adam's point, then, is that the more "secure" they are in this third sense, the less "secure" they are likely to be in the first. In Francis Quarles's words, "the way to be safe is never to be secure."[7]

Mulder's failure to notice this critical extension of the original pun may well be the result of a mistaken assumption he makes at the very beginning of his analysis, namely that the only ambiguous element in the word is the prefix se. The Latin securus, he notes, "is a combination of se and cura. The latter is 'care,' but the seventeenth century was less sure of the meaning and derivation of se" (p. 87). In fact, the seventeenth century was not at all sure of the meaning of cura either, for like "care" it had two radically different senses, one negative ("anxiety," "worry," "trouble") and one positive ("attention," "heed," "alertness"). Security, therefore, could signify either a blissful absence of anxiety or a morally reprehensible lack of due concern, and the ambiguity is clearly reflected in the dictionaries of the period. Robert Cawdrey, John Bullokar, and Henry Cockeram, for instance, all gloss secure with the equally ambiguous "careless" while Thomas Cooper, Francis Holyoke, and Christopher Wase include both "safe" and "negligent" among the English equivalents of securus.[8]

It is, of course, upon this latter stage of the pun rather than upon the former, as Mulder claims, that the disagreement between Adam and Eve "finally turns." Despite its etymological deftness, many readers find the gyration a rather violent one. As Low remarks, most commentators on Paradise Lost "have seen a sudden and surprising shift in these lines," and it is not hard to see why.[9] After mustering an increasingly forceful series of arguments against Eve's proposal that they should work separately, Adam abruptly changes his mind and provides her with a plausible reason for disregarding all his previous objections. On the face of it at least, Low appears to be quite justified in claiming that Adam's eventual permission is "exactly the opposite of what he seems to be building up to — a prohibition. It reverses the whole line of his argument."[10]

How, then, are we to account for this extraordinary volte-face? Low believes that "since direct argument has proved useless [Adam] is trying reverse psychology."[11] Other, less charitable, critics maintain that he is simply throwing in the towel. "What . . . was Adam's motive in giving way?" enquires E. M. W. Tillyard in a seminal discussion of the scene. "Perhaps," he replies, "mistaken chivalry. When he saw Eve yielding, he could not bear not to meet her half way," and as a result failed to exercise "the authority it was his duty to assert."[12] Fredson Bowers also finds Adam guilty of "an effeminate abdication of his male responsibility" but suggests that it was motivated by "hurt feelings that Eve must want to work apart from him because she is tired of his company."[13] John C. Ulreich is even more reproachful. According to him, Adam "knows his decision is mistaken," and takes it only "because of the insecurity of his love, from his fear of not being loved, out of concern for himself rather than for Eve."[14] The hero of *Paradise Lost*, it thus appears, was fondly overcome with female charm long before the actual Fall. In Bowers's view "the two episodes are identical," and Dennis H. Burden concurs. "Adam's uxoriousness [consists] not only in his eating the fruit when it was offered to him," he argues, "but also in his yielding to his wife's arguments that they should garden separately."[15]

As Tillyard's initial question reveals, the basic premise underlying these interpretations of the scene is that Adam's last minute change of heart requires more explanation than the text itself provides. His ostensible reason for letting Eve have her way, they all assume, is not to be taken seriously. Tillyard dismisses it as "specious," and Bowers calls it a "pseudo-rationalization" comparable with those which Adam offers later in favor of eating the forbidden fruit. So great is the "irrationality of Adam's permission," Bowers argues, that no one could believe he was "actually convinced of the truth of the reasons he gave when he allowed Eve to depart."[16] From which it follows, presumably, that Adam's so-called "last reasoning words" (IX, 379) were nothing of the kind. His concern for avoiding a third, and potentially harmful, form of "security" was merely a piece of face-saving sophistry, a hastily improvised attempt to conceal his surrender to conjugal infatuation.

I would like to suggest that far from concealing anything, Adam's etymological reflections articulate the fundamental moral principle which has informed his debate with Eve from the very outset, namely, the importance of paying attention. The whole point of Eve's opening speech, after all, is that the pleasure they take in each other's company may distract them from the task at hand, and so induce them to be physically (if not morally) negligent:

> For while so near each other thus all day
> Our taske we choose, what wonder if so near
> Looks intervene and smiles, or object new
> Casual discourse draw on, which intermits
> Our dayes work, brought to little, though begun
> Early, and th' hour of Supper comes unearn'd.   (IX, 220–25)

In order to keep their minds on the job, she concludes, they would be better advised to divide their labors. So long as they continue to work together, they run the risk of neglecting their horticultural duties.

Adam's response to his wife's suggestions has often been described as indecisive, and so in a way it is. For at this stage of his development he is still engaged in what Barbara Lewalski has called the process of "human growth by trial and error." In the state of innocence, she argues, the first pair habitually "respond to a new situation by one or two false starts or false guesses before they find or are led to the proper stance."[17] Among the false starts that Adam makes in the present scene is the disastrous suggestion that Eve is incapable of resisting temptation without his assistance. Although he could perhaps yield to a "short absence" (IX, 248), he tells her, "other doubt possesses me, least harm / Befall thee sever'd from me" (IX, 251–52) — not, as Eve could hardly fail to notice, lest harm befall *me* severed from *thee*. He may go on to reassure her that if they remain together "each / To other speedie aide might lend at need" (IX, 259–60), but the lop-sided form of his initial doubt has already made it clear that in his view she is the only one who is likely to need help.

When Adam eventually finds the proper stance, as he does shortly afterward, it turns out to be a variant of the point that Eve had made in her opening speech. After reminding her of Satan's subtlety (as evidenced by his ability to seduce angels) and cautioning her against rejecting "others aid" (IX, 308), Adam confesses:

> I from the influence of thy looks receave
> Access in every Vertue, in thy sight
> More wise, more watchful, stronger, if need were
> Of outward strength; while shame, thou looking on,
> Shame to be overcome or over-reacht
> Would utmost vigor raise, and rais'd unite.   (IX, 309–14)

Whereas Eve had begun the debate by arguing that if they worked separately they would be less likely to neglect their physical tasks ("our dayes work," IX, 224), Adam now maintains that if they remain together they will be in a better position to fulfil their moral duties ("good workes," IX, 234), specifically their obligation to resist the Devil's assaults. Since Satan "watches" (IX, 257) for a chance to do them harm, they too must keep their eyes open. The "looks" (IX, 222) which Eve feared might intermit their day's work will serve rather, Adam insists, to intensify his resistance to evil. If he is "more watchful" (IX, 311) in her presence, he concludes rather plaintively, why shouldn't she be more alert in his?

By now, unfortunately, Eve has got the bit firmly between her teeth. Still preoccupied with Adam's suggestion that her "faith" (IX, 286) might prove to be less firm than his, she replies that unless they are "endu'd / Single with like defence" (IX, 324–25) their virtue is meaningless:

> And what is Faith, Love, Vertue unassaid
> Alone, without exterior help sustain'd?
> Let us not then suspect our happie State
> Left so imperfet by the Maker wise,
> As not secure to single or combin'd.
> Fraile is our happiness, if this be so,
> And Eden were no Eden thus expos'd.   (IX, 335–41)

In view of the emphasis upon individual self-sufficiency in these lines it is hard to see how Mulder can maintain that "Eve's 'secure' obviously means *sine cura* 'free from care'" (p. 87) rather than *se cura* "in one's own care." For to be left "in her own care" is precisely what Eve is demanding here. Confident of her ability to resist temptation without any help from her husband, she claims, in effect, that if they are not "secure" in the sense of *se cura* then they are not "secure" in the sense of *sine cura* either. It is Eve, not Adam, who insists that "the two senses are interdependent."

The point of Adam's rejoinder, in turn, is not that "man in paradise is 'secure' or 'free from fear of external harm' *because* he is 'secure' or 'in his own care'" as Mulder would have us believe (p. 88). It is, rather, that *although* man may be free of external harm he is still vulnerable to internal threats to his well-being. Security in the second of the senses Mulder has identified is no guarantee of security in the first, Adam informs his wife, for there is always the danger of being betrayed by what is false within:

> Against his will he can receave no harme.
> But God left free the Will, for what obeyes
> Reason, is free, and Reason he made right,
> But bid her well beware, and still erect,
> Least by some faire appeering good surpris'd

> She dictate false, and misinforme the Will
> To do what God expressly hath forbid.   (IX, 350–56)

The key element here, it seems to me, is not so much the theme of moral illusion, important though that is, as the repeated warnings against being "surprised," that is, against the third kind of security. In his preceding speech Adam had asserted that he was "more watchful" (IX, 311) in Eve's presence than he would be on his own. Now he gives another reason why being "watchful" is so essential. It is not simply that they have an enemy who "watches" (IX, 257) for an opportunity to corrupt them. It is also that reason may "fall into deception unaware" (IX, 362) if she fails to keep "strictest watch as she was warnd" (IX, 363). In order to ensure that they remain "ware," therefore, he proposes that "I should mind thee oft, and mind thou me" (IX, 358). As A. J. A. Waldock has rightly emphasized, attention is of the essence: "Our task is to keep our reason in good condition, braced up and alert; it is our duty not to allow it to be caught napping."[18] The price of innocence in Eden is the same as the price of liberty outside it.

It is at this juncture of the argument that Adam introduces the prospect of a "trial unsought" (IX, 370), gives his pun on "secure" an additional twist, and offers to let Eve go off on her own after all. Despite the variety of explanations they have put forward to account for his "permission" (IX, 378), the commentators whose opinions I summarized earlier seem to be in general agreement on three points: first, that Adam's decision was sudden; second, that it was prompted by considerations other than those acknowledged in his speech; and third, that it was a mistake. As regards the first point, John Peter seems to me to be exaggerating only slightly when he claims that "far from being sudden, [Adam's] decision is almost inevitable."[19] For the past seventy lines or so Adam has been insisting, with Hamlet, that "the readiness is all" (*Ham.* V, ii, 215), that watchfulness is the only guarantee of their well-being. If, as he has just come to suspect, their watchfulness is likely to be heightened by Eve's departure, it is hard to see how he could fail to approve their separation. The only reason he had withdrawn his original offer to yield to a "short absence" (IX, 248) was the proximity of their "malicious Foe " (IX, 253). Now that the foe appears to pose a greater threat when they are together than when they are apart, it is only reasonable to renew his consent to a "short retirement" (IX, 250). His decision to pursue the course of action that minimizes the risk of succumbing to "security" is the logical culmination of his entire argument.

The second point (concerning Adam's motivation) is more difficult to contend with, for it consists of little but conjecture. Certainly, none of the motives that has been imputed to Adam has any basis in the actual text. There is no reason to suppose, with Tillyard, that he gives way because he thinks Eve is about to yield. Nor is there any evidence to support the view that Adam feels either "hurt" (Bowers), "unloved" (Ulreich), or "uxorious" (Burden) at this juncture of the poem. On the contrary, everything we have learned about him during the preceding five books would lead us to believe that he consents to Eve's departure for no other reason than the one he adduces. In the state of innocence, as I have remarked elsewhere, the whole person speaks in unison.[20] Not until the forbidden fruit has been tasted does there appear to be a disjunction between what Adam and Eve say and what they mean. To assume that Adam is being less than completely sincere in the explanation he offers for allowing Eve to leave him is to blur the distinction between pre- and postlapsarian discourse.

About the rightness or wrongness of Adam's decision to let his wife go off on her own there is, perhaps, more room for disagreement. The mere fact that Eve yielded to temptation so soon after her departure may well persuade us that Adam's consent was, in Bowers' words, "a fatal blunder," though there is more than a hint of the *post hoc ergo propter hoc* fallacy in such a line of argument.[21] A more substantial objection to Bowers's view, however, is that it commits us to accepting the demeaning estimate of Eve's moral status which Adam offers in Book X:

> But for thee
> I had persisted happie, had not thy pride
> And wandring vanitie, when lest was safe,
> Rejected my forewarning, and disdain'd
> Not to be trusted, longing to be seen
> Though by the Devil himself, him overweening
> To over-reach, but with the Serpent meeting
> Fool'd and beguil'd, by him thou, I by thee,
> To trust thee from my side, imagin'd wise,
> Constant, mature, proof against all assaults,
> And understood not all was but a shew
> Rather then solid vertu, all but a Rib
> Crooked by nature. (X, 873–85)

The problem with this is obvious: if Eve was created "crooked by nature," then she cannot be held morally accountable for eating the forbidden fruit. We should not be surprised if a "fair defect Of Nature" (X, 891), as Adam calls her shortly afterward, acts defectively. Unless Eve was "sufficient to have stood" (III, 99), her Maker has only himself to blame for her Fall.

But there is no reason to suspect that Eve's virtue was "but a show" in the state of innocence. For even granting that Adam had, in Satan's words, a "higher intellectual" (IX, 483) than his wife, it does not follow that she was morally and rationally incompetent. She may have been the "weaker" partner (IX, 383) without being incapable of standing on her own feet. Indeed, the last words she hears from her husband before the temptation are a ringing affirmation of her moral self-sufficiency. "God towards thee hath done his part," Adam assures her, "do thine" (IX, 375).

Finally, those critics who find fault with Adam for allowing Eve to leave him are not only implicitly acquiescing in Adam's false assumptions about Eve's prelapsarian moral nature. They are also acquiescing in the rebuke which Eve herself directs at her husband during the course of their mutual recriminations immediately after the Fall, namely that Adam was not "firm and fixt" (IX, 1160) in his dissent. Thus Waldock comments after quoting Eve's reproaches: "The amusing thing is that Eve is perfectly right in her contention; her position, on Adam's tenets and on Milton's own, is absolutely unassailable."[22] It seems extremely doubtful, however, whether Milton would have put his own considered opinion of Adam's behavior in the mouth of an angry and recently fallen Eve. Before we accept what in the context is a thoroughly self-serving interpretation of Adam's conduct, we would be well advised, surely, to consider other possibilities as well, including the possibility that Adam was quite right to give his consent.

And indeed, as soon as we consider it in the context of what precedes it rather than what follows it, Adam's decision appears to be perfectly defensible. We have already seen that the prospect of being caught off guard by an unexpected temptation has alerted him to the possibility of being "secure" not only in the sense of being "safe" or "in one's own care" but also in the sense of being "negligent." The more "secure" they are in this third sense, his pun implies, the less "secure" they are in the first. The question is: how does the second sense relate to the other two? Should Eve decide to remain with Adam, and so forego the possibility of being "in her own care," is she likely to be "safer" or "more negligent" as a consequence? The way Adam poses the question suggests that she will be "more negligent," but events, of course, prove him wrong. Eve, it turns out, would have been "safer" had she remained with Adam. She becomes "more negligent" when she is "in her own care." It is difficult to see how Adam could have anticipated this outcome, however. For if, in the words of Archbishop Sandys, "men are commonly nearest unto peril, both corporal and spiritual, when their minds are furthest from thinking of preventing it,"[23] then Adam has every reason to assume that Eve will be more vigilant when she is on her own, and thus expects to be tempted, than when she is in his company, and thus believes herself to be safe. It is not that Adam "abandons reason, fails in his responsibilities to advise and govern Eve, and thus plays into Satan's hands," as Low asserts.[24] It is simply that he thinks they may be safer if they work separately. Tillyard rejects this argument as "false" because "both of them are now thoroughly warned and there is no reason why the effect of the warning should wear off in each other's company."[25] But there is. As Adam has pointed out more than once, the Devil is less likely to tempt them when they are in each other's company, and they are therefore more likely to be caught off guard if he does. On the other hand, now that Eve has been so thoroughly warned, she may reasonably be expected to be on her mettle. Indeed, with Adam's warnings ringing in her ears, she is never likely to be more alert than she is at this moment. So once again I would propose a modification of Mulder's thesis. The wordplay in *Paradise Lost*, he wrote, "was intended to keep the reader's mind ever vigilant as he follows the poet's quick intelligence" (p. 88). In this particular instance, I believe, it was intended to keep Eve's mind ever vigilant in her encounter with the tempter's quick intelligence.

Bentley, whose opinion of both the poet's and the reader's intelligence was rather lower than Mulder's, thought the wordplay was merely confusing, and proposed to replace "securer" in line 371 by "less heedful."[26] It is a measure of Eve's perspicacity that she gets the point immediately and without the aid of an emendation. Unconfused by her husband's *triple entendre*, she correctly glosses "securer" as "less prepared" when she replies:

> With thy permission then and thus forewarnd
> Chiefly by what thy own last reasoning words
> Touchd onely, that our trial, when least sought,
> May finde us both perhaps farr less prepar'd,
> The willinger I goe.
>
>   (IX, 378–82)[27]

The dissonance set up in the intervening line by Milton's observation that Eve "persisted, yet submiss" has thus been resolved both aurally and morally. Thanks to Adam's "permission," Eve can leave her husband without disobeying him, and thus remain technically "sinless" (IX, 659) until the Fall itself.

As it turns out, however, the effect of Adam's warning is tragically short-lived. For no sooner has Eve acknowledged the need to keep her guard up than she lets it down again. In her very next breath she announces that she does not "much expect / A foe so proud will first the weaker seek" (IX, 382–83), thereby not only conceding the point she had devoted so much energy to defending in her earlier speeches but also relaxing the attention that Adam has been at such pains to sustain. Ironically, Adam's warning has produced exactly the opposite effect from the one he intended; believing, as she does, that they will be more alert, and thus safer, if they separate, Eve has already lapsed into "security." As Adam puts it later:

> But confidence then bore thee on, secure
> Either to meet no danger, or to finde
> Matter of glorious trial.   (IX, 1175–77)

As a result, when Satan first spies her among the flowers, Eve is not merely "separate" (IX, 424) as he hoped; without a partner to "mind" her, she is already "mindless" (IX, 431) — so much so, indeed, that she doesn't "mind" (IX, 519) the serpent's initial attempts to catch her eye. Worse still, when he has finally succeeded in engaging her in conversation, she is so "amaz'd" (IX, 552, 614) to hear him speak that she does not seem to listen to what he is saying. She may reply to his flattery by saying that "Such wonder claims attention due" (IX, 566), but her subsequent behavior reveals that "attention due" is precisely what she does not pay it. On the contrary, as Milton points out shortly afterward, she remains fatally "unwarie" (IX, 614).

Her unwariness can readily be measured, I think, by comparing her response to Satan with Satan's earlier response to her. In a scene which has not attracted as much critical comment as it deserves, the devil was momentarily disarmed by Eve's sheer beauty:

> her Heav'nly forme
> Angelic, but more soft, and Feminine,
> Her graceful Innocence, her every Aire
> Of gesture or lest action overawd
> His Malice, and with rapine sweet bereav'd
> His fierceness of the fierce intent it brought:
> That space the Evil one abstracted stood
> From his own evil, and for the time remaind
> Stupidly good, of enmitie disarm'd,
> Of guile, of hate, of envie, of revenge;
> But the hot Hell that always in him burnes,
> Though in mid Heav'n, soon ended his delight,
> And tortures him now more, the more he sees

Of pleasure not for him ordain'd: then soon
Fierce hate he recollects, and all his thoughts
Of mischief, gratulating, thus excites.   (IX, 457–72)

Confronted with the serpent, Eve stands, as it were, abstracted from her
own good, stupidly evil, disarmed of innocence, of faith, of bliss. The crucial difference is that whereas the tempter reacts by recollecting his "fierce
hate" (IX, 471) and exciting "all his thoughts of mischief" (IX, 471–72),
Eve conspicuously fails to offer any real resistance to her moral metamorphosis. Unlike her adversary, she does not return to her true self. As
the serpent begins to speak, instead of remembering Adam's warnings
about specious objects by the foe suborned, she is totally "credulous" (IX,
644). Now that she needs it most, the intellectual acumen she displayed
in her earlier exchanges with Adam seems to desert her completely, and
the tempter's blatant nonsequiturs, self-contradictions, and misrepresen-
tations win "too easie" (IX, 734) entrance into her heart. Indeed, it is
almost as if she hasn't been listening. So when Adam reproaches her in
Book X for being "unwarie" (947) he is accurately diagnosing her fatal
weakness. John Chrysostom's observation in his sermon *Quod nemo laeti-
tur* applies to Milton's Eve with particular force. "The Dyuell," he wrote,
"dyd not hurte [man], but his own necligence [*sic*] while he watched not
to keep the commaundement."[28] Eve falls very largely through sheer inattentiveness. In *Paradise Lost* as in *Macbeth*, "security is mortals' chief-
est enemy" (III, v, 32–33).

It is her negligence, moreover, which establishes Eve's moral culpa-
bility despite the fact that she was "much deceived" (IX, 404). Normally
we do not hold people morally responsible for their mistakes, and given
Milton's insistence on the tempter's guile it may appear at first sight that
Eve has committed an intellectual error rather than a mortal sin. As Adam
had predicted, her reason, surprised by a fair appearing good, has dictated false and misinformed her will. But although Satan's words were
"impregn'd / With Reason, to her seeming, and with Truth" (IX, 737–38),
Milton insists that she is nonetheless responsible for her actions. Eve simply
should not have *allowed* herself to be taken in. Milton would have agreed,
I think, with William James's definition of a moral act as consisting in
"the effort of attention by which we hold fast to an idea which but for
that effort of attention would be driven out of the mind by other psychological tendencies that are there."[29]

But we do not have to rely on modern psychological theories to illustrate the point. For what Stanley E. Fish has called "the imperative
of Christian watchfulness" was a commonplace of seventeenth-century

ethical thought.[30] To take just one instance, the Protestant casuist Henry Hammond points out that in order to determine whether one has committed a forgivable sin of infirmity, as opposed to an unforgivable sin of willfulness, the sinner should enquire whether "thy understanding and the grace of God in it, being thus layed asleepe as it were, by some naturall, sinlesse, or at least invincible and so excuseable frailty, or else (as in a drowzy fit) not perfectly awake, there be not some meanes prescribed and presented to thee by God, which if thou hadst used, thou mightest have wakened thy understanding, or fortified thy will or weakened the temptation." If so, he continues: "and thou hast through negligence, or confidence, or spirituall security, or pride, omitted to make use of them, then will this still amount to a wilfull sinne or a sinne against strength."[31] One could hardly wish for a better analysis of Eve's sin in *Paradise Lost*. Even though Adam had provided her with the "meanes" which should have wakened her understanding, through negligence she omitted to make use of them. After all Adam's warnings about the dangers of "security," she should not have *permitted* her reason to be surprised. Her failure was ultimately a failure of will. In Empson's words, the Fall "is due to carelessness."[32]

As Hammond's emphasis on "spirituall security" suggests, then, Milton's seventeenth-century readers would have had no difficulty in identifying the cause of Eve's fall or in locating the responsibility for it. Indeed, the sermons and ethical treatises of the period positively bristle with injunctions against moral inattentiveness. "Man's life is a warfare," declared Archbishop Edwin Sandys in a famous sermon preached at York. We must, therefore

keep our standing and watch, lest we be unawares both assaulted and surprised. We have both many and mighty and fierce adversaries; the devil who is violently and greedily set as a hungry lion, that roareth for his prey; the world, which hath infinite sleights to deceive us; the flesh which mightily striveth and wrestleth against the Spirit. There is no place of security left for a Christian soldier, there being so many great dangers. There is nowhere any place wherein it is safe to be secure.[33]

The association of security with the world and the flesh was confirmed by many other writers of the Renaissance. William Fulbecke, for example, fulminated against "the secure and voluptuous Epicure" whose idleness made him a ready prey to sensuality, while Richard Brathwayt identified the epicure's home as "the cave of sensualitie and securitie."[34] Nowhere are the debilitating moral and spiritual effects of inattentiveness more vividly depicted, however, than in the opening stanza of Ben Jonson's great ode *To Himself*:

> Where doest thou careless lie,
> Buried in ease and sloth?
> Knowledge that sleeps doth die;
> And this security,
> It is the common moth
> That eats on wits and arts, and oft destroys them both.

Security was still more closely associated with the first of the adversaries mentioned by Sandys: the Devil. "Security," declared Brathwayt, "is rightly termed the divels opportunitie" and in his influential treatise *The Christian Warfare* (1609) John Downame applied this axiom directly to the Fall itself. Noting that the Devil "setteth upon us when we are most secure," he went on to point out that "thus he assaulteth our first parents in paradise, when they securely promised unto themselves the continuance and increase of their happiness."[35] Like Milton's Samson, they were "proudly secure, yet liable to fall" (55) — liable to fall, one might say, *because* proudly secure. In the moral theology of the sixteenth and seventeenth centuries, with its emphasis on the strenuousness of the good life, security thus came to be regarded as a form of *accidie*, or spiritual sloth. Among the epithets that Joshua Poole applies to it in his *English Parnassus* (1657), for instance, are "easie, sluggish, sleepy, carelesse, supine, and negligent." In Robert Cawdrey's memorable phrase, security was nothing less than "the highway to destruction."[36]

With the single exception of Downame, all the moralists I have quoted so far have been concerned with the danger of security in our postlapsarian world. The importance of Downame's analysis (and, to a still greater extent, of Milton's) is that they demonstrate why security was such a particular danger *before* the Fall. For although one might have expected the state of innocence to be exempt from this kind of threat, Milton's double-barreled pun emphasizes that even in Eden the life of virtue was hot and sweaty. As I said earlier, a "secure" person might be engaged in one or other of two possible activities: either enjoying a blissful absence of anxiety or displaying a morally reprehensible lack of due concern. By locating his pun where he does, at the pivotal point between innocence and sinfulness, Milton reveals that the two activities are intimately related to each other. To be carefree, he implies, is to run the risk of being careless. Paradoxically, then, security is Adam's and Eve's greatest blessing and at the same time the source of their greatest peril.

To rephrase Mulder for the last time, man in paradise is in danger of being "secure" or "off-guard" because he is "secure" or "free from [fear of external] harm." Far from being the fatal Cleopatra for which he lost the world, Adam's quibble on "security" could have been the watchword by means of which he saved it.

Stanford University

NOTES

1. John R. Mulder, *The Temple of the Mind* (New York, 1969), p. 87.

2. IX, 339. All quotations from *Paradise Lost* are from *The Works of John Milton,* ed. Frank Allen Patterson et al. (New York, 1931–38). Hereafter cited in the text.

3. Characteristically, Adam slips from "both" to "thou" as he contemplates their prospective trial. See below.

4. IX, 347–48. "Secure" has meant "safe" throughout the rest of the poem, moreover. See: I, 261, 638; II, 359, 399; IV, 186, 791; V, 638, 736; VI, 541, 672. The one apparent exception is at V, 238: "He swerve not too secure," where it means "confident, assured" (cf. XI, 196). This is close to the sense here in IX, 371, but the equivalence depends on the "too." Without it there would be no pejorative overtones.

5. In his article, "Adam, Eve, and the Fall in *Paradise Lost,*" *PMLA,* LXXXIV (1969), 264–73, Fredson Bowers raises the possibility that Adam's argument was "intended to be so far-fetched . . . as to bring Eve to her senses" (p. 271), but ultimately rejects it. Anthony Low, on the other hand, seems to believe that Adam was in fact using reverse psychology ("The Parting in the Garden in *Paradise Lost, PQ,* XLVII [1968], 30–35).

6. Richard Bentley, *Milton's "Paradise Lost": A New Edition* (London, 1732), note on lines 370–72. Patrick Hume glosses "secure" in IX, 339, as "safe" but provides no note on IX, 371, in his *Annotations on Milton's "Paradise Lost"* (London, 1695). Jonathan Richardson and son render it as "less upon our Guard" in their note to IX, 370, in *Explanatory Notes and Remarks on Milton's "Paradise Lost"* (London, 1734).

7. Francis Quarles, *Enchiridion* (London, 1644), iv, 63.

8. Robert Cawdrey, *A Table Alphabeticall* (London, 1604); John Bullokar, *An English Expositor* (London, 1616); Henry Cockeram, *The English Dictionarie* (London, 1623); Thomas Cooper, *Bibliotheca Eliotae* (London 1548); Francis Holyoke, *Dictionarium Etymologicum* (London, 1648); Christopher Wase, *Dictionarium Minus* (London, 1662), *A Copious Dictionary* (Cambridge, 1664). Neither Thomas Blount's *Glossographia* (London, 1656), nor Edward Phillips's *The New World of English Words* (London, 1658), contains an entry for *secure,* which may suggest that by mid-century the meaning of the word was well established as a result of its popularity in the works of Puritan divines and moralists. In the seventeenth century, of course, *careless* could mean "carefree" as well as "remiss" (the *NED* gives examples of both). Milton uses it in the first sense in *PR* IV, 450, and in the second in *PR* IV, 299. The word does not occur in *PL.*

9. Low, "The Parting," p. 31. In "The Crisis of *Paradise Lost,*" in *Studies in Milton* (London, 1951), E. M. W. Tillyard, for instance, writes that "Adam, who could now be

firm with impunity, whom Eve expects to be firm, suddenly weakens" (p. 19). Bowers remarks that "after this firm assertion of his hierarchical duty to command . . . [Adam] suddenly appears to cave in" ("Adam, Eve," p. 270). And Millicent Bell declares that "Adam, at the very climax of his most forceful argument, suddenly collapses" ("The Fallacy of the Fall in *Paradise Lost*," PMLA, LXVIII [1963], 869).

10. Low, "The Parting," p. 31.

11. Ibid.

12. Tillyard, "The Crisis," p. 20.

13. Bowers, "Adam, Eve," p. 272.

14. John C. Ulreich, "'Sufficient to Have Stood': Adam's Responsibility in Book IX," MQ, V (1971), 39.

15. Bowers, "Adam, Eve," p. 273; Dennis H. Burden, *The Logical Epic* (London, 1967), pp. 90–91.

16. Tillyard, "The Crisis," p. 20; Bowers, "Adam, Eve," p. 273.

17. Barbara K. Lewalski, "Innocence and Experience in Milton's Eden," in Thomas Kranidas, *New Essays on "Paradise Lost"* (Berkeley and Los Angeles, 1971), p. 100.

18. A. J. A. Waldock, *"Paradise Lost" and Its Critics* (Gloucester, Mass., 1959), p. 32.

19. John Peter, *A Critique of "Paradise Lost"* (New York, 1960), p. 117. I disagree with Peter, however, about the reason for Adam's decision. "First," Peter writes, "he is unnerved by the thought which has just struck him, that their trial will come when it is least expected. If this is so, then Eve may as well go off at once, while she is freshly warned and on her mettle. Secondly, his wife's gentle persistence has forced him to acknowledge, to her and to himself, that her complaint at 285–9 was justified. He feels guilty for mistrusting her, and tries to make up for it by letting her have her way" (p. 117). In fact, as I shall argue below, Adam has been emphasizing the importance of being on their mettle from the outset of the discussion.

20. J. M. Evans, *Paradise Lost, Books IX–X* (Cambridge, 1973), p. 31.

21. Bowers, "Adam, Eve," p. 270.

22. Waldock, *PL and Its Critics*, p. 35.

23. Edwin Sandys, "A Sermon Made at York," in *The Sermons*, ed. J. Ayre, for the Parker Society, vol. II, (Cambridge, 1841), p. 211.

24. Low, "The Parting," p. 35.

25. Tillyard, "The Crisis," p. 20.

26. Bentley, *PL*, note on lines 370–72.

27. Eve's paraphrase is not entirely accurate, however. Adam's cautious condition "if" has become a statement of fact "that," and his relatively neutral "unsought" has become the superlative "least sought." In much the same way "securer" has been intensified to "far less prepared."

28. *A compendious Treatise of saynte John Chrisostom provingue that no man is hurte but of him selfe*, trans. Charlys Chanalary (London, 1541), sig. A4v.

29. William James, "The Will," in *Talk to Teachers on Psychology* (London, 1899), p. 187.

30. Stanley E. Fish, *Surprised by Sin: The Reader in "Paradise Lost"* (London, 1967), p. 12.

31. Henry Hammond, *Of Sinnes of Weaknesse, of Wilfulnesse* (Oxford, 1645), pp. 8–9.

32. William Empson, *Some Versions of the Pastoral* (Norfolk, Conn., 1960), p. 172.

33. Sandys, *Sermons*, II, p. 210.

34. William Fulbecke, *A Booke of Christian Ethicks or Moral Philosophie* (London, 1587), sig. B1; Richard Brathwayt, *Natures Embassie: or, The Wilde-Mans Measures* (London, 1621), p. 77.

35. Brathwayt, *Natures Embassie*, p. 155; John Downame, *the Christian Warfare* (London, 1609), p. 94.

36. Joshua Poole, *The English Parnassus* (London, 1657), under "security" (see also Abraham Fleming, *A Monomachie of Motives in the mind of man* [London, 1582], p. 127, where the reader is cautioned to ensure that "Slothfull Idleness" does not carry him "headlong into securitie and carelessnes"); Robert Cawdrey, *A Treasurie or Storehouse of Similies* (London, 1600), p. 718.

PRETEXTS AND SUBTEXTS
IN "THAT FAIR FIELD OF *ENNA*"

George deForest Lord

AT T H E heart of what may be the most famous extended simile in English, Milton introduces, in an epic voluntary, the fatal heroine of *Paradise Lost* and the *locus amoenissimus* she and her uxorious mate will soon be compelled to leave, having tasted — she under the seductions of the grisly king of the underworld and he out of despair at the prospect of life without her — the fruit of that forbidden tree.

The simile's fourteen lines offer with apparently dégagé opulence a succession of Sicilian, Middle Eastern and African paradises that cannot "strive" with this true biblical Eden. Like so many of the major similes in *Paradise Lost*, it is what I have come to think of as a "dissimile," what Widmer calls a dismissive simile — a trope developed from Homer in which characters and places, often of exotic and legendary power, are invoked only to be discarded as false or inferior by comparison with Milton's "true" mythical version.[1] The strategy of expanding the differential ratios of the simile beyond its referential ones is to a large extent dictated by the poet's compelling need throughout *Paradise Lost* to establish the unique truth of his epic in contrast to the fabulous or feigned impositions of his precursors. The need is all the greater in view of the central event of the poem — Eve's rash acceptance of Satan's false myth for God's true one. Thus, in his crucial introduction of our "grand parents," Milton repeatedly denies the beauty of countless pagan paradises in comparison with Eden, while tacitly employing their strong mythical associations to enhance and embellish its incomparable perfections:

> Not that fair field
> Of *Enna*, where *Proserpin* gath'ring flow'rs
> Herself a fairer Flow'r by gloomy *Dis*
> Was gather'd, which cost *Ceres* all that pain
> To seek her through the world; nor that sweet Grove
> Of *Daphne* by *Orontes*, and th' inspir'd
> *Castalian* Spring might with this Paradise
> Of *Eden* strive; nor that *Nyseian* Isle
> Girt with the River *Triton*, where old *Cham*,

127

Whom Gentiles *Ammon* call and *Lybian Jove*,
Hid *Amalthea* and her Florid Son,
Young *Bacchus*, from his Stepdame *Rhea's* eye;
Nor where *Abassin* Kings thir issue Guard,
Mount *Amara*, though this by some suppos'd
True Paradise under the *Ethiop* Line
By *Nilus* head, enclos'd with shining Rock,
A whole day's journey high, but wide remote
From this *Assyrian* Garden, where the Fiend
Saw undelighted all delight, all kind
Of living Creatures new to sight and strange. . . .[2]

The sentence runs on for another twenty-two lines to describe Adam and Eve for the first time in the poem. The lines quoted, as is well known, are based on Ovid's accounts of the rape of Proserpina in the *Metamorphoses* and *Fasti* and also draw on Claudian's epic *de Raptu Proserpinae*. *Enna*, *Proserpin*, and *Dis* are sufficient to mark the false Hesperian fable from Sicily that Milton dismisses before enumerating and dismissing various oriental paradises as inferior to his Eden. The passage may also draw on Milton's familiarity with other accounts of the fable in Natalis Comes, in Sandys' commentary on the *Metamorphoses*, in Apollodorus and in Pausanias. He probably would have known allusions in the *Helen* of Euripides and surely would have known references to Persephone and Demeter in the culminating episode of *Oedipus at Colonus*, one of the models for *Samson Agonistes*. Unlike Chapman, who had to use Latin trots to translate Homer, Milton's rare mastery of Greek would have made him equal to the task of reading the original version of the tale of Persephone in the Homeric *Hymn to Demeter*, the only version that brings together nearly all the allusions to the archetypal myth in his simile.

Yet his choice of a late and degenerate Latin version of the myth as pretext artfully conceals the vital, pristine subtext in the pseudo-Homeric hymn that was transcribed at about the time when the *Iliad* and the *Odyssey* attained their final written form in the eighth century B.C., more than seven centuries before Ovid. The ghostly presence of the ancient, primordial subtext, with its rich etiological resonances not to be found in the versions of Ovid and Claudian, Milton conceals and dismembers. The ghostly presence of the hymn helps to endow the great simile of *Paradise Lost* with a large measure of the force and poignancy that has reverberated in the imaginations of generations of readers. Let me say here that I am positing Milton's knowledge of the archetype fully aware of the observation of N. J. Richardson, a recent editor of the *Hymn to Demeter*, that "as the manuscript of the Hymn was not apparently known to the world in general until the end of the eighteenth century, the Hymn exercised no influence over Renaissance literature. A paper was once written which endeavoured to identify Milton's debts to the Hymn." This, he concludes sternly, "should serve as a warning against the perils of any such attempts to trace literary influences."[3]

Before I consider how Milton may have known — or may have reconstituted — the details of this crucial subtext, the only manuscript of which we know today having been catalogued in Moscow in 1777, and the only one of the thirty-three Homeric hymns not included in the editions of 1525, 1535, 1557, and 1660, let us examine some of the ways in which the *Hymn to Demeter* makes its presence felt in Milton's simile. Here are the opening lines:

Now shall I sing of rich-haired Demeter,
a holy goddess, and of her slim-ankled daughter
whom Aïdoneus seized as a gift from Zeus
the Thunderer, who sees all, while she played
with the buxom daughters of Ocean, far from Demeter   5
of the golden blade, bearer of rich fruit,
gathering flowers in a soft meadow — roses, crocuses,
lovely violets, irises, hyacinths, and the narcissus
Earth made flourish as a bait for the flowerlike girl,
as Zeus willed, to please the Host of the Many —
a gleaming wonder that awed all who saw it,   10
whether men or gods. From its root
a hundred blossoms grew; they smelled so sweet
that all wide heaven above and all the earth
and the briny swell of the sea smiled with delight.
Amazed, the girl stretched out both her hands   15
to grasp the lovely toy. Wide earth gaped
there, in the Plain of Nysa and the Host of the Many,
with his deathless horses, sprang on her,
the Son of Kronos, the Lord of Many Names.
   He caught her up in his golden chariot
and bore her off lamenting, against her will.
She cried aloud, calling her father, the Son of Kronos,   20
who is supreme and powerful. Neither god nor mortal heard
her cries, nor did the rich-fruited olive tree;
only gentle Hecate, the bright-coifed daughter of Persaeus,   25
heard the girl from her cave, and the Lord Helios,
bright Son of Hyperion, as she cried to her father, son of Kronos.
But he was aloof, sitting apart from the gods,
in his temple, where many pray, accepting their sweet offerings.
And so the many-named Son of Kronos,

Ruler and Host of Legions, by the will of Zeus, her father's own brother, was carrying her off against her wishes with his immortal horses. 30

    As long as the goddess still saw earth and starry heaven
and the flowing sea filled with fish, and the sun's rays, and hoped still
to see her dear mother and the tribes of immortals, 35
hope calmed her great mind for all her grief . . . ,
and the mountain ridges and the depths of the sea
Echoed her immortal voice, and her queenly mother heard her.
    A bitter pang seized her heart, and with her hands she tore apart 40
the veils that covered her lovely hair, and throwing the dark cloak
from her shoulders, she flew like a bird over land and sea,
seeking. But no one, divine or mortal, would tell her the truth, 45
nor would the birds of omen. For nine days queenly Deo
wandered over the earth with torches in her hands so grieved
that she never tasted ambrosia or sweet nectar, nor did she bathe. 50
But when the tenth dawn came, Hecate, bearing a torch,
met her and told her news:
    "Lady Demeter, bringer of seasons and rich gifts,
what heavenly god or what mortal has seized 55
Persephone and grieved your heart?
I heard a voice, but saw not who it was.
But let me tell you briefly all I know."
    Thus spoke Hecate. The daughter of rich-haired Rhea
did not answer, but sped off with her, holding torches in her hands, 60
and they came to Helios, the seer of gods and men,
and stood before his horses, and the bright goddess asked:
    "Helios, you at least should respect me, goddess as I am,
if ever by word or deed I have cheered your heart. 65
Through the barren air I heard the loud cry of the girl
I bore, the sweet scion of my body, lovely in form,
as of one seized violently, but I didn't see her with my eyes.
But you, who look over all the earth and sea
from the bright heavens with your brilliant glance, 70
tell me truly of my dear child, if you have seen her anywhere,
what god or mortal has violently seized her against her will and
mine and so fled?"[4]

    The pathos of the search that "cost Ceres all that pain" depends, of course, on the functional limitations the bereaved mother suffers, as most of the Olympians do, despite their divinity. That she could hear her daughter's cry without seeing what was happening to her makes her passionate grief all the more poignant, especially in contrast with Zeus' omniscient detachment, which is much like that of Milton's God, who

From the pure Empyrean where he sits
High Thron'd above all highth, bent down his eye,
His own works and their works at once to view.   (III, 57–59)

Obviously Milton's orientation to the Middle East rather than to Ovid's Sicily or to the hymn's Attica for the *fons et origo* of his true myth of Creation was determined by his Old Testament sources — Genesis especially. Enna, in the center of Sicily, a halfway point in the westward movement of empire and culture, was by his standards a scene fabulous and corrupt and hence a ground of pagan delusions to be readily and firmly rejected, even while, as we shall see, he used some of the Ovidian legend's associations to enhance his own. The Attic original, however, contributes even more to the proleptic intimations of the seduction of Eve and goes far beyond the later versions in intimating that the heroine's apparently fatal experience is a sort of *felix culpa*.[5]

Ovid's most complete version, in the *Metamorphoses*, is set in a thematic context of erotic love that reduces the archetypal myth of Proserpina's loss and recovery to an Olympian social comedy, entertaining but doggedly inconsequential, while the *Hymn to Demeter* accounts for the birth of agriculture and achieves a vision of the interdependence of life and death that forms the etiological model for the oldest, the longest-lasting, and the most influential cult of religious mystery in the pre-Christian West. The Eleusinian Mysteries, indeed, were vital enough to be regarded by Clement and other church fathers as challenging the hegemony of Christianity. Originating before the Trojan War, Eleusis thrived even under Roman occupation, until Alaric's hordes and Christian monks destroyed it in the fifth century.

That Sophocles, Socrates, Plato, Alcibiades, Solon, Peisistratus, and Kimon were among the initiates into the Greater Mysteries; that in Roman times the cult continued for four hundred years with undiminished prestige, as the initiation of Cicero, Hadrian, Marcus Aurelius and his empress attests; that Alcibiades and Aeschylus narrowly escaped death for allegedly revealing Eleusinian secrets; and that Nero, according to George Mylonas, "abstained from initiation" are indications of the unique and cosmopolitan character of the rituals and the myth they celebrate. Political and military achievements of the highest order were held to be inadequate without the crowning *epopteia*, and so Octavius hastened to Eleusis after the Battle of Actium to enter into "the beatitude of those who have seen these mysteries" (*Hymn* 480).[6]

The theme of restoration and beatific vision at the heart of the Mysteries is all the more important in relation to *Paradise Lost* because of the myth's preponderant emphasis on the roles of women in the cultural and agricultural well-being of the community, in a serene awareness of the interdependence of life and death or of growth and decay in the biological and spiritual life of mankind. If the *Hymn to Demeter* has suffered a *sparagmos* at Milton's hands, as he casually disjoins and dismisses vital elements of the archetype, our task will be, like Isis recovering the dismembered limbs of Osiris, to show how these elements reconstitute themselves, explicitly and implicitly, in *Paradise Lost*.

The rape of Proserpina/Persephone at Enna/Eleusis by Dis/Hades as she is gathering flowers, and her unwilling trip to the underworld, where she becomes consort of the lord of death is proleptic of Eve's seduction/abduction by Satan, the father of death, after she has tasted a forbidden fruit that may bind her to the realm of mortality forever. Eve, a fertility figure (mother of mankind) like Persephone/Proserpina, has wedded herself and all her progeny to mortality. In the Old Testament version of the myth, she replicates her own seduction by the lord of death by seducing Adam into tasting the forbidden fruit, thereby altering the role of innocent Persephone and, in an ultimate betrayal, seducing Adam into assuming, with her, the deadly function.

Most of these elements of the myth are to be found in the opening lines of the *Hymn to Demeter* (1–73). For "that fair field of Enna," which Milton borrows from Ovid, the hymn specifies the *Nusion pedion* (1, 17), the Plain of Nysa, located (among many other sites) between Eleusis and Athens, where Persephone was abducted by the "Lord of Many Names," a euphemism for Hades, Pluto, Aïdoneus, and the counterpart of the Latin Dis. In the Miltonic passage, Nysa (an element in the name of Dionysus, of which more later) is transferred to "that Nyseian Isle," where "Amalthea's florid son," Dionysus, following one of many legends, was born. The originating myths about Dionysus or Bacchus are manifold, but all the myths concur in his being twice-born: Zeus concealed the infant in his thigh, according to one version, to protect him from "stepdame Rhea." In some versions of the Eleusinian myth Bacchus/Dionysus appears under the name Iacchus, the god of wine who functions in the myth as the child of Persephone and Pluto and, in the ritual, as the leader of the procession from Athens to Eleusis, while Rhea is entirely benign. Milton had no choice but to make the Nyseian isle of the Middle East Bacchus's birthplace, despite the multitude of places, Crete among them, where he was supposed to have been born and reborn. Yet it is impossible to exaggerate the importance of the Attic Plain of Nysa as the area in which the vine, like grain, was, perhaps, first cultivated, as the hymn suggests.

Another exotic place Milton picks up and discards is *"Daphne* by *Orontes,* and th' inspir'd *Castalian* Spring." Daphne, with its "sweet grove," about two-thirds of the twenty-kilometer journey from Athens to Eleusis along the Sacred Way, was a famous stopping point for the Eleusinian procession. As for other key landmarks, the Castalian Spring Milton mentions is a shadow of the prototype at Delphi, in easy walking distance, as Oedipus to his horror discovered, from nearby Corinth.

Let me sum up, briefly, the links between Milton's *Enna* simile and the *Hymn to Demeter.* Milton mentions and discards Enna, Proserpina, Dis, and Ceres, as constituents in a myth that lacks the beauty and verity of his own. The name of the sacred area where Persephone was carried off is relegated to an island in a middle-eastern river, the alleged birthplace and hiding place of Dionysus, who is a major figure in the Eleusis myth. The sacred grove of Daphne, again relegated to the Levant by Milton and his sources, is originally the main place of sojourn between Athens and Eleusis for the initiates in their progression along the Sacred Way. The famous Castalian Springs of Delphi, that play a major role in the mythical landscape of Eleusis and Delphi, Milton also relocates (as he must, following his Old Testament geography) in Mesopotamia. The divine child, whose birth is held to have been the climax of the *epopteia* at Eleusis, born, according to some accounts, of Zeus and a mortal mother, but immortalized by his second birth, is huddled off to concealment in what is now Tunis and there kept effectually out of play. But Dionysus/Iacchos was ritually reborn at Eleusis as the son of Persephone and Pluto/Dis.

If we now add the major links between Ovid's version of the Proserpina story and Milton's simile, we shall find that, combined with the hymn, it supplies a rich background myth that influences and enhances Milton's. Milton prefaces his golden age account of Eden with the lines,

> The Birds thir choir apply; airs, vernal airs,
> Breathing the smell of field and grove, attune
> The trembling leaves, while Universal *Pan*
> Knit with the *Graces* and the *Hours* in dance
> Led on th' Eternal Spring. (IV, 264–68)

This is a deft adaptation of the lines with which Ovid introduces the story of Proserpina in *Metamorphoses* V:

> Haud procul Hennaeis lacus est a moenibus altae,
> nomine Pergus, aquae: non illo plura Caystros
> carmina cycnorum labentibus audit in undis.
> silva coronat aquas cingens latus omne suisque
> frondibus ut velo Phoebeos submovet ictus;
> frigora dant rami, tyrios humus umida flores:
> perpetuum ver est.

[Not far from Henna's high walls there is a deep pool of water, Pergus by name. Not Cayster on its gliding waters hears more songs of swans than does this pool. A wood crowns the height around its waters on every side, and with its foliage as with an awning keeps off the sun's hot rays. The branches afford a pleasing coolness, and the well-watered ground bears bright-coloured flowers. There spring is everlasting.][7]

Birdsong, the chiaroscuro of sun and leaves, and, most of all, Ovid's *perpetuum ver* contribute to Milton's synaesthetic, vital, and static "eternal spring," although Ovid could never reach (not that he tried to) the deep implications of Milton's eternal cycle of fecundity. While it would be too much to claim that the Homeric hymn had reawakened in Milton the mythological motifs latent in Ovid's belated version, the comparison of the Ovidian passage and its counterpart in *Paradise Lost* suggests some of the ways in which Milton was revitalizing a myth that had become decorative and vulgar.

Let us take a similar Miltonic adaptation from the *Hymn to Demeter*, one which also occurs shortly before the *Enna* simile:

> As when to them who sail
> Beyond the *Cape of Hope*, and now are past
> *Mozambic*, off at Sea North-East winds blow
> *Sabean* Odors from the spicy shore
> Of *Araby* the blest, with such delay
> Well pleas'd they slack thir course, and many a League
> Cheer'd with the grateful smell old *Ocean* smiles.   (IV, 159–65)

Looking back at the opening lines of the hymn, we find that Persephone, playing with the daughters of Ocean, is captivated by a narcissus whose fragrance makes heaven and earth and "even the briny swellings of Ocean smile" (14). In both cases the innocent harmonies of man and nature are to be broken by a fatal fruit or flower, and Milton's familiar intimacy toward "old *Ocean*" mimics the insouciance of the destined victim.

Unlike Eve, however, this victim is intrinsically innocent. As she collects the flowers of the narcissus (not included in Ovid), Persephone reaches both her hands out toward the "dolos" (lure, bait) that the earth, personified as Gaea, has fostered as Zeus willed (9). In her distracted delight, she is overtaken by Dis/Pluto, who catches her up with passion (*dilectaque rapta*, V, 395) and takes her off to the underworld as his bride.

As subtext, the hymn's elaborate account of the *narkissos* as the *dolos* that distracts Persephone and makes her vulnerable to the sudden onslaught of Aïdoneus is deeply significant. Like Eve she is *amazed* and stretches out her hands to the bait (15–16). And, like Eve, as she does so, the earth gapes or splits open and Death claims her:

> So saying, her rash hand in evil hour
> Forth reaching to the Fruit, she pluck'd, she eat:
> Earth felt the wound. (IX, 780–82)

Unlike Persephone, Eve's rash plucking is the fruit of her narcissism. The fruit she has taken from the tree of knowledge, later called "the bait of *Eve* / Us'd by the Tempter" (X, 551–52), functions symbolically as both the *dolos* of the narcissus and the pomegranate seeds that Persephone swallows beneath the earth (in the hymn, secretly given her by Hades) that confirm her commitment to the underworld. The pomegranate, as Richardson notes, "was symbolical of blood and death, but also of fertility and marriage" (p. 276). Clearly the *pomum* element of pomegranate would associate Eve's apple with Persephone's fruit, while the distinction between the young flower goddess who eats seeds (*grana*) and the mother who presides over the fruiting stage would be preserved.

George Sandys, whose commentary Milton knew well, pointed out that the younger goddess's Latin name, *Proserpina*, is derived from *proserpo* (to creep forth), which would be appropriate to her presiding over the germinal stage in which shoots appear from seeds. As Sandys observes, "*Ceres*, as we have said, is taken for corne: her *Proserpina* for the fertility of the seed, which of creeping forth is so called: begotten by *Jove*, that is by the aetheriall virtue and clemency; when corrupting and dying (for even that which groweth dies before it be quickened)."[8] Sandys almost makes the figurative connection between the serpentine Proserpina and Eve in a further comment: "But *Proserpina* having eaten seven graines of Pomegrannet (a fatal liquorishness, which retains her in Hell; as the Apple thrust *Evah* out of Paradise whereunto it is held to have a relation) . . . her hopes were made frustrate" (p. 256). Sandys is commenting on the following passage:

> frigora dant rami, tyrios humus umida flores:
> perpetuum ver est. quo dum Proserpina luco
> ludit et aut violas aut candida lilia capit

dumque puellari studio calathosque sinumque
inplet et aequales certat superare legendo
paene simul visa est dilectaque raptaque Diti.		(V, 390–95)

[The branches afford a pleasing coolness, and the well-watered ground bears bright-colored flowers. There spring is everlasting. Within the grove Proserpina was playing, and gathering violets or white lilies. And while with girlish eagerness she was filling her basket and her bosom, and striving to surpass her mates in gathering, almost in in one act did Pluto see and love and carry her away.]

Sandys' comment cannot fail to remind us of Eve's capacity to play the serpent, a role she learns instantly from Satan in Book IX and one signalized by Adam's devastating rejection of her in Book X: "Out of my sight, thou Serpent, that name best / Befits thee with him leagu'd, thyself as false / And hateful" (867–69). The Latin name of the young goddess enables Milton to suggest proleptically the serpentine rhetoric and "covert guile" (II, 41) she will employ on Adam. Of course the predominant impression of Milton's Eve/Proserpina juxtaposition is of feminine innocence and faith and beauty unwittingly reaching out for a beguiling bait while Death lurks close by her. This impression is reinforced by the powerful mutual affection that binds mother and daughter and drives Ceres to seek the vanished Proserpina through the world (and, one might add, through the underworld), a quest, as has often been observed, that anticipates Christ's redemptive role.[9] The name *Proserpina* may also remind us that Eve's act, though its direct consequences are mortal, will, like Proserpina's, entwine the forces of destruction and renewal. In the one forbidden fruit, Milton combines the *dolos* of the ambivalent narcissus and the equally ambivalent pomegranate seeds that bind Proserpina/Persephone to an annual sojourn with Death as her husband. Like the narcissus, it is an emblem of the narcissism that underlies Eve's rebellious act, and, like the narcissus, its fragrance is almost irresistible:

Meanwhile the hour of Noon drew on, and wak'd
An eager appetite, rais'd by the smell
So savory of that Fruit, which with desire,
Inclinable now grown to touch or taste,
Solicited her longing eye.		(IX, 739–43)

The hymn's narcissus, the narcotic and deadly properties of which are indicated by its inclusion in the wreath Pluto wears, according to Natalis Comes,[10] is "die verhängnisvolle Todesblume" in the words of Franz Bömer's commentary on the *Metamorphoses*, but, as he also points out, it forms the garlands worn "by the mother and daughter," presumably

Demeter and Persephone, in *Oedipus at Colonus*, 682.[11] The motifs of the narcissus' beauty, intoxicating and sometimes deadly power, narcissistic symbolism, and fragrance are combined with "the smell / So savory" (L. *sapor*, derived, like *sapientia*, from *sapio*) of pomegranate and apple as Eve "Greedily . . . ingorg'd without restraint, / And knew not eating Death" (IX, 791–94). "Knew not eating Death" puns on the latent paradox that from the *sapor* of this fruit Eve not only fails to acquire more *sapientia;* its mortal taste has diminished rather than increased knowledge.

Like Persephone, Eve is the victim of fraud, but while Persephone was the innocent victim of Pluto's guile, Eve participated willingly in the solicitations of "the spirited sly snake." Ovid's Proserpina wanders innocently through the underworld sampling the fruit:

> non ita fata sinunt, quoniam ieiunia virgo
> solverat et, cultis dum simplex errat in hortis,
> poenicum curva decerpserat arbore pomum
> sumptaque pallenti septem de cortice grana
> presserat ore suo, solusque ex omnibus illud
> Ascalaphus vidit.   (V, 534–39)

[Not so the Fates; for the girl had already broken her fast, and while, simple child that she was, she wandered in the trim gardens, she had plucked a purple pomegranate hanging from a bending bough, and peeling off the yellowish rind, she had eaten several of the seeds. The only one who saw the act was Ascalaphus.]

The fruit this tree bears, metaphorically speaking, is sterile. Ovid often empties old myths of their profounder qualities, and so here nothing would have come of Proserpina's indulgence in pomegranate seeds if Ascalaphus (who has no other function in the story) had not seen her eat them and blabbed about it.

Although Milton employs the associations of the Persephone/Proserpina myth chiefly to evoke the pathos that surrounds Eve and Eden in the introductory simile, the redeeming aspects of the myth — especially in the Greek version — reverberate powerfully in the "true" fable of *Paradise Lost*. The redemptive role undertaken by Demeter/Ceres, while presented in Ovid as the resolution of a difficult social contretemps, is represented in the hymn as a profoundly mystical reconciliation of apparently irreconcilable oppositions that seem to lie at the heart of the human situation. To be sure, the hymn is not without humor, as when Helios tries to cajole Demeter into accepting a brighter view of her daughter's marriage to Pluto by reminding her that he is, after all, Zeus' own brother and "no unfitting husband for your child" (83–84), since he reigns over a third of the universe, tactfully overlooking the fact that all his subjects, of course, are dead. Such humor is, nonetheless, subordinate to the divine comedy of the hymn.

In order to see this we must briefly survey the events that follow the rape of Persephone.After a fruitless ten days' search through the world, Demeter comes to the town of Eleusis disguised as an old woman. Here she is welcomed into the family of a leading citizen, Celeus, whose wife has given birth late in life to her first son, Demophoön. Demeter undertakes to nurse the child and, through secret rites involving the use of ambrosia and fire, plans to make the boy immortal, perhaps as a substitute for the gooddess-daughter she has lost. When the mother learns of these strange practices and reclaims her child, Demeter berates her, discloses her divine nature, and demands that the Eleusinians build her a temple. Having learned that her husband, Zeus, had helped to plot the abduction of their daugher by Pluto, she retires into the temple for a year and imposes a total blight on the land. When Zeus is finally forced to make concessions, he and his wife agree that Persephone will spend a third of each year with her chthonic husband and the rest in the upper world. In response, Demeter provides the Eleusinian Triptolemos with her dragon-drawn chariot and a supply of seed sufficient to provide abundant harvests. This part of the myth celebrates both seasonal rhythms of growth and dearth (with the very important, if mistaken, idea that the seed "dies" before it germinates — a mistake shared by St. John and St. Paul) and the birth of agriculture, which first occurred, according to Greek legend, on the Nysion Plain that extends from Eleusis eastward. Although the division of visiting rights differs in various versions of the myth, the eight months correspond to the normal growing season in Attica and approximate the period of human gestation. The rituals that are marked in the Attic calendar by the fall Boedromion and the early spring Anthesterion may reflect such key seasonal changes.

The climactic *epopteia* achieved in the vast *telesterion* at Eleusis seems to have involved a reenactment of Demeter's torchlit search for her daughter and a culminating pronouncement by the hierophant of the birth of the sacred boy: "The sublime one has borne a sacred boy, Brimo has given birth to Brimos."[12] In some versions, as we have noted, Brimos is identified with the infant Bacchus, a connection that would reinforce the vinicultural and agricultural concerns of the myth. At any rate it is this aspect of the mystery, the birth of the sacred boy, that St. Paul, recognizing Pluto's alternate function as god of riches, converts into the *ploutos tou Khristou*, the "unsearchable riches of Christ."[13] While Milton seems nowhere to suggest such a Christianization of the myth in *Para-*

dise Lost, his myth parallels that of the hymn in seeing the ultimate and restorative fruit as the divine child. It should also be emphasized that such an epiphany at Eleusis was accompanied by the initiates' sharing in a sacred drink, *ho kukēon,* whose mildly intoxicating qualities remind one of the communion wine, just as the blade of wheat that was displayed as in a monstrance obviously suggests the consecrated bread.[14]

We come now to the conclusion of the hymn and the reunion of Demeter (whose name is derived from the Greek word for mother) and Persephone:

> So then all day with one heart they cheered each other,
> and with many embraces they relieved their grief in mutual joy.
> Then bright-coifed Hecate approached them
> and often embraced Demeter's holy daughter,
> and from that time forth was her minister and companion.
> And all-seeing, deep-thundering Zeus sent fair-haired Rhea
> as messenger to bring dark-robed Demeter
> back to the tribes of immortals, and he promised
> to give her whatever honors she chose among the deathless gods
> and agreed that the Maiden should spend a third of each circling
> year in the misty gloom and two thirds with her mother and the
> other deathless gods.
> So he ordered, nor did the goddess disobey the message of Zeus,
> Swiftly she plunged from the peaks of Olympus
> and came to the Rharian Plain, once rich corn-land,
> but then entirely unfruitful, for it lay idle and leafless,
> because the white grain was hidden by the design of trim-ankled Demeter.
> But afterwards, as spring came on, it was soon rippling with long ears of corn,
> its rich furrows laden with cut grain or with grain in sheaves.
> These she first alighted from the fruitless air. Gladly
> the goddesses looked at each other, and their hearts were cheered.   (434–58)

Rhea proceeds in Homeric fashion to repeat Zeus's message verbatim and then continues:

> "But come now, my child, give way; don't be unrelentingly angry
> with the dark-clouded Son of Kronos, but rather increase quickly
> the fruit that gives men life."
> So she spoke, and fair-crowned Demeter did not disobey:
> she made fruit spring quick from the rich lands,
> and the whole wide earth was covered with leaves and flowers.
> Then she went to the kings who administer justice,
> Triptolemos and Polyxeinos and Diocles, the horse-driver,
> and mighty Eumolpus and Celeus and taught them all her mysteries—

awful mysteries that no one in any way may transgress or pry into or utter,
for deep awe of the gods checks the voice. Happy is he
of earth-borne men who has seen these mysteries,
but the uninitiated, who has no part in them,
never has the same good lot, once he is dead, down in the misty gloom.
    Then when the bright goddess had taught them all,
the three goddesses went to Olympus to the grave conclave,
and there they dwell beside Zeus who rejoices in thunder,
holy and wonderful goddesses. Blessed is he whom they freely love:
soon do they send Plutus as guest in his great house.
Plutus who gives wealth to mortal men.
    But now, queen of Eleusis and sea-girt Paros and rocky Antron,
lady, giver of good gifts, mistress of the seasons, queen Deo,
May you and your daughter, lovely Persephone,
for this song of mine cheer my heart,
and now I will remember you and remember another song as well. (467–95)

The adjudication of the central conflicts in the hymn is a sign of a peculiarly Attic genius for resolving in ways satisfactory to all the interested parties contesting claims that seem irreconcilable, in the course of which (as in the transformation of the Furies into Eumenides) major cultural advances are achieved. In the *Metamorphoses* the resolution is simply a recognition of contending interests. In the hymn the settlement, which on the surface appears to be a more or less arbitrary recognition of competing equities (the contending rights of Persephone, Demeter, and Pluto), gains its authority through the vital implications of the associated myth. Through its mystical vision, the apparent oppositions between mother and husband, underworld and upperworld, life and death, fertility and decay are seen as profoundly interdependent, and this vision of a divine *discordia concors* pervading the entire universe must have been close to the undisclosed *mysterion* at the heart of the ritual.

    To conclude this phase of the discussion, let me recapitulate the implications of the Demeter myth on *Paradise Lost*. The heroine is captured by the king of the underworld while she is preoccupied with flowers. She has moved away from her chief protector: Persephone from Demeter; Eve, the "fairest unsupported Flow'r, / From her best prop so far, and storm so nigh" (IX, 432–33), from Adam. Both flowerlike in their innocence and beauty, they both are "gathered" in the act of "gathering" blossoms and fruit of strong sensuous appeal. At the crucial moment "earth feels the wound," as Milton puts it, or, as the hymn says, "the earth yawned there on the Nysion Plain" ("chane de chthon . . . Nusion am pedion," 16–17). The plucking of fruit or flower thus opens earth to the power of death, and harsh weather and drought and blight ensue.

The abducted or seduced heroine has thus become the bride of Death—Persephone in fact and Eve figuratively. Adam sees this when he exclaims: "How art thou lost, how on a sudden lost, / Defac't, deflow'r'd, and now to Death devote?" (X, 900–01). Notwithstanding its rhetorical and alliterative excess, this statement associates Eve's experience with the kind of sexual violation suffered by Persephone. As bride of Death, Persephone inadvertently binds herself to periodic sojourns in the underworld when she eats a single seed of the deadly pomegranate, the death apple which, as we have seen, has the same "mortal taste" as Eve's. Not only does the narcissus share with the forbidden fruit associations with narcissism and narcosis; both fair objects are referred to as "bait," and both strike their rash gazers with *amazement:* Persephone *"d' ara thambesas orexato chersin am ampho"* ("in amazement put forth both her hands," 15–16); Eve's amazement is repeatedly emphasized in Book IX, both before and after she eats the fruit, and most notably in the following passage:

> Lead then, said *Eve.* Hee leading swiftly roll'd
> In tangles, and made intricate seem straight,
> To mischief swift. Hope elevates, and joy
> Bright'ns his Crest, as when a wand'ring Fire,
> Compact of unctuous vapor, which the Night
> Condenses, and the cold invirons round,
> Kindl'd through agitation to a Flame,
> Which oft, they say, some evil Spirit attends,
> Hovering and blazing with delusive Light,
> Misleads th' amaz'd Night-wanderer from his way
> To Bogs and Mires, and oft through Pond or Pool,
> There swallow'd up and lost, from succor far.   (IX, 631–42)

The simile constitutes a proleptic scenario of Eve's oblique physical and mental movement to the point where, like her counterpart, Persephone, by swallowing deadly fruit, she will be "swallow'd up and lost, from succor far." This simile implicitly refers to the possibly hallucinated visions "some belated Peasant sees, / Or dreams he sees" (I, 783–84) and confirms the impression that both Persephone and Eve are not only amazed but fooled, with possibly a further implied allusion to the hallucinogenic properties of the narcissus and the fruit of the tree of knowledge, both of them *lusūs naturae.*

At this point we should take note of a fundamental distinction between the ways in which the myths of these two divine comedies reach fulfillment. The essentially innocent Persephone accepts an accommodation ultimately worked out by her mother and father (Demeter and Zeus) between the demands of death and life. Her strong attachment to her mother was a way of avoiding or denying not only the claims of mortality but those of marriage and child-bearing, the latter position being ludicrously incompatible witih her destined career as a fertility goddess like her revered mother. If abduction by Death and marriage to him are seen, understandably, as repellent, the match in the long run, as Helios remarks, is not such a bad one. If the nubile goddess becomes queen of the dead, she nevertheless succeeds in producing life out of death both through her marriage and through her mysterious function as the divinity of the germinating seed. The marriage with Death thus converts her life from a perpetually unfruitful virginity, tied regressively to her mother's apron strings, into true fertility. The triptych of the three generations of women at the end of the poem — Rhea, Demeter, and Persephone — emphasize major stages in the life of a woman as bride, mother, and grandmother. Here we find, as it were, a *seasonal* emphasis on the human life-cycle that, since these are immortals, has a kind of perpetual stasis somewhat like the village folk represented on Keats's Grecian urn. In this respect it is worth noting that Persephone and Demeter are virtually indistinguishable in such Eleusinian works of art as the Niinion tablet. The Demeter myth, far from celebrating abstemiousness, as the Genesis myth does, celebrates a growth in *techné* and wisdom in this world as a prelude to happiness in the next. If *Themis* is violated, as it obviously is in the conspiracy of Zeus and Pluto, the offense can be compensated by arbitration, without anything like "the rigid satisfaction, death for death" that the justice of Milton's God requires. In fact the Eleusinian rites are remarkable for the virtual absence of blood sacrifices. Triptolemos, the Eleusinian agricultural hero, transformed from an Ares-like threefold warrior (tripolemos) to plougher of the triple furrow, left three commandments: "Honor your parents. Honor the gods with fruits. Spare the animals" (Kerényi, p. 128). One might add to what Kerényi tells us of Triptolemos, who became a kind of Johnny Appleseed in his universal distribution of grain and agricultural technology, that in drawing the triple furrow, he was, as W. F. Jackson Knight has shown, one of those archetypal city consecraters who were to sanctify the walls of Troy, Athens, and Rome.[15] He and the Eumolpids, who guarded the sacred city of Eleusis, lived on good terms with all their fellow-creatures. Nowhere in the hymn is there a vestige of male superiority. Nowhere, by the same token, despite the myth's evolution from the chthonic celebrations of the Earth Mother, so dazzlingly represented in the Hypogeum at Malta, and despite the fact that the principal figures of the myth and the cult are female, is there a suggestion that we have here to do with a matriarchy.

Carl Kerényi, who, with George Mylonas, has done more than anyone else to elucidate the implications of Eleusinian myth and ritual, says that the cult was important "not only because people continued" after the fall of Greece "to come from every corner of the earth to be initiated, as they had in the days of the Emperor Hadrian, but also because the mysteries touched on something that was common to all people. They were connected," he continues,

not only with the Greek and Athenian existence, but with human existence in general. And Praetextus clearly stated just this: "*bios*, life," he declared, would become "unlivable (*abiotos*)" for the Greeks if the celebration were to cease. Beyond a doubt the Greeks are here contrasted with the Christians. The sharpness of the formulation of the significance of Eleusis, which has no parallel in earlier documents, springs from the conflict between Greek religion and Christian. Nonetheless, it suffices to give the mysteries a special significance for us, which goes beyond any concern for the history of religions. If life was unlivable for the Greeks without the annual celebration of Eleusis, it means that this celebration was a part not merely of non-Christian existence but also of Greek life, of the Greek form of existence; and this is another reason why it is of concern to us. Despite the enormous amount of literature devoted to them, the Eleusinian mysteries have not been studied from the standpoint of Greek existence, nor has Greek existence ever been considered in the light of Eleusis. (P. 12)

That Praetextus, the proconsul of Greece, should have ignored the decree of the Emperor Valentinian ordering the termination of the Eleusinian observances is a further tribute to the power of the vision which attracted men and women throughout the civilized world to participate in them. Finally, it was the pale Galilean who conquered. As Kerényi remarks, "the men in dark garments who moved in with Alaric were monks" (p. 18). It took more than monks and Visigoths to extinguish the light from Eleusis, however. Church fathers such as Clement of Alexandria, Tertullian, and Psellos probably knew only a debased version of Eleusis established in Egypt under the Ptolemies with a decidedly "erotomorphic" character that failed utterly to suggest the unique character of the original, cosmogonic myth and the mysteries out of which it grew. Mysteries "thought to hold the world together" (Kerényi, p. 12) were degraded into lewd performances that, according to Lactantius, represented theatrically, among other things, Persephone's coition with Zeus and Alexander's with Thaïs under the direction of an Eleusinian expatriate, derided in Dryden's *Alexander's Feast,* named Timotheus.

Like Praetextus, Milton seems to have chosen to preserve the Mysteries, alluding to them only through debased Latin versions, while (the internal evidence strongly suggests) deploying all the elements of the Greek original as a vital subtext for *Paradise Lost*. His art is the art that conceals art, as the involutions in the gesture of artful authorial diffidence that introduces the *Enna* simile shows:

> But rather to tell how, if Art could tell,
> How from that Sapphire Fount the crisped Brooks,
> Rolling on Orient Pearl and sands of Gold,
> With mazy error under pendant shades
> Ran Nectar, visiting each plant, and fed
> Flow'rs worthy of Paradise which not nice Art
> In Beds and curious Knots, but Nature boon
> Pour'd forth profuse on Hill and Dale and Plain.   (IV, 236–43)

So involuted is the passage from which this is taken that we may not notice that Milton fails to supply a verb to govern the infinitive *to tell*, at the same time converting, through pastoral clichés, the Golden Age into the Age of Gilt. So this ornamental passage, which he slyly offers in his "Hesperian Fable true," further conceals the latent archetype from Eleusis that transforms the simile into true gold. The hidden Eleusinian subtext winds endlessly through the roots and branches of Milton's forbidden tree and, like that tree, will bear restorative fruit, implying by what Bagehot felicitously termed its "enhancing suggestions" the "essential gift" of "the ceremonies which no one may describe or utter" (Kerényi, p. 13). In dismissing Eleusis by dismissing its Ovidian version, Milton was obeying the dictates of his Christian and monotheistic myth. As scholars like John Steadman have shown, he characteristically dismisses classical models in an explicit way while reassimilating them selectively and tacitly.[16] The *Enna* simile may be the most significant example of artful innocence in *Paradise Lost*.

If Milton knew the entire myth of Demeter, internal evidence, as I have said, suggests very strongly that he knew it through the *Hymn to Demeter*, but there is to my knowledge no external evidence that he ever saw the poem. Is it therefore necessary to conclude, because the only surviving text of the hymn was found in Moscow in 1777, that he could not have seen a version during his Italian trip in 1638–1639? What was found was once lost, and the interest in Eleusis and in the *Hymn to Demeter* in antiquity suggests that the poem must once have existed in multiple copies. A wild surmise would connect his knowledge of the poem to his friend Marvell's long sojourn in Moscow in 1663–1665 as a member of the earl of Carlyle's diplomatic mission. In any event, however the myth of Demeter found its way into a consummately beautiful simile in *Paradise Lost*, we can only rejoice that it did.

Yale University

NOTES

I would like to acknowledge with thanks a searching critique of this essay by Glen Most of the Department of Classics at Princeton while we were at the American Academy in Rome. Professor Most questioned or corrected numerous details, much to the benefit of the final version.

1. Kingsley Widmer, "the Iconography of Renunciation: The Miltonic Simile," *ELH*, XXV (1958), reprinted in *Critical Essays on Milton from ELH* (Baltimore, 1969), p. 76.

2. IV, 268–87. The edition of *Paradise Lost* used throughout is from John Milton, *Complete Poems and Major Prose*, ed. Merritt Y. Hughes (Indianapolis, 1957). Hereafter cited in the text.

3. N. J. Richardson, *The Homeric Hymn to Demeter* (Oxford, 1974), p. 73.

4. 1–73. My version is based on the text and translation in Hesiod, *The Homeric Hymns and Homerica*, ed. Hugh G. Evelyn-White (Cambridge, Mass., 1914), and on the text and commentary of Richardson.

5. After writing this paragraph I found my conjecture about the *felix culpa* developed by Eliade: "In the last analysis, the rape — that is, the symbolic death — of Proserpina had great consequences for humanity. As a result of it an Olympian goddess temporarily inhabited the kingdom of the dead. She had annulled the unbridgeable distance between Hades and Olympus. Mediatrix between two divine worlds, she could thereafter intervene in the destiny of mortals. Using a favorite expression of Christian theology, we could say: *felix culpa!* Just so, the failed immortalization of Demophoön brought on the shining epiphany of Demeter and the foundation of the mysteries" (Mircea Eliade, *A History of Religious Ideas*, vol. I, *From the Stone Age to the Eleusinian Mysteries* [Chicago, 1978], p. 293). G. S. Kirk, although critical of what he regards as facile or repetitive in Eliade's work, finds a similar depth of significance in the hymn: "In the Greek canon the tale of Demeter and Persephone occupies a central place, and might be still more prominent in classical art and literature were it not restricted by its secret role in the Eleusinian mysteries" (*Myth: Its Meaning and Function in Ancient and Other Cultures* [Cambridge, 1970], p. 197).

6. Milton had the myth of Ceres and Proserpina on his mind for many years before the appearance of *Paradise Lost* in 1667. In a letter to Charles Diodati dated September 23, 1637, he writes: "Not with so much labour, as the fables have it, is Ceres said to have sought her daughter Proserpina as it is my habit day and night to seek for this idea of the beautiful, as for a certain image of supreme beauty, through all the forms and faces of things (for many are the shapes of things divine) and to follow it as it leads me on by some sure traces which I seem to recognize" (*The Works of John Milton*, ed. Frank Allen Patter-

son et al. [New York, 1931–38], XII, p. 27; Hereinafter cited as CM). His feeling for the beauty of the myth did not, however, extend to what he knew of the Eleusinian mysteries, as we see from the second edition of The Doctrine and Discipline of Divorce (1644): "We must be resolv'd how the law can be pure and perspicuous, and yet throw a polluted skirt over these Eleusinian mysteries, that no man can utter what they mean: worse in this than the worst of heathen superstition; for their filthines was hid, but the mystick reason thereof known to their Sages" (CM III, pt. iii, p. 446). When he composed this Milton may have known only of the debased rites practiced in the pseudo-Eleusinian mysteries in Alexandria.

    7. V, 385–91. Text and translation are quoted from Metamorphoses, ed. F. J. Miller (Cambridge, Mass., 1916).

    8. George Sandys, Ovid's Metamorphosis Englished by G.S., Mythologiz'd, and Represented in Figures: An Essay to the Translation of Virgil's Aeneis (Oxford, 1632), p. 254. The derivation has been questioned. See the Oxford Classical Dictionary s.v. Persephone.

    9. In Mystagogus Poeticus (London, 1648) Alexander Ross makes the identification of Christ and Ceres explicit: "Christ is truly Ceres; which having lost mankinde, being carried away by the Devil, he came, and with the Torch of his Word, found him out; and being drawn by the flying serpents of Zeal and Prudence, dispersed his Seed through the World, went down to Hell, and rescued us from thence" (p. 69).

    10. Natalis Comes, Mythologiae (1583), p. 175.

    11. P. Ovidius Naso, Metamorphosen, commentary by Franz Bömer (Heidelberg, 1976), II, p. 238.

    12. Carl Kerényi, Eleusis: Archetypal Image of Mother and Daughter (New York, 1967), p. 92. Hereafter cited in the text.

    13. Paul Schmitt, "The Ancient Mysteries in the Society of Their Times, Their Transformation and Most Recent Echoes" (1944), in The Mysteries: Papers from the Eranos Yearbooks (Princeton, 1955), p. 103.

    14. The use of psychotropic drugs in the Eleusinian rituals is the subject of The Road to Eleusis: Unveiling the Secret of the Mysteries, by R. Gordon Wasson, Albert Hofmann, and Carl A. F. Ruck (New York, 1978).

    15. W. F. Jackson Knight, in Cumaean Gates, a Reference of the Sixth Aeneid to the Initiation Pattern (Oxford, 1936).

    16. See esp. Milton and the Renaissance Hero (Oxford, 1967).

"NATIVE SOIL": THE RHETORIC
OF EXILE LAMENT AND EXILE
CONSOLATION IN *PARADISE LOST*

Christopher Fitter

> But longer in this Paradise to dwell
> Permits not; to remove thee I am come,
> And send thee from the garden forth to till
> The ground whence thou wast taken, fitter soil. (XI, 259–62)

THESE WORDS lock Adam into physical paralysis and make Eve cry aloud from her refuge. The utmost weight of the tragic vision in *Paradise Lost* falls here, in what must accordingly be one of the most crucial and carefully meditated experiences of the epic's imagination. Imminent banishment is the third and worst blow to fallen man: "O unexpected stroke, worse than of death!" Worse than the humiliating strife of mutual recrimination, harsher even than the agony of knowing that these parents had murdered all the children of the world, this final punishment is felt to be quite unendurable. Its calamity overthrows Adam and Eve's earlier healing in mind, their partial recovery of peace: Adam had affirmed prayer to be valid (XI, 148–155) and Eve had become resigned to hardship (XI, 180). The clipped legality of Michael's notification of eviction, the icy reasonableness of his "consolations" to Eve, tough talk unsympathetic to flowers and smells (recalling God's interdiction of remorse at XI, 105), make Adam's thanks to him — "gently has thou told" — deeply ironic.[1] For Eve has, since Michael began talking, entirely lost her new sense of fortitude, and Adam no longer believes prayer to be worthwhile:

> prayer against his absolute decree
> No more avails than breath against the wind,
> Blown stifling back on him that breathes it forth. (XI, 311–13)

It will be the contention of this paper, however, that Michael's continuing statements give greater comfort than might seem the case to us today: that they provided, in effect, precisely that consolatory substance which Milton's readers will have anticipated, and whose profundity they will have approved. My purpose is to recall, as vital to our reading of this section of *Paradise Lost,* the existence of an approved topos of exile consolation: descended from Hellenistic rhetoric; elaborated in Plutarch, Cicero and Seneca; and extended into Renaissance literature from sentential collections and proverbial lore. Moreover, from Michael's first words to the closure of the exile discussion in ascension of the hill (XI, 251–366), the section is throughout unusually active in echoes and borrowings, literary and theological, which heighten feeling and strengthen argument. The laments and consolations mobilize for their antithesis rhetorical commonplaces of Renaissance and classical "homeland" writing unremarked by Milton's editors and critics.[2] We miss today these assimilations which ripen feeling in their sudden, strategic pressures. We have inherited a bland climax.

Beside the momentous truths of atonement theology, the formulae of classical solace function as lesser principles, immediacies of support. The cardinal consolations emerge in the prophetic section. Here is promised "the paradise within thee, happier far" (XII, 587), landscaped by virtuous living, and here are foreseen the healing conclusions of providence: the second Adam who shall restore us (XII, 310–14), and the higher eschatological bliss of the final and universal paradise (XII, 463–65). While the panorama from the "specular mount" exhibits and qualifies the cosmic disaster of man's exile from innocence, the antecedent dialogue, in the darkened garden below, ponders the lesser, sharper heartbreak of losing one's home. It is an almost routine domestic atrocity in the age of eviction and enclosure: the era of the *Mayflower;* of European expatriates fleeing the wars of religion; of the dispossession in England of defeated enemies from their estates; of family homelands swallowed by enclosures or wasted by war. Michael's juridical language of "rapacious claim," "sentence," and "seizure" casts Death as urgent creditor, God as shielding, resourcefully clement judge, and himself as bailiff.

> O unexpected stroke, worse than of death!
> Must I thus leave thee Paradise? Thus leave
> Thee native soil, these happy walks and shades,
> Fit haunt of gods? Where I had hope to spend,
> Quiet though sad, the respite of that day
> That must be mortal to us both.   (XI, 268–73)

However, the protestation of love for ancestral grounds is itself an ancestral cry. Bitter plaints of exile and farewells to the homeland are extant in Homer, in Euripides and Sophocles, in Ovid and Virgil.[3] Vilification of far foreign lands provides a common antithesis.[4] The neo-Stoic poetry of rural retreat carries the sentiments of settled order and ancestral peace into the verse of Renaissance France and England.[5] In the England of country-house poetry and of Stuart proclamations commanding the gentry to return to their estates, an England of subversive geographic mobility and nostalgia for medieval "tryed estate," it establishes itself as a fashionable rhetoric. "Let no man for any transitory pleasure sell away the inheritance he hath of breathing in the place where he was born. Get thee home, my young lad; lay thy bones peacably in the sepulchre of thy fathers; wax old in overlooking thy grounds; be at hand to close the eyes of thy kindred. The devil and I are desperate, he of being restored to heaven, I of being recalled home."[6] This is from the journalism of Nashe, but the motif of paternal acres anywhere guarantees pathos — as Shakespeare demonstrates in *The Winter's Tale* (IV, iv, 446–48) and *Richard II* (I, iii, 306–07). Eve's plaint, then, draws poignancy, deeper still for contemporaries than for us, from the currency of dispossession as both an established literary pathos and as actuality.

Milton structures her speech along three centers of anguish, and two of these exert the dignity and heightened emotional impact of classical topoi. The immediate form in which her heartbreak finds expression is the plaint for paternal acres. She at once focuses the exile from an Eden that is "native soil," restating the "heartland" emotion, the moving propriety of quiet last days in the birthplace. Her following lines tap the wealth of a still richer and more popular vein of literary feeling, wreathing her misery with the ancient pathos of the lost golden world.

> O flowers,
> That never will in other climate grow . . .
> Who now shall rear ye to the sun, or rank
> Your tribes, and water from the ambrosial fount? (XI, 273–76)

The motif of reciprocal support between her flowers and herself echoes the intimacies of belonging in Virgil's *Eclogues* (I, 38, 69; IX, 19–20) and summons all the menaced sweetness of the pastoral tradition. Finally, she cries out to the forfeit "nuptial bower," home within home as the most secure recess of innocence: a lament which leads very naturally to the form of consolation offered her by Michael.

Adam's plaint typifies the stronger spiritual consciousness that differentiates his disposition: "He for God only, she for God in him" (IV, 299). While the separation she fears is from the beloved environment which is "fit haunt of gods," that which Adam fears is from God himself. In a fine touch, Eve had been the one, as closer to natural beauty, to sense nature's new impersonal harshness in the postlapsarian world: the morning "All unconcerned with our unrest, begins / Her rosy progress smiling" (XI, 174–75). Her lament wavers along desperate vocatives, as of one ignorant of the laws disposing her fate crying to the sole principles of her security. Eve's communing apostrophe is contrasted by Adam's objectifying substantives — "this happy place, our sweet recess . . . this mount . . . this tree . . . these pines." He pleads a love for Eden not as native soil but as holy ground.

> This most afflicts me, that departing hence,
> As from his face I shall be hid, deprived
> His blessed countenance; here I could frequent,
> With worship, place by place where he vouchsafed
> Presence divine, and to my sons relate;
> On this mount he appeared; under this tree
> Stood visible, among these pines his voice
> I heard, here with him at this fountain talked:
> So many grateful altars I would rear
> Of grassy turf, and pile up every stone
> Of lustre from the brook, in memory,
> Or monument to ages, and thereon
> Offer sweet smelling gums and fruits and flowers:
> In yonder nether world where shall I seek
> His bright appearances, or footstep trace?   (XI, 315–29)

However, for Milton as for Michael, the speaker is Adam Idolatrous. Milton's nonconformist devaluation of "hallowed" properties is well known. He deplored the "new-vomited Paganisme of sensuall Idolatry, attributing purity, or impurity, to things indifferent, that they might bring the inward acts of the *Spirit* to the outward . . . as if they could make *God* earthly, and fleshly, because they could not make themselves *heavenly*, and *Spirituall*," and he vigorously denied the sacrilegiousness of buying monastic lands.[7] Even Eden is annihilated in divine wrath "to teach thee that God attributes to place / No sanctity, if none be thither brought / By men who there frequent, or therein dwell" (XI, 836–38). (This conception of an associate hallowing of place, a formulation of Protestant rationalism, had been poetically expressed already, we may recall, by "sage and serious Spenser" in the July Eclogue.)

The case against religious misvaluation of outward forms had opened in *Paradise Lost* as early as the exordium, with the reminder that the spirit prefers the "upright heart and pure" to all temples. Even Bethal, we discover in Book III, is only provisionally numinous, an impermanently holy place, for the celestial connection turns out to be a retractable ladder

(516–17). By contrast, Eve, on falling from grace, worships the tree of knowledge on her knees in a burst of pure and heartfelt idolatry (IX, 835–36). Milton's refusal of sacred site extends beyond Michael's consoling statement of divine omnipresence: "in valley and in plain / God is as here" (XI, 349–50). In his portrayal of life in Eden he deliberately breaks with the tradition which held that a special area had been reserved for religious service near the two trees in Eden, and his Adam and Eve worship wherever and whenever they please without external restraints.[8] The "here I could frequent / With worship, place by place where he vouchsafed / Presence divine" passage closely recalls an attack upon misguided veneration from Milton's prose:

Where ever a man, who had bin any way conversant with the *Apostles*, was to be found, thither flew all the inquisitive eares, the exercise of right instructing was chang'd into the curiosity of impertinent fabling . . . with lesse fervency was studied what Saint *Paul*, or Saint *Iohn* had written then was listen'd to one that could say here hee taught, here he stood, this was his stature . . . and O happy this house that harbour'd him, and that cold stone whereon he rested, this Village wherein he wrought such a miracle, and that pavement bedew'd with the warme effusion of his last blood . . . by this meanes they lost their time, and truanted in the fundamental grounds of saving knowledge. ("Of Prelatical Episcopacy," YP I, pp. 641–42)

Adam's plaint has thus advanced the exile theme in three ways. As is recognised, the "necessary errors about local devotion . . . provoke Michael's instruction" concerning omnipresence.[9] Additionally, the near-idolatrous form such piety takes colors the passage with the urgent feeling of topical controversy. Moreover, this is a self-disqualifying plea: the "veneration" of paradise proposed by Adam would be a desecration of it. The lament demonstrates corrupted man's unfitness to command in the garden of innocence: exile is extenuated as spiritually imperative.

Turning from the plaints to the formulae of solace which Michael extends to Adam and Eve, we may observe that, as the very substance of his overt exile consolation speeches, Milton imports a widely respected rhetoric. His two arguments approximate, I would suggest, to set pieces, visible and quickening to his contemporaries, each drawing on a long established consolatory formula.

> Thy going is not lonely, with thee goes
> Thy husband, him to follow thou art bound;
> Where he abides, think there thy native soil.
> (Consolation to Eve: XI, 290–92)

Adam, thou know'st heaven his, and all the earth.
Not this rock only; his omnipresence fills
Land, sea, and air, and every kind that lives,
Fomented by his virtual power and warmed.
All the earth he gave thee to possess and rule,
No despicable gift; surmise not then
His presence to these narrow bounds confined
Of Paradise or Eden: this had been
Perhaps thy capital seat, from whence had spread
All generations, and had hither come
From all the ends of the earth, to celebrate
And reverence thee their great progenitor.
But this pre-eminence thou has lost, brought down
To dwell on even ground now with thy sons:
Yet doubt not but in valley and in plain
God is as here, and will be found alike
Present.   (Consolation to Adam: XI, 335–51)

At the close of the first century A.D., Plutarch wrote to a friend in banishment the epistolary essay or διατριβή entitled περὶ φυγῆς, "On Exile."[10] Here he outlined a number of exile consolations. The first sketches a philosophic redress in the theory of determinative disposition (599 C–D, 600 D–E). It argues that, in contrast to the fixed intrinsic qualities of material phenomena, the character of any human circumstance is generated by the evaluative response of the individual experiencing it: it is morally supplied, by the interpretative action of personal conception. This variability to estimation of personal fortune represents for Plutarch not a confining doctrine of solipsism, but rather the ground of optimism. Coupled with an ultimately providential and celestial vision of man's destiny, it makes possible the accommodation of adverse fortune through an active remaking of it in the reformation of opinion consistent with a truly rational perspective. This exile consolation of reformed opinion is Plutarch's major argument, realized in particulars of rational reconceiving throughout the remainder of his essay. Further to this argument Plutarch recommends the consolatory dilution of evil by remaining goods: "misfortunes . . . can be blended with whatever is useful and comforting in your present circumstances: wealth, friends, freedom from politics" (600 A, D). What distinguishes this whole line of argument is the appeal to the personal imagination of circumstance, and this is what stamps Michael's consolation to Eve: it is less an exposition of external facts of cheer than an appeal to her corrective, deepest values, the attempt to steer her interpretative sensibility: "Think there thy native soil."

Plutarch provides a second major consolation in the argument of the universal home. The entire universe is our native land (600 E–601 D). Socrates called himself not a Greek but a Cosmian (κόσμιαν). Plutarch scorns the trivial particularism of local attachment, of commitment to zone, as a mere sublunary matter, and urges the insignificance of terrestrial placement. Locality is irrelevant in his cosmic perspective of global minuteness. Further, on earth, "no one is either exile or foreigner or alien; here are the same fire, water and air; the same magistrates and procurators and councillors — Sun, Moon, and Morning Star; the same laws for all, decreed by one commandment and one sovereignty — the summer solstice, the winter solstice, the equinox, the pleiades, Arcturus, the seasons of sowing, the seasons of planting; here one king and ruler 'God, holding the beginning, middle, and end of the universe'." "But we, when like ants or bees we have been driven out of one anthill or beehive, are dismayed and feel strange, possessing neither the knowledge nor the instruction that would teach us to take and consider the whole world to be our own, as indeed it is" (601 A–B, C). The note of rebuke is as clear as Michael's, and so is the similarity of the reasoning. Plutarch's mockery of those who "on coming to a foreign land . . . fail to recognise this earth, the sea, the air, the sky, as though they were distinct and different from those familiar to us" (601 C), perhaps suggested Adam's intimidated myopia:

> all places else
> Inhospitable appear and desolate,
> Nor knowing us nor known,   (XI, 305–07)

forgetful of the universal providence of "earth's great altar" (IX, 195) and of Raphael's reminder anyway that "man . . . dwells not in his own" (VIII, 103).

It is almost certain that Milton was acquainted with this essay. Plutarch was highly popular in the seventeenth century as moralist, historian, and educator. "The Education of Children" was misattributed to him; Jacques Amyot, French scholar and cleric, translated the *Moralia* into French in 1572; Philemon Holland Englished it in 1603, and a new edition of this version was published in 1657. As early as 1609 a fluent Ben Jonson character, one Truewit, is petulantly addressed: "Foh! Thou hast read Plutarch's Morals now, or some such tedious fellow; and it shows so vilely with thee, 'fore God, 'twill spoil thy wit utterly."[11] North's translation of the *Lives* was published in 1579, with later editions in 1595 and 1603. Milton's canon makes many references to the *Moralia*, and it seems clear that eclectic Plutarch appealed to syncretic Milton. Milton recommends him for school instruction in his "Tractate on Education" as a wholesome classical author; and the two overlap in many points of view and curiosity. Plutarch nowhere disparages Christianity (in his time still a minor affair of scattered communities), attacks both Epicureanism and Stoicism, and significantly presents himself as a convinced Platonist. Like Milton, he opposes the condemnation of matter as the source of evil, and has a keen speculative interest in the visitation of spirits or "daimones." His ultimate Platonic perspective of home in eternity dominates the consolation structure, and the celestial homeland likewise lends the comforting closes to his "Consolation to his Wife" and to "On Tranquility of Mind." Although this leads him to adopt the absolute position of affirming exile a delusion, there being no such thing as a native land, the thrust, tenor, and majority of his arguments in the περὶ φυγῆς do not contradict the Christian viewpoint. Indeed, his accent upon human self-determination, and belief in man's educability and potential goodness, present corruption notwithstanding, would have endeared him to Milton. The essay's exhortation of the banished to cheerful, industrious resettlement accorded well both with the Protestant tendency to especial favor of diligent enterprise, and the praise in Psalm cvii of a God who guides his people from exile into colonizing action.

The "diatribe" form in which Plutarch wrote, introduced by the Academy and developed by the Stoics and Cynics, specialised in the provision, within the form of a letter, of a synthesis of philosophic commonplaces. For his composition on exile Plutarch accordingly draws consolations garnered from many minor Greek writers: from Bion, Ariston of Chios, Musonius, and Teles.[12] Recent editors have noted common ground with Favorinus and Epictetus.[13] Indeed, in the *Tusculan Disputations*, Cicero had noted a *topos* of exile consolation (III, 34.81). He himself essays a brace of commiserations, invoking the Socratic "Cosmian" and affirming the universal homeland of the sage (V, 37.108). The wise man, we find Seneca agreeing a century later, is at home everywhere: for the scheme of natural providence everywhere environs us. Moreover the ills of loss lie only in opinion. "Every evil is only as great as we have reckoned it to be. In our hands we have a remedy."[14] We may redress privation through an interpretative readjustment of the mind, a revaluation of judgment in accord with a rational conception of circumstance. "Omne solum forti patria est," declares Ovid: "To a wise man the whole world is fatherland" (*Fasti*, I, 493). There pertains, it thus appears, a wide currency to the consolatory motifs. They are diffused throughout the philosophic sensibility of antiquity. The logic they present moves not within a local philosophic insularity, but constructs the master themes of the Cynic-Stoic tradition, put to consolatory purpose in redress of a spectrum of grievances: poverty, bereavement, confiscation of property, as well as exile. The "City of the World" is among the most widely celebrated of Stoic doctrines, and the beneficent and universal god or goddess of nature was "one of the last religious experiences of the late-pagan world. She possesses inexhaustable vitality."[15]

As we might expect, the themes recur in Boethius' compendium of philosophic comforts, where the exile consolation of reformed conception is twice given.[16] Augustine's *Confessions* confirms the unimportance of burial in a country of exile, and the passage debates a commonplace misgiving and reassurance, recalling Teles and Favorinus (IX, 11).[17] And by the Renaissance, such sentiments are fast in proverbial lore. Tilley records twelve instances of the Stoic-descended formula "A wise man makes every country his own" between 1571 and 1666, and several of the related proverb "A man's country is where he does well." Baldwin quotes, in a gloss of *Richard II:*

> Unto a valiant hart there is no banishment,
> All countreys are his native soil beneath the firmament.
> As to the fishe, the sea, as to the fowle, the ayre,
> So is like pleasant to the wise, eche place of his repayre.[18]

The themes have likewise established themselves in sentential collections, as Baldwin elsewhere has remarked. Under *exilium* in the quotation books is filed the admirable sage who is everywhere at home; and the *Fasti*, in which Ovid's popular compression occurs, is regular grammar-school reading. Correlative with this, Erasmus in the *Adagia* gives under *patria:* "Patria est ubicumque est bene," attributed to Seneca: "One's country is where it is well with one." He records this again in *De conscribendis epistolis*, a textbook on the writing of epistles which enjoyed widespread grammar-school use.[19] Milton quotes the English version of this himself, with approval, in one of the *Familiar Letters*.[20] Robert Burton, in the *Anatomy*, cites both this and the Ovidian "omne solum forti patria" in a section devoted to "Remedies Against Discontents," including that of exile, for which he draws on Alcinous' influential epitome of Platonic philosophy.[21] Pierre Charron deploys the same persuasions in his chapter "Du Bannissement et exil."[22]

Contemporary literature is likewise pervaded by the ancient themes which Milton deploys for his two exile consolations: the Stoic universalist natural scheme, and the redress of adversity through the rationally reformed imagination. The former theme is found in Perdita: "the selfsame sun that shines upon his court / Hides not his visage from our cottage, but / Looks on alike" (IV, iv, 436–38) in a charged pastoral encounter where the rhetoric of quiet death in the ancestral home also reappears:

> You have undone a man of fourscore-three
> That thought to fill his grave in quiet, yea,
> To die upon the bed my father died,
> To lie close by his honest bones.   (IV, iv, 445–48)

Richard II gives the theme in its exile context: "All places that the eye of heaven visits / Are to a wise man ports and happy havens"(I, iii, 275–76). "It is the mynd that maketh good or ill" is of course a commonplace of the age, and the application of this to geographic location is fertile. Extant examples include Lovelace's "stone walls do not a prison make" and Hamlet's dialogue with Rosencrantz on Denmark as a prison: "There is nothing either good or bad, but thinking makes it so. To me it is a prison. . . . O God, I could be bounded in a nut shell and count myself a king of infinite space, were it not that I have bad dreams" (II, ii, 249–50; 253–55). But it is again *Richard II* that gives the convention full value:

> Teach thy necessity to reason thus— . . .
> Think not the King did banish thee,
> But thou the King. Woe doth the heavier sit
> Where it perceives it is but faintly borne. . . .
> Look what thy soul holds dear, imagine it
> To lie that way thou goest.   (I, iii, 277–87)[23]

There is one further and highly influential mediator of the exile consolations redeployed by Milton, the source indeed of Shakespeare's acquaintance with them. John Lyly, in *Euphues* (1578), gives a substantial free version of Plutarch's letter in "Euphues to Botonio, to take his exile patiently." Here we congregate again with the old favorites, Cosmian Socrates and the internationalist wise man (who "lyveth as well in a farre country as in his owne home"). Here again are exile as delusory, the dilution of ills by remaining sources of strength, and the remedial sovereignty of the mind over circumstance: "It is not the nature of the place but the disposition of the person that maketh the lyfe pleasaunt." And here once more flourishes the generous global fundamental: "*Plato* would never accompt him banished yt had the Sunne, Fire, Aire, Water, and Earth, that he had before, where he felt the Winters blast and the Summers blaze, wher ye same Sunne and the same Moone shined, whereby he noted that every place was a countrey to a wise man, and all partes a pallaice to a quiet minde."[24]

It seems sure, then, that the archangelic solaces of Milton's poem

summon a popular rhetoric, that they comfort estrangement with resonances of familiarity. The case for a direct Plutarchan influence on Milton is strong, if circumstantial. If Milton was also familiar with Cicero's
and Seneca's exile writings, Plutarch remains closer to the Eden dialogue
in providing both the consolations, of revaluation and of global belonging, within one concentrated work: the two Latin writers omit the former argument in their brief exile treatments, expressing the principle more
generally elsewhere. It may be that Milton had in mind all those references to the endurance of banishment which I have outlined. Certainly,
as I have said, his letters quote the "patria" formula; and it is hard to
see how he could have been unaware of the *Euphues* section and its Shake-
spearian echoes. There appears to be no exact imitation of Plutarch's language and images, although two further thematic similarities represent
possible influences. One has already been mentioned: Adam states the
position Plutarch parodies, of failing to recognize that the same primary
features of Nature are at work in the wider world. The other concerns
the exile consolation of the choice of homeland. "The exclusion from one
city is the freedom to choose from all," Plutarch points out in the *Moralia*.
"The Kings of the Persians were called happy for spending the winter
in Babylon, the summer in Media, and the most pleasant part of Spring
in Susa" (604 B–C). Lyly reiterates the same point and imagery, and Burton recalls "the pleasure of peregrination, variety of objects will make
amends." (2.3.4). This may well have suggested Michael's turn of phrase
in his remark to Adam: "this had been / Perhaps thy capital seat" (XI,
342–43). It must certainly have been intended to contribute to the richness of the spell, the pathos yet strange freshness, of the close of *Paradise
Lost:* "The world was all before them, where to choose / Their place of
rest, and providence their guide."

I think we may observe that Milton adapts these models to an im-
peccable thematic belonging. The wise consolation lyveth as well in the
farre country of the Puritan epic as in his classical and proverbial home.
The pagan themes are accommodated to the poem by becoming, as it
were, both "Christianized" and "Miltonized" — harmonized, that is, both
with scriptural and patristic accounts of the Fall and with prominent features of Milton's distinctive portrayal of Adam, Eve, and Eden.

In the tradition of philosophic consolation, Michael has exhorted Eve
to a restorative revaluation of circumstance, through the active exercise
not only of patience and reason but of her rational imagination, centered
on a prime remedial truth: the continuing presence of Adam. The "Teach
thy necessity to reason thus" convention is given, somewhat sharply, in
"think there thy native soil." This not only contrasts with the pastoral

trope of reciprocal support (she will live in truer symbiosis with Adam than with her flowers), it also extends scriptural perspective. The tone of rebuke and command in "him to follow thou art bound" recalls the Son's judgment recently passed on her, the Genesis subordination of post-lapsarian woman. And the motif of the superlative valuation of the lover recalls Augustine's interpretation of the priorities actuating the Fall, in the *City of God:* Adam had fallen not "because he believed that the woman spoke the truth," but "because they were so closely bound in part-nership" (his motive is the "socialis necessitudo").[25]

And there is of course a further accommodating dimension of fa-miliarity here. The lover as effectually a homeland, the summative, tran-scending, and eclipsing valuation of the lover, is a commonplace of Re-naissance love literature. From Donne we learn that "Love, all love of other sights controls, / And makes one little room an everywhere."[26] From Shakespeare we recall Helena discomfiting Demetrius with:

> Nor doth this wood lack worlds of company,
> For you, in my respect, are all the world.
> Then how can it be said I am alone
> When all the world is here to look on me?
>   . . . .
> I'll follow thee, and make a heaven of hell.
>
> (*MND* II, i, 223–26, 243)

Romeo similarly declares "There is no world without Verona walls . . . heaven is here / Where Juliet lives" (III, iii, 17, 29–30). While Romeo is banished and insects buzz near Juliet, "More validity, / More honour-able state, more courtship lives / In carrion flies than Romeo" (III, iii, 33–35).[27] This sufficiency of happiness in the company of the beloved is absolutely integral to sexual portrayal in *Paradise Lost*. Adam expresses it with regard to Eve, both in having her ("so lovely fair, / That what seemed fair in all the world, seemed now / Mean, or in her summed up," VIII, 471–73) and in projected loss ("How can I live without thee, how forgo / Thy sweet converse and love so dearly joined, / To live again in these wild woods forlorn?" IX, 908–10 — a precisely inverse form of Helena's words to Demetrius). It has been stated by Eve, in her majestic nocturnal love-song (IV, 639–56), and is repeated in the courageous mood of reconciliation at the poem's close. It is felt even by Satan ("She most, and in her look sums all delight," IX, 454), who bitterly perceives the pair "Imparadised in one another's arms / The happier Eden" (IV, 506–07). And this sexual allness is, of course, but one example of *Para-dise Lost*'s overarching drive, the demonstration that the ground of spiritual contentment eclipses and transcends physical and historic circumstance. Home is, indeed, where it is well with one, inward, evaluative, and personal, and the structure of the epic offers almost a comedy of eclipse in respect of the external and topographic Eden. The exposition of the truth that the "mind is its own place" (I, 254) is systematic — Eden is waived by Adam in love, and by Satan in hate, the mind continually transforming, resisting, or transcending outward circumstance.[28] Indeed Milton's portrayal of Eden is distinguished by the pains he takes to show the love of Adam and Eve as spiritual and rational, rather than as primarily physical and domestic — "Union of mind, or in us both one soul" (VIII, 604) — and he is unique in presenting theirs as a crucially religious relationship, mutually supportive in the worship of God.[29] The exile consolation of reformed conception is given final integration in a sharp textual twist. For the forfeit "native soil" of Paradise, Michael suggests compensation in the "native soil" of Adam's presence: Eve, we know, has been literally composed from the ground of her husband's flesh. The solace of the right thinking imagination is clinched by the cogent literalness of an Archangelic pun.

Finally, Milton's introduction of the Cynic-Stoic exile consolation of global belonging into the expulsion scene in *Paradise Lost* has some further implications. Most obviously, the pagan comfort of the universal scheme of providential nature is smoothly assimilated to the Christian doctrine of divine omnipresence. Plutarch's essay, of course, had suggested in the conception of geographic homeland an erroneously sublunar and punctual definition of man's context, whereas Christian orthodoxy maintained that the charmed circle of Paradise was the incomparable true homeland of man. Milton did not subscribe to the postulate of certain contemporary theologians that Paradise had comprised the whole earth.[30] His poem asserts that expulsion from Eden is genuine exile, and he dispossesses his consolation of our familiar proverb of the wise man anywhere at home. In application to fallen man, the "pagan" exile consolation of joy in the universal frame thereby acquires an ironic element, a further dimension of pathos accessible to contemporaries and usually lost upon moderns.

However, the Protestant spirit of confidence in a beauty and holiness extending through creation, its militant understanding of omnipresence, so harmonious with the tenor of the pagan assurance, is nonetheless secure in this poem of the felix culpa. Human involvement in the world beyond Eden, perceived in terms of adventure and dignity, "no despicable gift," has long informed the poem's consciousness, just as the outreach of direct supernatural force from the sacred boundaries of the paradise garden into contemporary life, into creation at large, had intrigued the minds of contemporary poets. Herbert in *Decay* and Vaughan in *Corruption* and *Religion* are excited by the perpetuation in the earlier historic world, indeed the sheer contingent ease, of celestial encounter, by scriptural angels once met casually in landscape. The chapel windows of University College, Oxford (1641), exhibit this same imagination of man's intercourse with the heavenly as only gradually receding: the picture of Abraham's reception of the visitant angels is placed *between* the Expulsion and the Toil windows.[31]

For Milton, then, though the commitment to earthly location is valid at the human level, actualized, as in the case of Eve, through the bonds of biography and cultivation, at the highest level we learn the primacy of universal goodness over geographic sentiment, an exhilarating perspective reconciled even with the scriptural ascendancy of Eden in the balancing appraisal of Michael. Even as Milton refutes the absolute conception of the global home, a further effective devaluation of Paradise ensues as Michael establishes the exact degree and kind of loss: it would have proved only — and one notes the reductive secular terminology — Adam's "capital seat." In conclusion, then, the familiarity and momentum of an ancient consolatory tradition works, in a passage typical of much seventeenth-century sentiment, to strengthen the distinctive courage and equipoise of Milton's version of the Fall of Man, his indomitable vision of a felix culpa.

St. John's College, Oxford

NOTES

1. Milton is quoted from *The Poems of John Milton*, ed. John Carey and Alastair Fowler (London, 1980).

2. The omission is all the more surprising, unrectified as it remains after Louis Martz's *Milton: Poet of Exile* (New Haven, 1964).

3. *Odyssey* I, 57–59, and IX, 31–36; *Alcestis* 248–49; *Philoctetes* 1452–1463; *Tristia* III, 10, 1–78, and III, 4, 1–62; *Eclogues* I and IX. All references to classical texts are given in the Loeb Classical Library editions.

4. Virgil's *Eclogues*, I, 64–71; *Aeneid* I, 198–209; Ovid's *Tristia* III, 10, 1–78, and III, 4, 1–62; Seneca, *De consolatione ad Helviam* IX, 1.

5. *Georgics* II, 510–31; Joachim Du Bellay, "Heureuse, qui comme Ulysse," (*Les Regrets*), in *Oevres morales*, ed. Henri Chambard (Paris, 1908), pp. 76–77; Honorat de Racan's *Stances* ("Thirsis, il faut penser"), in *Poesies Lyriques*, ed. Louis Arnold (Paris, 1930), pp. 176–85. In *England's Helicon*, ed. Hugh Macdonald (1600; rpt. London, 1949):

Thomas Lodge, *Olde Damons Pastoral*, p. 19; William Byrd, *The Heard-Mans; Happie Life*, p. 144. Typical too is Richard Barnfield's *The Shepherd's Content*, in *The Poems of Richard Barnfield*, introd. Montague Summers (London, 1936), p. 25.

6. *The Unfortunate Traveller*, in *The Works of Thomas Nashe*, ed. R. B. McKerrow, rpt. with corrections by F. P. Wilson (Oxford, 1966), II, pp. 302–03.

7. *Of Reformation in England*, in *Complete Prose Works of John Milton*, ed. Don M. Wolfe et al. (New Haven, 1953–82), I, p. 520 (hereafter cited as YP). On Milton and the nonconformist contempt for veneration of consecrated ground see Keith Thomas, *Religion and the Decline of Magic* (London, 1973), pp. 58–59, 65–67, 114–21.

8. The tradition was supported, among others, by Archbishop Ussher, Lancelot Andrewes, and John Gregory. See Joseph E. Duncan, *Milton's Earthly Paradise* (Minnesota, 1972), p. 164.

9. Carey and Fowler, *Poems of John Milton*, note to *PL* XI, 315–33.

10. Quotations are from *Moralia*, trans. Phillip H. de Lacy and Benedict Einarson, Loeb Classical Library (Cambridge, Mass., 1959), VII.

11. *The Silent Woman* I, i, 62–64. For this reference, and a general study of the influence of Plutarch's thought, see D. A. Russell, *Plutarch* (London, 1972), pp. 143–58. For a list of sixteenth-century versions of *Moralia* in Latin and in vernacular languages, see R. Aulotte, *Amyot et Plutarque* (Geneva, 1965), pp. 325–37, 340–45.

12. See C. A. Giesecke, *De philosophorum veterum quae ad exilium spectant sententiis* (Leipzig, 1891), who concludes an ultimate descent of these ideas from Bion and Ariston. However, Jean Hani, editor and translator of the more recent *Oeuvres morales* (Paris, 1980), dissents, finding constant reminders of the Stoic tradition and of such contemporaries as Epictetus and Seneca (pp. 139–40).

13. See A. Barigazzi, *Favorino opere* (Florence, 1966). See also note 12.

14. Seneca, *De consolatione ad Helviam* in *Moral Essays*, Loeb Classical Library (Cambridge, Mass., 1932), II: VIII, 5–6; IX, 2; IX, 7. Also *De consolatione ad Marciam*, ibid., XIX, 1.

15. E. R. Curtius, *European Literature and the Latin Middle Ages* (London, 1953), p. 107.

16. *The Consolation of Philosophy*, trans. V. E. Watts (Middlesex, 1969), pp. 48, 63.

17. See Plutarch, *On Exile*, 604 D (Russell, p. 551 and note d).

18. M. P. Tilley, *A Dictionary of the Proverbs in England in the Sixteenth and Seventeenth Centuries* (Ann Arbor, 1950), M 426 and M 468. T. W. Baldwin, *William Shakespeare's Small Latine and Lesse Greeke* (Urbana, 1944), II, p. 427, glossing *Richard II* I, iii, 275–76.

19. See T. W. Baldwin, *Parallels Between "Soliman and Perseda" and Garnier's "Bradamante,"MLN*, LI (1936), 237–41. Although Tilley and Baldwin have recorded the proverbial and sentential background to these sentiments, and the Lyly-Plutarch basis of the *Richard II* consolations has been registered since Malone's edition, scholars do not appear aware of the scale of exile consolation writing as a topos, subsuming Boethius, Augustine, Alcinous, and Burton in addition to Plutarch and Lyly; neither has the tradition been extended in application from Shakespeare to Milton.

20. *Familiar Letters*, in *The Works of John Milton*, ed. Frank Allen Patterson et al. (New York, 1931–38), XII, p. 115.

21. Alcinous, *Epitoma disciplinarum Platonis* (Rome, 1469). The *Epitoma* was translated from the second-century Greek by Petrus Balbus and published with the works of Apuleius. This respected work, soon afterward translated by Ficino, was published in various forms in Italy, France, Holland, and Germany. See R. E. Witt, *Albinus and the History*

of *Middle Platonism* (Cambridge, 1937). Robert Burton, *The Anatomy of Melancholy*, ed. Holbrook Jackson (London, 1972), pp. 174–75, section 2.3.4. I am indebted for this reference to the vigilant scholarship of Mr. Amlan das Gupta.

22. Charron, *Oeuvres* (Paris, 1635), ch. 24, p. 143.

23. Cf. *Coriolanus* III, iii, 125, 137. All Shakespeare quotations and references are from *The Complete Works of William Shakespeare*, ed. Peter Alexander (London, 1951).

24. Lyly, *Euphues: The Anatomy of Wyt*, in *The Complete Works of John Lyly*, ed. R. Warwick Bond (Oxford, 1902), I, pp. 313–16.

25. *The City of God*, trans. David Knowles (Middlesex, 1972), XIV, 11.

26. *The Good Morrow* 10–11.

27. See also *Othello* V, ii, 147.

28. See also IV, 20–23, 75; IX, 467–68, 1125–26; XII, 495, 587.

29. See Duncan, *Milton's Earthly Paradise*, pp. 177, 185–86.

30. Such theologians as Vadianus, Goropius Becanus, Lodovico Nogarola, Juan de Pineda, and Johann Bronchorst. See ibid., pp. 199–202.

31. See Louis Martz, *The Paradise Within* (New Haven, 1964), pp. 147–48.

CREATION IN GENESIS AND
IN *PARADISE LOST*

Philip J. Gallagher

S HORTLY BEFORE the Restoration, Milton wrote, apropos of the translation of the Bible into various vernacular languages, "Therefor are the Scriptures translated into every vulgar tongue, as being held in main matters of belief and salvation, plane and easie to the poorest."[1] The author of *Paradise Lost*, however, knew also that the plain and perspicuous in all things needful to salvation may not be self-evident in all things: what is dark in God's word must be illumined, as witness (for example) the tortuous process by which Milton's Adam comes to divine the full import of the protevangelium (Gen. iii, 14–15).[2] Adam's exegetical struggle is paradigmatic of fallen man's relationship to Holy Writ: biblical hermeneutics is a difficult and tricky business, replete with pits into which lame faith, leading understanding blind, is all too likely to fall. Nevertheless in *Paradise Lost* Milton plunges unhesitatingly into the arena of biblical commentary, anticipating many of the discoveries of modern exegesis — and this, necessarily, without availing himself of the extraordinary explanatory power of the documentary hypothesis.[3] Consistent with his intention to "justify the ways of God"[4] down to their last recorded syllable, Milton habitually clarifies vexed passages, especially from the first two chapters of Genesis. In the process he often divagates from what appear to be more or less self-evident biblical implications, seeking always to accommodate the details of the received narrative to a pious interpretation. Moreover, as Irene Samuel has observed, "the direction of Milton's [biblical] nonconformities was never toward greater mystery, greater miracle, but rather always toward greater rationality, greater availability as a guide in living."[5] Indeed, as I hope to show, the epic bard invests a good deal of creative energy in demonstrating that the archaic creation myths of Genesis are thoroughly rational and mutually compatible, a demonstration whose efficacy certain modern scholars have underestimated.[6] My method will mimic Milton's: just as he takes up biblical problems in Genesis seriatim, as he encounters them verse by verse in chapter i, so shall I examine his solutions, proceeding chronologically from day to day and, as it happens, from the relatively simple to the infinitely complex.

163

I. Genesis i, 1–5 and 14–19

"In the beginning," the King James Bible reads, "God created the heaven and the earth."[7] This translation is problematical in at least three ways: (1) it implies creation *ex nihilo*, a common but illogical interpretation (for nothing comes from nothing — nothing ever could) nowhere supported by the Hebrew Scriptures; (2) it involves the Creator in apparently shoddy workmanship, for what ensued after verse 1 was chaos (i, 2a), which consequently demanded his immediate attention; and (3) it implies that the original creative gesture (i, 1) was anomalous, the God of Genesis i having created everything *except* the heaven and the earth by the power of the word ("Let there be light," i, 3, "Let there be a firmament," i, 6, "Let the waters," i, 9, etc.). These difficulties are nowhere present in *Paradise Lost*, however. Milton eliminates the first two by relying on the doctrine of creation *ex Deo*.[8] Contrary to the Authorized Version, our poet believes that Moses taught the ancient Jews "In the Beginning how the Heav'ns and Earth / Rose," not out of nothing, but "out of *Chaos*" (*PL* I, 9–10), a portion of whose contents "th' Almighty Maker . . . ordain[s] / His dark materials" (II, 915–16) to shape into the visible universe.[9] Unfallen Adam seems intuitively to recognize this state of affairs and to dismiss *ex nihilo* creation as unthinkable. His curiosity aroused perhaps by a reminiscence of Raphael's allusion to the "one first matter all" (V, 472) whence all nature proceeds,[10] Adam wants to know "When" our world began, "whereof created, for what cause" (VII, 64). He thus affirms in a single stroke his belief in a world made in time, of preexistent matter, and teleologically. Whence did the matter of Chaos derive? From God, clearly, *ex Deo* (VII, 168–73). Who differentiated part of the chaotic mass "Of neither Sea, nor Shore, nor Air, nor Fire" (II, 912) into the elemental heaven and earth of Genesis? Although Satan assigns such creative efficacy to Chaos itself ("*Space* may produce new Worlds," he heretically alleges, I, 650, emphasis mine), Milton attributes the world's beginning to the word of God, which he hypostatizes, on the analogy with John i, 1–18, as the instrumental cause: "As by his Word the mighty Father made / All things" (V, 836–37).

So committed is Milton to a logos-cosmogony that, boldly extrapolating from the opening chapters of Genesis and John, he traces to an originative verbal gesture even Hell itself, "which God by curse / Created evil" (II, 622–23).[11] Consequently, it should come as no surprise that, even before Raphael has illuminated their darkness, unfallen Adam and Eve can intuit that God "out of Darkness *call'd up* Light" (V, 179, emphasis mine); nor should the reader be perplexed to find Milton eliminating the anomaly of Genesis i, 1 by asserting that *all* God's creative acts, including the making of heaven and earth, are effected by the spoken word: "ride forth," the Father tells the Son, "and bid the Deep / Within appointed bounds be Heav'n and Earth" (VII, 166–67). According to the Archangel Uriel, God's word became flesh

> when at his Word the formless Mass,
> This world's material mould, came to a heap:
> Confusion heard his voice, and wild uproar
> Stood rul'd, stood vast infinitude confin'd.   (III, 708–11)

Rather than being *ex nihilo*, then, creation in *Paradise Lost* entails the verbal imposition of form upon an already present material matrix. The making of heaven and earth proceeds in three well-defined stages, two of which are divine speech acts. Before riding into Chaos, Messiah prepares the region to receive him by the power of his word: "Silence, ye troubl'd waves, and thou Deep, peace, / Said then th' Omnific Word, your discord end" (VII, 216–17). Whereupon he enters the abyss, takes in hand compasses that Milton found in Proverbs viii, 27, and with them circumscribes a spherical universe (218–29), saying the while: "Thus far extend, thus far thy bounds, / This be thy just Circumference, O World" (230–31). Where, therefore, the Authorized Version can assert simply (but problematically) *that* "God created the heaven and the earth," Milton can investigate "*how* this World / Of Heav'n and Earth conspicuous first began" (62–63, emphasis mine). Raphael, aided by the witness of the eye, can characterize the *how* and conclude definitively, "Thus God the Heav'n created, thus the Earth" (232). So much is required in *Paradise Lost* to make Genesis i, 1 safe for Miltonic orthodoxy.

Next, whereas Genesis i, 2a ("And the earth was without form, and void; and darkness *was* upon the face of the deep") appears to describe a new-found chaotic situation brought into being *ex nihilo*, for Milton the verse merely records the consequence of God's bounding what was previously chaotically unbounded (233–34); and whereas Genesis continues, "And the Spirit of God moved upon the face of the waters" (2b), Milton greatly expands this cryptic half-verse to assure the purposefulness of the Deity's so moving and to render explicit the biblical implication that God is hovering over the new-made world much as a bird would brood over an egg.[12] Moreover, the opening invocation of *Paradise Lost*, like Genesis, makes it appear that God is impregnating the Chaos that has resulted from the supposedly creative activity of i, 1: "with mighty wings outspread" the Spirit "Dove-like satst brooding on the vast Abyss / And mad'st it pregnant" (I, 20–22); but Raphael's more extended narrative confirms that we are involved rather with the further differentiating of an already-made heaven and earth:

> but on the wat'ry calm
> His brooding wings the Spirit of God outspread,
> And vital virtue infus'd, and vital warmth
> Throughout the fluid Mass, but downward purg'd
> The black tartareous cold Infernal dregs
> Adverse to life; then founded, then conglob'd
> Like things to like, the rest to several place
> Disparted, and between spun out the Air,
> And Earth self-balanc't on her Centre hung.   (VII, 234b–42)

These lines have no warrant in Genesis, though the notion of an earth self-suspended centrally within the circumference of the world's great circle derives from Job xxvi, 7, where it is said that God "hangeth the earth upon nothing." If we may regard Uriel's brief account as an anticipatory gloss upon Raphael's, Milton is probably describing the creation of the five elements and the separation of the four earthly from one another and from their heavenly counterpart:

> Swift to thir several Quarters hasted then
> The cumbrous Elements, Earth, Flood, Air, Fire,
> And this Ethereal quintessence of Heav'n
> Flew upward.   (III, 714–17a)[13]

The "Ethereal quintessence" or fifth element to which Uriel refers is the *aether*, which emerges from Chaos to form the indestructible substance of the supralunary world, most notably the sun. It therefore implies the creation of light, which returns Milton at last to Genesis i, 3 ("And God said, Let there be light: and there was light"), which he paraphrases as follows:

> Let there be Light, said God, and forthwith Light
> Ethereal, first of things, quintessence pure
> Sprung from the Deep, and from her Native East
> To journey through the airy gloom began.   (VII, 243–46)[14]

The poet's nonbiblical reference to the birthplace of light explains why between verses 2 and 3 of Genesis i he describes the differentiating of the world's chaotic contents into the several elements that hasten to occupy their proper places therein: Chaos being a region "Without dimension, where length, breadth, and highth, / And time and place are lost" (II, 893–94), God's aboriginal circumscription of part of the region into a "hollow Universal Orb" (VII, 257) and his separation of earth, water, air, fire, and the *aether* from one another comprise the creation of dimensionality and place, enabling Milton to posit "her Native East" as light's point of origin. Moreover Milton importantly describes light as *moving* from its indigenous abode to traverse the "airy gloom" of the new world as a discrete parcel of radiance. This unbiblical detail effectively registers the creation of time, which Aristotle defines as the measure of motion according to the spatially prior and posterior.[15] Genesis merely assumes time's existence by mysteriously asserting that God somehow "divided the light from the darkness. And God called the light Day, and the Darkness he called Night" (i, 4b–5a). Unlike the Bible, however, Milton can tell us *how* God separated these antipodes into temporal categories: "light from darkness *by the Hemisphere* [he] / Divided" (VII, 250–51, emphasis mine) into day and night — that is (on the analogy with the apparent diurnal movement of our sun across the firmament), by specifying the half of Milton's spherical world that moving light illuminates as it circumnavigates it. Consequently, whereas Genesis concludes simply *that* "the evening and morning were the first day" (i, 5b), the poet of *Paradise Lost* can again aver that "*Thus* was the first Day Ev'n and Morn" (VII, 252, emphasis mine), by which he implies not only how God spent the first creating day, but also how he created day one itself.

At the same time Milton eliminates a final biblical crux issuing from the fact that in Genesis God creates light on day one (i, 3) but the sun on the fourth day (i, 14–19): this paradox is deftly resolved by having light sojourn "in a cloudy Tabernacle" (VII, 247–49) until, on day four, the "greater" portion God "Transplanted from her cloudy Shrine" into "the Sun's Orb," which hitherto was "unlightsome . . . , / Though of Ethereal Mould" (355–61).[16]

The reconciliation of this biblical crux concludes Raphael's elegant elaboration of Genesis i, 1–5 and 14–19. Eleven richly suggestive but problematic biblical verses have prompted from Milton a poetic recension including such spectacular modifications of the Authorized Version as creation *ex Deo*, a tripling of the *inquit* formula of Genesis i, 3, and a disquisition on how light could "as with a Mantle . . . invest / The rising world of waters dark and deep" "Before the Sun" existed (III, 8–11). As we shall now see, similar (but increasingly complex) hypotactic strategies are characteristic of Milton's retelling of the biblical narratives of creation.

II. Genesis i, 11–13 and ii, 5–6; Genesis i, 20–25a and ii, 19a[17]

The two passages from *Paradise Lost* that I am about to discuss reconcile certain chronological inconsistencies between the creation accounts of Genesis i and ii. First, at i, 11–13 all vegetation is said to have been created on the third day—that is, fully three days prior to the making of man (i, 26–28); at Genesis ii, 4–9a, on the other hand, God forms Adam first and only then creates the plant kingdom, when there is a man to care for it. The biblical contradiction is explicable as such if one accepts the hypothesis of separate and independent composition for the narratives; but Milton, ignorant of the conclusions of biblical higher criticism, found it necessary to reconcile the two versions.[18] He accepts the formulation of Genesis i, 11–12a, which he repeats almost verbatim (with appropriate expansions) at VII, 309b–28a: in both the Bible and in *Paradise Lost*, on day three "th' Earth / Put[s] forth the verdant Grass, Herb yielding Seed, / and Fruit Tree yielding Fruit" (309–11) in the sequence "grass . . . herb . . . tree" (i, 11–12a). But whereas the scriptural version concludes with the formulaic utterance "God saw that *it was good.* And the evening and the morning were the third day" (i, 12b–13), Milton, in the interest of harmonization, at this point interpolates into his narrative selected materials from Genesis ii, 4–9a, which read as follows in the Authorized Version (I have italicized those portions that Milton incorporates):

[4] These are the generations of the heavens and of the earth when they were created, in the day that the LORD God made the earth and the heavens, [5a] *And every plant of the field before it was in the earth, and every herb of the field before it grew:* [5b] *for the LORD God had not caused it to rain upon the earth, and there was not a man to till the ground.* [6] *But there went up a mist from the earth, and watered the whole face of the ground.* [7] And the LORD God formed man of the dust of the ground, and breathed into his nostrils the breath of life; and man became a living soul. [8] And the LORD God planted a garden eastward in Eden; and there he put the man whom he had formed. [9] And out of the ground made the LORD God to grow every tree that is pleasant to the sight.

These details Milton repeats, omitting, however, verse 4 (which in context would imply that God created the heavens and the earth on day three), verses 7–8 (which would imply that God made man on the third day), and verse 9a (which would imply that the trees were formed after Adam):

> Earth now
> Seem'd like to Heav'n, a seat where Gods might dwell,
> Or wander with delight, and love to haunt
> Her sacred shades; [5b] though God had not yet rain'd
> Upon the Earth, and man to till the ground
> None was, [6] but from the Earth a dewy Mist
> Went up and water'd all the ground, [5a] and each

> Plant of the field, which ere it was in the Earth
> God made, and every Herb, before it grew
> On the green stem.   (VII, 328b–37a)

Having relocated part of the *disjecta membra* of Genesis ii, 4–9a immediately after his lengthy paraphrase of i, 11–12a, Milton now completes the transplantation by looping back, in conclusion, to the terminal formulaics of i, 12b–13: "God saw that it was good: / So Ev'n and Morn recorded the Third Day" (VII, 337–38).[19] The net effect of Milton's omissions (of ii, 4, 7, 8, and 9a), interpolations (of ii, 5–6 between i, 12a and 12b), and rearrangements (of ii, 5–6 into the sequence 5b, 6, 5a) is to make chapter ii conform to the normative chronology of chapter i, a goal Milton pursues even to the point of substituting the concessive conjunction *though* (VII, 331) where King James utilizes the causative *for* (i.e., *because*, ii, 5b). This apparently minor adjustment is really a major instance of the poet accomplishing great things by small: for whereas Genesis ii implies that the plants came *after* man *because* there was at first no farmer to till the ground, *Paradise Lost* insists—so determined is Milton to remake chapter ii in the image of its predecessor—that the vegetation came *before* man *even though* no gardener was yet available.[20]

Turning now to a second chronological inconsistency that Milton takes pains to eliminate, at Genesis i, 20–23 the "fowl *that* may fly above the earth" are said to be born from the sea on day five, and at i, 24–25a all the land animals—"cattle, and creeping thing[s], and beast[s] of the earth"—are said to be born autochthonously during the first portion of day six: both bird and beast therefore antedate man's creation, which occupies God during the second half of the sixth day. At Genesis ii, 19a, on the other hand, the nonhuman sentient inhabitants of both air and land are described as earth-born creatures formed after Adam, not before him. Milton mediates these biblical discrepancies artfully and expeditiously, relying once again on a strategy of interpolation and omission. First he composes a greatly expanded version (VII, 387–448) of the three verses (i, 20–23) that Genesis devotes to day five, confirming chapter i's contentions about the aquatic origin of birds on that day. Milton next turns—as does the Bible—to the events of the sixth day. After repeating the autochthonous narrative of i, 24 ("Let the earth bring forth the living creature after his kind"), however, he deftly subjoins to it a similar passage from Genesis ii, 19a: ("And out of the ground the LORD God formed every beast of the field, and every fowl of the air"), omitting, for the sake of consistency, the phrase "every fowl of the air" (for they have already been created from the sea on day five):

> [i, 24] God said,
> Let th' Earth bring forth Soul living in her kind,
> Cattle and Creeping things, and Beast of the Earth,
> Each in their kind. The Earth obey'd, and straight
> Op'ning her fertile Womb teem'd at a Birth
> Innumerous living Creatures, perfet forms,
> Limb'd and full grown: [ii, 19a] out of the ground up rose
> As from his Lair the wild Beast where he wons
> In Forest wide, in Thicket, Brake, or Den.   (VII, 450b–58)

By thus pulling verse ii, 19a into the orbit of i, 24 (and deleting the problematical reference to birds), Milton disposes of the half-verse's chronological disproportions; having done so, he may now conclude his redaction of the first half of day six by attending to Genesis i, 25a. Actually
the poet has already begun to do so, for lines 456b–58 echo the first part
of i, 25a ("And God made the beast of the earth after his kind") as much
as they do ii, 19a. At lines 459–92, therefore, Milton incorporates the rest
of verse 25a, completing, for chronological consistency's sake, another
set of adjustments to the biblical text.[21] He is not yet quite done with verses
24–25, however, for three additional (and only partly chronological) difficulties remain in the Authorized Version's redaction of the creation of
the land animals. As we shall see in the next section, reckoning with them
required the poet to exercise his utmost art.

III. Genesis i, 24–25 and iii, 1a

Anyone who has read Genesis i–iii *en bloc* is struck with the arrest-
ing notice, at the outset of the third chapter, that "the serpent was more
subtile than any beast of the field which the LORD God had made" (iii,
1a). But what sort of animal is this special creature? The Authorized Version implies that it is not a beast of the field (for were it the translators
would have written "the serpent was more subtile than any *other* beast
of the field," a distinction not lost on the lynx-eyed editors of the Revised
Standard Version).[22] Nor, obviously, is the animal fish or fowl or cattle
or — as the curse on it at iii, 14, so clearly implies — creeping thing. Not
knowing the serpent's *differentia specifica* creates moreover a second difficulty: on which day was it created? Genesis i nowhere mentions the
beast — not surprisingly, for its authors, as the documentary hypothesis
amply demonstrates, themselves know nothing of the animal's complicity in the tragic fall of man and so have no reason to take special note
of it. Milton, however, could not construe the matter by referring to independent authorship of chapters ii and iii; nor, given his homocentric
bias, could he afford to ignore what the Bible ignores in his expansion

of chapter i. Instead he found it convenient to graft the serpent-lore of iii, 1a onto his elaboration of i, 25a, a transplantation easier for Milton to accomplish than for me to analyze.

To justify affiliating the two verses Milton must, consistent with the zoological categories of i, 25a, declare the serpent to be either beast, cattle, or creeping thing. He naturally chooses the first, by having Raphael "correct" (albeit all unwittingly) the stylistic "infelicity" of the Authorized Version: when the angel speaks of "The Serpent subtl'st Beast of all the field" (VII, 495), his substitution of the superlative ("subtl'st") for the Bible's comparative ("more subtle than") effectively includes the animal among the nonbovine noncreeping field dwellers.[23] Happily, moreover, the language of iii, 1a ("beast of the field") closely resembles that of i, 25a ("beast of the earth"); this fortuitous circumstance makes it seem more natural for the poet to intertwine biblical verses that derive from otherwise quite alien contexts.

Nevertheless, a third problem remains: although it is appropriate, for the reasons just given, for Raphael to cite the serpent in his discussion of day six, the question remains: at what point ought he to do so? Genesis itself offers a likely solution, one implied in a stylistic eccentricity of i, 24–25a:

And God said, Let the earth bring forth the living creature after his kind, *cattle*, and *creeping thing*, and *beast of the earth* after his kind: and it was so.
And God made the *beast of the earth* after his kind, and *cattle* after their kind, and *everything that creepeth upon the earth* after his kind.

(Emphasis mine)

What strikes me about this passage is the way that verse 25a chiastically reverses verse 24b: thus the last sort of land animal whose existence God commands is the first to be made (though last in expression, the beast of the earth is first in execution). This fact is not lost on Milton: following the biblical paradigm with a care that borders on scrupulosity, he first repeats the order of i, 24 ("Cattle and Creeping things, and Beast of the Earth," VII, 452) to articulate God's command that the earth bring forth such animals; then, in a more leisurely narrative of the parturitional process itself, Milton emulates the chiasmus of i, 25a, describing seriatim the birth of "the wild Beast" (457), "The Cattle" (460), and lastly "whatever creeps the ground" (475). One would therefore expect Raphael to mention the serpent early in his narrative of the land animals, by inserting Genesis iii, 1a at lines 457ff., where other beasts of the field are dutifully itemized.

Nevertheless, as my reader will already know, the angel says nothing about the serpent at this juncture. Given that animal's contribution to the fall of man, the fact that Raphael's narrative exists for Adam's sake, and the further facts that in Genesis i last is best[24] and in Genesis iii the serpent is the best (because the subtlest) nonhuman sentient creature — for all these reasons, it would be decidedly anticlimactic for the angel to discuss the beast in an antepenultimate position, but decidedly appropriate for Raphael to engage in comment on serpents at the very end of his lengthy expansion of i, 24–25a (VII, 450–92) as a last climactic concern. This, of course, is precisely what happens in *Paradise Lost*, and without any violation of the sequential imperatives of Genesis i, 25.[25] Consistent with that verse, at lines 456b–92 Raphael moves from wild beasts through cattle to creeping things, which he subdivides into "Insect or Worm" (476). To the two members of this third category he pays the closest attention: after briefly characterizing first the one (476–79), then the other (480–81), the angel distinguishes creeping worms according to size (481–84). He next gives equal time to insects, both those that creep — citing the provident ant (484–89) — and those that can also fly — citing the exemplary bee (489–92). Finally, Raphael summarily concludes his elaborate redaction of i, 24–25a by observing that "the rest [of whatever creeps the ground] are numberless" (492), an observation that any entomologist or worm-lover would despairingly second.

Now the significance of Raphael's taxonomic efforts resides in what he says of the larger creeping worms, for his language there is the middle term that enables him and Milton to achieve an effortless transition from creatures that creep to the most important noncreeping beast of the field — "the Serpent sly / Insinuating [that] wove with Gordian twine / His braided train" (IV, 347–49): "not all" worms, says Raphael, are

> Minims of Nature; some of Serpent kind
> Wondrous in length and corpulence involv'd
> Thir Snaky folds, and added wings.   (VII, 481–84)

The topic at hand is, I repeat, things that creep — just as Genesis i, 25a says it ought to be; but as is obvious, the angel's diction also reverberates with echoes of iii, 1a and therefore suggests not only serpentine creeping worms but also beasts of the field in general and the serpent in particular. These echoes jog Raphael's memory — not that they remind him of Genesis iii, 1a, which he has not read, but that they cause him to think of the serpent, whom he mentions ten lines later as a relevant afterthought arrived at by free association:

nor unknown
The Serpent subtl'st Beast of all the field,
Of huge extent sometimes, with brazen Eyes
And hairy Mane terrific.   (494b–97a)

The context of Raphael's remarks — at the conclusion of his extended paraphrase of Genesis i, 25a — enables the angel simultaneously to imply (1) the
snake's identity as a beast of the field, (2) its creation on the sixth day,
and (3) its special stature as the last-created nonhuman animal; thus, in
a single stroke of considerable poetic compression, Milton disposes of the
three difficulties in the Authorized Version's account of the land animals
with which I began this section.

One additional problem remains, however — or rather, in the process of resolving the three difficulties in his received text, Milton introduces into *Paradise Lost* a fourth crux evidently absent from Holy Writ:
he has Raphael append to his description of the serpent a disclaimer that
the beast is terrifying and indeed the counterassertion that serpents are
"to thee [i.e., Adam] / Not noxious, but obedient at thy call" (497b–98).
Now on the one hand the angel's point is well taken: for although both
Milton's and the Bible's Adam know that man has "Dominion . . . /
Over . . . / . . . every living thing that moves on the Earth" (532–34,
echoing Genesis i, 26b and 28b); and although Milton's God assures Adam
that *all* the animals will "pay thee fealty / With low subjection" (VIII,
344–45); and although *no* "Beast . . . durst enter" (IV, 704) the "blissful
Bower" (690) of our grandparents — "Such was thir awe of Man" (705) —
still, Raphael's adverting in admiration to the serpent's "brazen Eyes /
And hairy Mane terrific" might make the animal *appear* something less
than man's best friend. Ever the "affable Arch-angel" (VII, 41), Raphael
therefore assures Adam of the serpent's docility even before our father
can have begun to infer the (erroneous) opposite impression from the
angel's words. But on the other hand, given our knowledge of the subtle
beast's ultimate instrumentality in the mortal deception of Eve, it is difficult for us not to construe Raphael's disarming of Adam and Eve ("whatever you do, DON'T beware of serpents," he seems to be saying) as at
best a sardonic dramatic irony that implicates him — and God and Milton too — in the fall of man (though of course, since Raphael does not know
that Satan will use the serpent as the instrument of fraud, the irony is
lost on him).

Time serves not now to show that on the contrary Raphael's words
actually support Milton's intention to justify God's ways vis-à-vis the trans-

gression of Eve — for my theme is creation in Genesis and in *Paradise Lost*, not creation and fall.[26] Suffice it to say that our poet has arranged for Raphael to speak as he does in deference to the ethics (albeit not to the idiom) of Genesis i, 25b, which in context reads: [25a] "And God made the beast of the earth after his kind, and cattle after their kind, and every living thing that creepeth upon the earth after his kind: [25b] *and God saw that it was good*" (emphasis mine). Milton deals with the first half of verse 25 by subjoining to it Genesis iii, 1a; but then, as if to compensate for this interpolation, he deletes verse i, 25b ("and God saw that *it was* good") from Raphael's narrative — or rather he substitutes a kindred expression that would appear to render the same ethical verdict periphrastically by denying its opposite (the serpent is "Not noxious, but obedient at [Adam's] call," where the phrase "is *Not* noxious" may be construed as equivalent to "*is* good").

Very well, but why should Milton make Raphael resort to a nonscriptural periphrasis at precisely this juncture? The poet of *Paradise Lost* is not one to modify his inspired source on a whim, even when — as in the arbitrary chiasmus of Genesis i, 24–25a — the Authorized Version permits itself a modicum of seemingly whimsical vicissitude. What characterizes i, 25b, moreover, is not its stylistic whimsicality but rather its studied predictability as the penultimate instance of a semantic unit first introduced at the end of day one ("And God saw the light, that *it was* good," i, 4a), repeated verbatim fully five more times as the creation proceeds apace, and reiterated a final time, in a climactic variation of the original phraseology ("And God saw everything that he had made, and behold, *it was very* good," i, 31a, emphasis mine), at the conclusion of the six days' work. Milton faithfully reproduces six of the Bible's seven exemplars;[27] why, at i, 25b, should he opt for the anomalous circumlocution "it was *Not* noxious" over the familiar apothegm "it *was* good"?

That Milton does so can be traced to the enormously problematical consequences of his having previously adopted the position that not the serpent but rather Satan in the serpent tempts Eve at Genesis iii, 1–6a. Again it is beyond the scope of the present study to rehearse all the difficulties vis-à-vis the problem of theodicy that Milton encounters (and adjudicates) by affiliating himself with the traditional but exegetically unparsimonious opinion that "Th' infernal Serpent" (I, 34a) and not "The Serpent subtl'st Beast of all the field" (VII, 495) first seduced Eve. I must, however, essay to engage a number of these matters in order fully to account for Milton's periphrastically rendering the biblical notice "God saw that *it was* good," for his reasons derive exclusively from the Satan-serpent displacement.

Baldly stated, the poet's problem was to find a way to mediate the contradiction created by his confirming on the one hand the scriptural assertion that every thing that God had made was very good (Gen. i, 31a; *PL* VII, 548–49), and by his deducing on the other hand (from the biblical curse on the serpent at iii, 14–15) that the poor beast becomes entirely bad—"vitiated in Nature" (X, 169a)—notwithstanding its unwitting (and therefore also unwilled) complicity in the fall of Eve.[28] Certain Renaissance biblical commentators had sought to reckon with this dilemma by noticing that whereas God blesses the fish and fowl created on the fifth day, and whereas he similarly blesses man and woman after their creation at the conclusion of day six, enjoining irrational and rational animal alike to "Be fruitful, and multiply" (i, 22a, 28a), no such blessing climaxes the formation of the land animals. This omission was ingeniously explained by some exegetes in terms of Genesis iii, 1a. Deducing therefrom (as does Milton) that the serpent was among the beasts of the field created on the sixth day, they concluded that God could not properly bless the animal because he was ultimately to be cursed as the sad instrument of all our woe.[29] Milton's way of handling the enigmatic status of the serpent pivots not, however, on some such "simple" omission as this (although Milton too omits to have God bless the land animals) but rather on his transforming the Bible's notice *the land animals were good* into Raphael's observation *the serpent is not bad*. To understand how this can be the case we must look ahead to the poet's account of the curse on the subtle animal.

In *Paradise Lost* Milton "justifies" God's punishing the serpent for a crime it never committed ("Conviction to the Serpent none belongs," Messiah himself declares, X, 84) by deliberately and flamboyantly begging the entire question.[30] After Eve (repeating Gen. iii, 13b) alleges that "The Serpent me beguil'd and I did eat" (X, 162), we are told that

> without delay
> To Judgment God proceeded on th' accused
> Serpent though brute, unable to transfer
> The Guilt on him who made him instrument
> Of mischief, and polluted from the end
> Of his Creation; justly then accurst,
> As vitiated in Nature.   (163b–69a)[31]

That Milton believed the curse on the serpent to be just I do not for a moment doubt; but that he thought his explanation of God's justice in thus anathematizing the animal to be other than finespun sophistry— false rules prankt in reason's garb—would be a death to think: a mere brute is somehow justly accursed, though falsely accused, and cursed moreover without delay, because the Lord God Almighty is unable to transfer the guilt onto Satan, the truly guilty malefactor. This casual casuistry does not compute, nor does Milton mean it to, as he proceeds at once to make clear: "more to know / Concerned not Man (since he no further knew) / Nor alter'd his offense" (169–71). Here the question-begging parenthesis (an evident circularity) subverts the pseudological progress of the larger unit in which it occurs, challenging the reader to accept the curse on the serpent for what it must seem to be to anyone who believes, as Milton does, that Satan tempted Eve: an inexplicable (but divine and therefore just) fiat.

Now bear with me, reader, for I am about to demonstrate the relevance of this discussion to Milton's requiring Raphael to substitute the periphrastic "to thee / Not noxious" for the biblical "God saw that *it was good.*" As we have just seen, the poet cannot logically mediate the contradiction *all creatures are entirely good, the* (sinless) *serpent is entirely bad.* He can, however, render this puzzling state of affairs poetically palatable (and has so rendered it for me at any rate) by asserting the serpent's God-given goodness on the one hand while simultaneously discrediting the beast on the other (through oxymoronic innuendo) *even before* Satan pollutes him. Thus, from the very beginning we encounter a Janus-like serpent in *Paradise Lost:* in Book IV Milton writes of him,

> close the Serpent *sly*
> *Insinuating,* wove with Gordian twine
> His braided train, and of his *fatal guile*
> Gave proof unheeded.   (347b–50a, emphasis mine)

What makes these lines ominous for Adam and Eve and prejudicial to the serpent is not so much the reader's prescience, conferred on him by the Book of Genesis, that the animal will soon occasion the fall of man, as it is the pejorative connotations of the words I have italicized. Where the Authorized Version uses the encomiastic adjective *subtile* to characterize the serpent's intelligence, Milton calls the beast *sly,* which also implies its evasiveness, furtiveness, and duplicity; moreover *Insinuating,* while etymologically meaning "to move by windings and turnings" — and so used by Milton to describe the serpent's harmless meanderings — also connotes "slyly hinting or suggesting, usually in order to ingratiate oneself or to defame another." As for *fatal,* it derives from the Latin *fatum,* "to have spoken." In the context of *Paradise Lost,* therefore, it implies creation by the Word of God and has the force of "God-willed" or "God-destined" (thus the Deity can aver that "what I will is Fate," VII, 173b).

On one level, then, Milton is merely observing that the *guile* (i.e., the craftiness) of the serpent is God-willed and so entirely good; but *fatal* also means "disastrous" or "lethal" (as in a fatal blow), and *guile* often implies deceptive cunning in dealing with others.[32] The net effect of Milton's diction—in Book IV and elsewhere—is thus to describe a creature that is at once the quite innocent (for such God made him, from sin and blame entire) "Serpent subtl'st Beast of all the field" (VII, 495) that Raphael so admiringly calls to Adam's attention, but that is also—here and now—the quite nocent "wily Snake" (IX, 91b) that he will assuredly become after Satan discerns, in the unpolluted animal's "wit and native subtlety" (93), reasons to adjudge him the "Fit Vessel, fittest Imp of Fraud" (89a). The moment therefore that Satan—that "Inmate bad" (495)—decides to enter the creature, Milton drastically accelerates the rhetorical discrediting that he has begun as early as Book IV, swiftly transforming the good/bad serpent of a week ago into a thoroughly perverse "spirited [i.e., possessed by the Devil] sly Snake" (613), a "wily Adder, blithe and glad" (625), even a "dire Snake . . . that into fraud / Led Eve our credulous Mother" (643–44). Finally, Satan's deceptive scheme having been consummated, Milton abandons any pretense of retaining even vestiges of the equivocal language of Book IV: the richly ambiguous "Serpent sly / Insinuating" of unfallen Paradise becomes now, thanks to Satan, the unequivocally "guilty Serpent" of the postlapsarian world, that "Back to the Thicket slunk" (784–85).

We have at last sketched out the necessary context in which to comprehend why, at the conclusion of his discussion of the land animals, Raphael calls the serpent "Not noxious" instead of echoing the explicit biblical language "*it was* good": unbeknownst to the angel, his diction is the precise middle term whereby Milton negotiates the oxymoronic terrain staked simultaneously by the conflicting claims of "all creatures are good" in Genesis i and "the serpent is bad" in Genesis iii. When Milton remarks, a split-second before Satan expropriates the beast, that the serpent is "Not yet in horrid Shade or dismal Den, / Nor nocent yet" (185–86), readers familiar with the poet's ambiguous manipulation of negative particles throughout *Paradise Lost* will beware of prematurely assuming that they have encountered a straightforward litotes, which they may proceed blithely to paraphrase by affirming the contrary of what Milton has denied, namely, that the Edenic serpent resides innocently in open fields, far from deceit and guile; for while I concede that such a reading would be true as far as it goes, it would altogether eviscerate the semantic force of Milton's strategy of negation. The poet wants his utterance to participate, as much as it possibly can, in the very reality it supposedly serves to deny: the serpent is "Not *yet* in horrid Shade . . . / Nor nocent *yet*," but the pathetically weak disclaimer effected in the repeated doublet "Not yet . . . / Nor . . . yet" is itself a virtual litotes signifying the quite opposite notion: "Not yet in horrid Shade — but almost," Milton implies, "Nor nocent yet — but almost nocent." How nigh the serpent's change approaches! — and how fittingly Milton's language mimics the animal's altogether equivocal status. The beast occupies the center of a circle of ethical indifference; it moves about in worlds not realized, in a twilight zone midway between good and evil; neither good nor bad, the animal is strangely both at once. Milton's language therefore oscillates between two universes, one (the unfallen) about to give way to the other (the fallen), which is, however, *not yet* quite ready to be born.

Now just this state of affairs pertains in Book VII, wherein Raphael tells Adam that the serpent is "Not noxious": for while this phrase assures Adam (and us) of what the beast is *not*, it does not provide any unequivocal assurance of what the animal *is* (in this light, it is stunningly appropriate that Raphael should begin his disquisition on serpents by telling Adam "*nor unknown* / The Serpent subtl'st Beast of all the field" [VII, 494–95, emphasis mine]). Moreover, while it is possible that "Not noxious" is the semantic equivalent of "entirely good," so that (as I have said) the phrase may be construed as doing in *Paradise Lost* what verse 25b does in Genesis i, to the prescient reader the phrase has precisely the force of "Not noxious . . . *yet*," even though Raphael, unaware that the serpent will be corrupted, can nowise be permitted to think this adverb, much less to utter it. In short, the angel's periphrasis is seen to be an artful adjustment of the biblical text that, taken in conjunction with its stylistic equivalent at *Paradise Lost* IX, 185–86, serves the not insignificant purpose of mediating the contradiction between Genesis i, 24–25 and iii, 1a. It is, if I may venture to repeat myself, another stroke of considerable — nay, infinite — poetic compression.[33]

IV. A First Conclusion

Having, therefore, in the space of some three hundred lines, adjusted or expanded whatever portions of Genesis i, 1–5 and 14–19 require clarification in relation to themselves and to one another; and having, moreover, eliminated the chronological inconsistencies between Genesis i, 11–13 and ii, 5–6, on the one hand, and between i, 20–25 and ii, 19a, on the other; and having, finally, adjudicated the chronological, taxonomic, and ethical ambiguities of i, 24–25 in relation to iii, 1a; our poet has earned the richly deserved right to conclude his recension of these verses by proffering a six-line recapitulation of the six days' work:

Now Heav'n in all her Glory shone, and roll'd
Her motions, as the great first-Mover's hand
First wheel'd thir course; Earth in her rich attire
Consummate lovely smil'd; Air, Water, Earth,
By Fowl, Fish, Beast, was flown, was swum, was walkt
Frequent. (499–504a)

It is an artful summation; nevertheless Milton's work is not yet done, any more than his God's is: "and of the Sixt day yet remain'd" (504), the poet writes, alluding of course (1) to the creation of man at Genesis i, 26–29; (2) to the quite different account of this event at ii, 7 and ii, 15–25; and (3) to the problematic institution of the Sabbath at ii, 1–3. Milton, as I shall now demonstrate, attends to these matters with spectacular success.

V. Genesis i, 26–29 and ii, 7–9a; Genesis ii, 16–17

In a recent stylistic analysis of Milton's paraphrase of Genesis, Ernst Häublein has suggested that the "technique of blending [by which Milton describes the making of man] entails a radical transformation and condensation of the Bible unique within the paraphrase. It seems that the last act of creation was viewed by [the poet] as a challenge for his utmost craftsmanship."[34] I am not sure that Milton's rewriting of Genesis i, 26–29 is *unique* relative to his treatment of verses 1–25, but I quite agree that *Paradise Lost* VII, 505–47 proceeds from the hand of a master craftsman. In the Authorized Version, Genesis takes up the creation of man with the words, "And God said, Let us make man in our image, after our likeness: and let them have dominion over the fish of the sea, and over the fowl of the air, and over the cattle, and over all the earth, and over every creeping thing that creepeth upon the earth" (i, 26). Milton, however, begins his account with a twelve-line prolegomenon (505–16) that renders explicit what is only implicit in Genesis — namely, that man is "the Master work, the end / Of all yet done" (505–06). He then attends to a notorious crux created by his source's enigmatic use of the plural ("Let us") to describe the contemplative activity that immediately precedes the making of man. God's hortatory gesture has been said to smack of everything from polytheism to proto-Trinitarianism;[35] Milton (as might be expected, given the Johannine logos-Christology that informs his account of the six-days' work) opts for a reading that allows his non-Trinitarian God to be nevertheless the one and the many. Man being "chief / Of all his works," the Father himself descends to oversee his creation; thus, where Genesis has it simply that "God said," Milton writes:

> [i, 26a] th'Omnipotent
> Eternal Father (For where is not hee
> Present) thus to his Son audibly spake.   (515–18)

This passage neatly resolves the biblical crux by eliminating the ambiguity of "us." It also emphasizes the actual (as opposed to the merely virtual) participation of the Father in man's making ("to his Son" he "audibly spake"), which in turn implies the special dignity of man (his creation is not delegated), the ubiquity of God ("he also went / Invisible, yet stay'd [such privilege / Hath Omnipresence]," 588–90), and the subordination of the Son (unlike his ubiquitous Father he must return to Heaven, whence he came into Chaos to create).

Having made these four points in fewer than three lines, Milton now repeats the rest of Genesis i, 26 almost verbatim (519–23); but whereas the Bible exhibits a possible redundancy in the phrase "in our image, after our likeness," Milton's God says "Let us make now Man in our Image, Man / In our similitude" (519–20). If the scriptural *likeness* is not a mere tautological reflex of *image*, it may imply a distinction between the soul and the body and so emphasize that in both respects man is God-like. Milton perhaps detected such a nuance, which he may have heightened (by substituting "In our similitude" for "after our likeness") in order to distinguish the human "mind / And inward Facultie" on the one hand from man's "outward" and bodily features on the other (VIII, 541–43).[36]

But this is to conjecture; what happens next in Genesis is not a conjecture, however: moving uninterruptedly from deliberation to execution, "God created man in his own image, in the image of God created he him" (i, 27a). Milton's God does the same thing, when Raphael declares that he "form'd thee, *Adam*, thee O Man" (VII, 524). The angel's words bear some resemblance to i, 27a, but their primary referent is Genesis ii, 7, "And the Lord God formed man *of* the dust of the ground, and breathed into his nostrils the breath of life; and man became a living soul." In order to make chapter ii appear to conform once again to the normative chronology of its predecessor, Milton now weaves all of ii, 7 into his redaction; and in order to make his stitching and unstitching seem a moment's thought, he systematically staggers his references, quoting now from the one chapter, now from the other, in the event effecting a pleasing synthesis of the two:

> [i, 27a and ii, 7a] This said, he form'd thee, *Adam*, thee O Man
> [ii, 7a] Dust of the ground, and in thy nostrils breath'd
> The breath of Life; [i, 27a] in his own Image hee
> Created thee, in the Image of God
> Express, [ii, 7b] and thou becam'st a living Soul.   (524–28)

By adding the word "Express" to the Bible's "in the image of God," Milton now assures us unequivocally that Adam and Eve resemble God corporeally as well as intellectually — thus confirming what we have learned in Book IV, wherein even Satan can discern that "in thir looks Divine / The image of thir glorious Maker shone" (291–92), and still earlier, when a blind Milton nostalgically laments his inability to visualize man's "human face divine" (III, 44). Otherwise the lines serve the self-evident but not inconsiderable purpose of fusing two quite different creation stories "Easier than Air with Air" into a seamless "Union of Pure with Pure" (VIII, 626–27).

Paradise Lost next essays a less than self-explanatory return to the second half of Genesis i, 27 ("male and female created he them") and to all of i, 28, wherein God begins to apportion man prerogatives over the rest of the terrestrial world: "And God blessed them, and God said unto them, Be fruitful, and multiply, and replenish the earth." These verses Milton repeats — not, however, without making a subtle adjustment in the biblical wording:

> [i, 27b–28a] Male he created thee, *but thy consort*
> *Female for Race;* then bless'd Mankind, and said,
> Be fruitful, multiply, and fill the Earth.
>
> (VII, 529–31, emphasis mine)

Whereas, in typical paratactic fashion, Genesis merely *implies* a relationship between gender and procreation, the reader being required to infer it from the collocation of i, 27b and the command to "be fruitful and multiply," Milton renders explicit the procreative rationale of sexual differentiation (woman is "Female *for Race*"). At the same time, he disabuses his audience of the misogynistic opinion that Eve was made primarily for reproductive purposes: God did not make Adam's "consort / . . . for Race," but rather his "consort / *Female* for Race." Evidently she exists primarily for other reasons, a point to which I shall return.

At this juncture *Paradise Lost* turns once again to Genesis ii, continuing the pattern of oscillating interfusion that characterizes the entire narrative of man's creation. According to ii, 8–9a, "the LORD God planted a garden eastward in Eden" consequent upon Adam's creation. He then "put the man whom he had formed" into the garden, and only then "made the LORD God to grow every tree that is pleasant to the sight, and good for food." Milton, to be sure, agrees that the Deity did all these things, but the context in which he reports them implies a different chronology from the Bible's:

> [ii, 8] Wherever thus created, for no place
> Is yet distinct by name, thence, as thou know'st

> He brought thee into this delicious Grove,
> This Garden, [ii, 9a = i, 29] planted with the Trees of God,
> Delectable both to behold and taste.   (535–39)

In this passage Milton fuses the notice "God planted a garden" with its analogue "made the LORD God to grow every tree," thereby metamorphosing the Bible's simple preterites ("planted," "made to grow") into the past participial phrase "This Garden, *planted* with the Trees of God": consistent with the poet's view that the vegetable world antedates the creation of man by three days, his grammatical transformations suggest (contrary to Genesis ii, 8–9a) that Adam is brought into an already created garden replete with already planted trees. To reinforce the point Milton now returns to Genesis i again (and so to its chronology), a transition rendered the more smooth by the fact that the just cited notice at ii, 9a about the delectable loveliness of the plant world closely resembles the passage at i, 29 where God decrees man's vegetarianism. After paraphrasing this latter verse (540–42), Milton turns yet once more to chapter ii, so that Raphael can repeat God's sole command regarding the tree of prohibition (ii, 16b–17). Since verse 16b ("Of every tree of the garden thou mayest freely eat") echoes the generous sentiments of i, 29 ("I have given you . . . every tree, in the which *is* the fruit of a tree yielding seed"), the transition again seems utterly effortless; happily so, for by skillfully interjecting the forbidden fruit near the conclusion of his narrative of the six days' work, Milton enables Raphael to reserve for the climactic position certain redundant facts (the phrase "as thou know'st" at line 536 has already declared what follows to be ancient history for Adam) that nevertheless serve those vital admonitory purposes for which the angel has descended in the first place:

> [i, 29 = ii, 16b] freely all thir pleasant fruit for food
> [God] Gave thee, all sorts are here that all th' Earth yields,
> Variety without end; [ii, 17] but of the Tree
> Which tasted works knowledge of Good and Evil,
> Thou may'st not; in the day thou eat'st, thou di'st;
> Death is the penalty impos'd, beware,
> And govern well thy appetite, lest sin
> Surprise thee, and her black attendant Death.   (540–47)

On this cautionary note Raphael concludes his redaction of Genesis i, 26–29. In his version of man's creation Milton settles a number of perplexing biblical questions, ranging from the apparent plurality of gods in the Bible through the wherefores of human sexuality. The most striking characteristic of *Paradise Lost* VII, 505–47, however, is the subtle art that insinuates Genesis ii, 7–9a and 16–17 into the temporal context of i, 26–29 without a trace of Procrusteanism. Milton's technique of interfusion is not unlike what we have seen him do elsewhere, but the degree of blending effected in the passage just discussed has no parallel in Book VII: within the brief space of forty-three lines the poet shifts back and forth between his source's divergent creation accounts an astonishing seven times, splicing eight and one-half biblical verses into an esemplastic unity whose grateful vicissitude evidences in no small measure Milton's integrative artistry.[37]

There remains, nevertheless, a cluster of verses from Genesis ii so manifestly at odds with chapter i as steadfastly to resist the sort of reconciliation we have thus far encountered; I refer of course to the creation of Eve at ii, 18–25. With its idiosyncratic chronology, its emphasis on etiology, its anthropomorphic Deity, and the atmosphere of morally problematic interiority with which it suffuses both God and man, chapter ii stands in diametric opposition to its more succinct analōgue at i, 26–29, an opposition heightened by the intimate juxtaposition of the one with the other. Fully sensitive to the radical incompatibility of the two versions, Milton wisely declines essaying to conflate them into a single, internally consistent linear formulation. Instead he tears the two narratives quite asunder, relegating the details of Eve's birth to Adam's recollections in the second half of *Paradise Lost* VIII. The interposition of some 425 lines between Raphael's terse paraphrase of i, 26–29 and Adam's more leisurely exfoliation of ii, 18–25 mitigates the intrinsic incoherence of the two versions when viewed — as they must be in the Bible — as adjacent episodes in a narrative continuum. Milton's buffering also enables him to confer upon the latter story a certain degree of chronological autonomy. Freed thereby for once from the vexatious and troublesome bondage of temporal coincidence, Milton can, at the minimal expense of a modest anachronism, attend to more substantive cruxes in the creation of Eve, and most notably to eliminating the programmatic misogyny wherewith the patriarchal authors of Genesis ii sought to institutionalize their conviction that a woman's proper place is as a fruitful vine in some obscure corner of her spouse's home.

Because the problems I am about to address are of such magnitude and because they require correspondingly complex Miltonic solutions, I will divide the following discussion into two parts: section VI will repeat certain relevant portions of Raphael's version of the creation of man in order to consider them further in the light of Genesis ii, 15–17 and *Paradise Lost* VIII: section VII will then zero in on the problem of Eve.

VI. GENESIS I, 26–29 AND II, 7–9; GENESIS II, 15–17

Even though, as we have seen, Raphael modifies Genesis i, 26–28 by filling its interstices with the autochthonous details of ii, 7 (VII, 516–34), he does not alter the overriding impression — sustained throughout his narrative of the six days' work — that we are still very much in the stylized, scrupulously symmetrical cosmos of the first chapter. Consistent with this primary source, Raphael asserts that God made man — both "Male" and "Female" — simultaneously, as separate but equal reflections of the same divine image, and only "*then* bless'd Mankind" (529–30; emphasis mine) by decreeing Adam's and Eve's hegemony over the whole earth. The angel then rehearses certain supposedly subsequent details from chapter ii: God next brought man and woman into the garden of Eden and gave them leave to touch and to taste all the fruit thereof, interdicting only the Tree of Knowledge (535–44). Now the sexual egalitarianism and the chronological sequencing with which Raphael affiliates himself faithfully mirror Genesis i,[38] but they are contradicted by the implications of ii, 15–25, the view that Milton himself partially adopts, in startling departure from his habitual tendency to prefer the protocols of chapter i. Milton mediates the contradiction by separating Raphael's account from the later Adamic variant (so that the angel's may sound authoritative at the moment of its utterance), and by denying Raphael an omniscient point of view vis-à-vis the work of the sixth day (so that Adam's narrative may sound authoritative at the moment of *its* utterance).

According to Raphael he was not an eyewitness to the creation of man (VIII, 229–46). Without a doubt his absence that day reflects Milton's concern to observe the grand masterpiece, decorum: Adam is eager to tell his story (198–216) — not that he feels competent to do so adequately, but that he seeks a pretext to delay his angel visitor's departure (250–53) — and Raphael, providentially ignorant of the details, is equally eager to hear them: "Say therefore on" (228), he decorously urges, "for I attend, / Pleas'd with thy words no less than thou with mine" (247–48). But beyond averting the narrative inconvenience that would attend Adam's reciting and Raphael's hearing a twice-told tale, the angel's ignorance also enables us to adjust his brief report at VII, 505–47 in the retrospective light of Adam's more accurate version — without, however, accusing the "affable Arch-angel" (VII, 41) of either inadvertency or disingenuousness, for he speaks the truth as far as he knows it. Moreover, the transition from his version to Adam's is further mediated by the close family resemblance between the two.

Thus Adam explains that he was created outside the garden of Eden

(VIII, 253–91) and thence by God led into it (292–311). After identifying himself (312–18), God proceeded, just as Raphael has said, to transfer the garden and its fruits to Adam "To till and keep" (320), excepting only "the Tree whose operation brings / Knowledge of good and ill" (323–24). This sounds isomorphic with Raphael's version, but it differs in two crucial respects, as comparison with its source at Genesis ii, 15–17 will make evident:

> And the Lord God took *the man*, and put him into the garden of Eden to dress it and to keep it.
> And the Lord God commanded the man, saying, Of every tree of the garden thou mayest freely eat:
> But of the tree of the knowledge of good and evil, thou shalt not eat of it: for in the day that thou eatest thereof thou shalt surely die. (Emphasis mine)

The point, of course, is that the God of Genesis ii puts *man only* in the garden, for from its authors' point of view woman has yet to be made. Milton agrees with their formulation, a decision whose ramifications are legion; the first of them requires the poet quite simply to disagree with the view of Genesis i, 28–29 — a view erroneously seconded by Raphael (VII, 530–34) — that outside the garden, directly after their creation, God blessed man and woman alike. On the contrary, as ii, 15–17 imply, the benediction that the Bible records was uttered inside Paradise, after man alone was created, and therefore in Adam's presence only — not indeed to exclude Eve from the aboriginal land grant, but rather to balance Adam's recapitulation of God's "Sternly . . . pronounc'd" and "dreadful" "rigid interdiction" (VIII, 333–35) with a signal instance of the Deity's more characteristically "gracious purpose" (337):

> [Genesis i, 28] Not only these fair bounds, but all the Earth
> To thee and to thy Race I give; as Lords
> Possess it, and all things that therein live,
> Or live in Sea, or Air, Beast, Fish, and Fowl.   (338–41)

At this point Milton concludes his second redaction of Genesis i, 26–29, this time in the authoritative light of ii, 15–17.[39]

VII. Genesis ii, 18–25

Having thus for once — and only once — adjusted Genesis i to bring it within the chronological penumbra of chapter ii, Milton proceeds to confront the far more formidable burden of transubstantiating the admittedly subtle but morally dubious chauvinist etiologies of ii, 18–25 into a thoroughly rational justification of God's ways to man — and to woman too. To grasp the nature of the task before him, we must see the passage in its entirety:

[18] And the LORD God said, *It is* not good that the man should be alone; I will make him a help meet for him.

[19] And out of the ground the LORD God formed every beast of the field, and every fowl of the air; and brought *them* unto Adam to see what he would call them: and whatsoever Adam called every living creature, that *was* the name thereof.

[20] And Adam gave names to all cattle, and to the fowl of the air, and to every beast of the field; but for Adam there was not found a help meet for him.

[21] And the LORD God caused a deep sleep to fall upon Adam, and he slept: and he took one of his ribs, and closed up the flesh instead thereof.

[22] And the rib, which the LORD God had taken from man, made he a woman, and brought her unto the man.

[23] And Adam said, This *is* now bone of my bones, and flesh of my flesh: she shall be called Woman, because she was taken out of man.

[24] Therefore shall a man leave his father and his mother, and shall cleave unto his wife: and they shall be one flesh.

[25] And they were both naked, the man and his wife, and were not ashamed.

I will not pause to engage in protracted scrutiny of this extraordinary passage; it has, of course, been the object of infinite commentary, and I happily refer my reader to the recently published (and in my view unsurpassable) analyses of Robert Alter.[40] At the risk of oversimplifying, I wish merely to itemize what I believe Milton perceived as its nine problems.

To begin with a chronological matter, (1) the passage describes creation according to the sequence *man, land animals, fowl,* and finally *woman,* whereas Genesis i, adopting a roughly evolutionary developmental progression, moves along what would later be denominated the great chain of being, from *fowl* through *land animals* to *man* and *woman;* (2) the biblical God seems not to foreknow the proper names of the animals, which he brings (in ignorance?) to Adam "*to see* what he would call them"; (3) the names the animals acquire seem to be purely arbitrary signifiers contingent only upon the first man's whimsy (for "*whatsoever* Adam called every living creature, that *was* the name thereof"); (4) the passage suggests divine inadvertency, God first providing the animals to satisfy Adam's need for "a help meet," then learning (only *ex post facto*) that they will not suffice, and only *then* hastening to remedy the situation by creating Eve; (5) therefore, as Alter has appropriately observed, the narrative misogynistically "imagines woman as a kind of divine afterthought, made to fill a need of man, . . . made, besides, out of one of man's spare parts" (p. 141), and made, to that extent, radically imperfectly; (6) in Genesis i *nothing*, adventitious or otherwise, is permitted to intervene between God's deliberative and executive acts ("God said, . . . and it was so"); here, on the other hand, the creation of inferior creatures interposes between the Deity's stated intention to ameliorate man's single imperfection and his fulfilling that promise; (7) once created, Eve is brought to Adam to be named just as the animals have been: she seems therefore scarcely better than they and no less subject to man's dominance, not to say his despotic power; (8) verse 24 indulges in a gross hyperbole when it suggests that marriage can make a man and woman "one flesh" — an exaggeration immediately (and inconsistently) undercut by the grammatical plurality of verse 25 ("*they* were *both* naked, the man *and* his wife"); and finally, (9) it can be inferred from the naked unashamedness of Adam and Eve that they are childlike and indeed innocent — or rather ignorant — of human sexuality, a peculiar circumstance for presumably rational creatures enjoined in Genesis i to "be fruitful and multiply."

Now *Paradise Lost* reckons with these nine problems brilliantly, and for the most part within the brief confines of Adam's autobiography. I will discuss Milton's solutions in a series of triads.

As to the first three cruxes in Genesis ii, 18–25 (1) we know that in Book VII Milton follows the chronological order of chapter i; he therefore omits Genesis ii, 19a from Adam's story, describing instead how God brings the *long-since* created "Bird[s] and Beasts" (VIII, 342), of whose prior existence Adam has likewise known long since (263–65), to his onomastic attention (342–48); (2) although Milton's Adam does indeed name the animals at God's behest (342–45; cf. VI, 73–76), he does not do so independently of God's providential prescience: "I named them," he tells Raphael, "with such Knowledge *God* endu'd / My sudden apprehension" (352–54, emphasis mine); (3) nor, therefore, are the names conferred upon the animals merely conventional epithets. "I named them," says Adam, "and understood / Thir Nature" (352–53), an echo of Raphael's instancing that "thou thir Natures know'st, and gav'st them Names" (VII, 493): in the prelapsarian cosmos of *Paradise Lost* we discern a causal nexus between *signum* and *res* rather than a merely casual contiguity.[41]

Turning now to the second triad, (4) as to the more damaging charge of divine inadvertency vis-à-vis God's proffering the animals as companions for Adam, and as to its implications, namely, that (5) Eve is an expendable commodity built with "second thoughts" — just as Satan would believe the entire visible universe to have been built (IX, 99–102), and that (6) God's inadvertency necessitates an embarrassing delay in the swift, sure realization of the divine will, Milton eliminates these difficulties in a single poetic stroke. In *Paradise Lost* God arranges for "each Bird and Beast" to be christened in pairs—"Approaching two and two" is how Adam puts it (VIII, 349–50). By means of this quite unbiblical detail, Milton's Deity intends to apprise Adam of his anomalous solitude. Indeed his stratagem works: "in these / I found not what methought I wanted still" (354–55), Adam tells Raphael, both his desire for companionship and the inadequacy of the animals being inferred after the fact, to be sure, but by Adam, not by God. What follows next is an elaborate debate between God and man, with the Creator playfully urging his latest image to find solace among the beasts (369–75, 399–411), and with Adam retorting (deferentially, of course) that only rational fellowship will suffice (379–97, 412–33). The debate concludes when God, in what amounts to a reconstructive commentary on Genesis ii, 18–22, explains that he has orchestrated the whole scenario as a test of Adam's self-knowledge:

> Thus far to try thee, *Adam*, I was pleas'd,
> And find thee knowing not of Beasts alone,
> Which thou hast rightly nam'd, but of thyself,
> Expressing well the spirit within thee free,
> My Image, not imparted to the Brute,
> Whose fellowship therefore unmeet for thee
> Good reason was thou freely shouldst dislike,
> And be so minded still; *I, ere thou spak'st,*
> *Knew it not good for man to be alone,*
> *And no such company as then thou saw'st*
> *Intended thee,* for trial only brought,
> To see how thou couldst judge of fit and meet:
> What next I bring shall please thee, be assur'd,
> Thy likeness, thy fit help, thy other self,
> Thy wish, exactly to thy heart's desire.
>
>   (437–51, emphasis mine)

It is characteristic of Milton's genius that here, as elsewhere, he makes a virtue of the necessity (forced upon him by the inconveniences of Genesis) to depart radically from the received text. He assures us that, far from being inept, the biblical God presciently "Knew it not good for man to be alone" and that, appearances to the contrary notwithstanding, he never "Intended" that Adam seek "fellowship" among the beasts. Eve, therefore, far from being an afterthought, was foreordained for Adam *ab ovo*: as Genesis i implies, man (both male and female) was always first in intention though last in execution—even if unfallen Adam erroneously concludes that God's omega cannot also be his alpha (he believes that Eve was not "intended first, [but] after made / Occasionally," 555–56); nor does her having been derived from man's "spare" rib derogate from her perfection — even if fallen, self-extenuating Adam misogynistically calls her a "fair defect / Of Nature" (X, 891–92) made from a "Rib / Crooked," "sinister," and "supernumerary" (884–87) to boot. Milton's Eve, on the contrary, is perfect, both without (in a logical solecism the poet calls her "the fairest of her Daughters," IV, 324) and within (unfallen Adam insists that she was "Created pure," V, 100 and that she remains free "from sin and blame entire," IX, 292). Nor, finally, does Milton retain the disparity in Genesis between God's *verbum* — "I *will* make him a help meet for him" (where the modal auxiliary implies determination as well as simple futurity) — and *factum* — "*but* for Adam there was *not* found a help meet for him" (where the adversative conjunction is as much a reluctant and discouraged concessive as it is a factual adversative). Whereas in Genesis two verses describing the creation and naming of the animals (ii, 19–20a) intervene between the Bible's mournful litany "a help meet" (18b) / "not . . . a help meet" (20b), in *Paradise Lost* Milton relegates verse 19a to Book VII, 456–58, begins his account of the making of Eve by expanding ii, 19b–20a (VIII, 338–436), and only then attends to the *inclusios* "help meet" / "not . . . meet" — reversing, however, the biblical order of insertion: after declaring (not finding) that the "fellowship" of the animals was always "unmeet" (442) for Adam, God explains that the lengthy colloquy attendant upon the just completed naming ritual was educative and exemplary, God's intention having been to determine whether *Adam* (not God) "couldst judge of fit and meet" (448). Having successfully educed "the spirit within [Adam] free" (440) in ample manifestation of the first man's "complete / Perfections" (V, 352–53), God now — and only now — repeats the promise of Genesis ii, 18b (VIII, 449–51), a promise he proceeds at once — for "Immediate are the acts of God" (VII, 176) — to fulfill (VIII, 452–77). The effect of Milton's artful reconstruction is to eliminate the quantum gap in Holy Writ between divine intention and execution, an effect I will highlight by summarizing Milton's rearrangement of the relevant verses of Genesis ii:

[19b = *PL* VIII, 338–56] and [God] brought [the animals] unto Adam to see what he would call them; and whatsoever Adam called every living creature, that *was* the name thereof.

[20 = VIII, 352–444] And Adam gave names to all cattle, and to the fowl of the air, and to every beast of the field; but for Adam there was not found a help meet for him.

[18 = VIII, 444–51] And the LORD God said, *It is* not good that the man should be alone; I will make him a help meet for him.

At this point Milton's God does just that (ii, 21–22 = VIII, 452–490), there being no untidy biblical gap between *his* word and deed.[42]

We come now to the third and final triad of cruxes in the biblical creation of Eve, those deriving from Genesis ii, 21–25, wherein God finally gets round to forming her. To do so, as Robert Alter felicitously observes, he works in "the anthropomorphic métier of a sculptor in the medium of flesh and bone" (p. 29):

> [21] And the Lord God caused a deep sleep to fall upon Adam, and he slept; and he took one of his ribs, and closed up the flesh instead thereof.
>
> [22] And the rib, which the Lord God had taken from man, made he a woman, and brought her unto the man.
>
> [23] And Adam said, This is now bone of my bones, and flesh of my flesh: she shall be called Woman, because she was taken out of man.

Since (like the animals) Adam's spouse is brought to him by God, whereupon Adam names her (just as he has the animals), does it not logically follow (7) that Eve stands in relation to her husband precisely as the animals do — namely, as his decided inferior ripe for subjugation? This inference gains plausibility from the fact that Genesis ii, 21–22 resembles the well-known passage in the Babylonian creation epic, the *Enuma Elish*, wherein the god Marduk forms man out of the remains (and so in the image) of a just slain god, but only to be a slave "charged with the service of the gods / That they might be at ease."[43] Since Eve, too, will be cursed to subjugation once fallen ("thy desire *shall be* to thy husband, and he shall rule over thee," iii, 16b), does not the Bible's allusion to its Near Eastern analogue proleptically indict Adam's future "help meet" as the guilty occasion of his mortal transgression?

Perhaps so, but even if this reading seems congenial, it would never have occurred to Milton, who of course knew nothing of Genesis' Mesopotamian literary antecedents. Unlike the ignoble and ignominious ritual servitude that the *Enuma Elish* enjoins on both man and woman, the God of *Paradise Lost* forms Eve no less than Adam "upright with Front serene" freely to "Govern," not slavishly to serve (VII, 509–10), in fulfillment of his promise to bring the first man "Thy likeness, thy fit help, thy other self" (VIII, 450). While, therefore, it is true that Adam and Eve are "Not equal, as thir sex not equal seem'd" (IV, 296), it does not follow — as self-deprecating Eve humbly alleges — that her husband "Like consort to thyself canst nowhere find" (448): for Eve is Adam's "likeness" (VIII, 450), and both of them reflect "The image of thir glorious Maker" (IV, 292).

Consequently Milton graciously endues Eve — on the analogy with

Genesis ii, 19b–20a — with an exquisite onomastic facility not unlike her mate's: witness fallen Eve's nostalgically apostrophizing the "flow'rs" that she "bred up with tender hand / From the first op'ning bud, *and gave ye Names*" (XI, 273–77, emphasis mine). By thus conferring upon woman the status of *anthropos onomastikos*, Milton delicately mitigates whatever innuendo of tyrannical male domination may be thought to surface in Genesis ii, 21–23; he also takes advantage, for the sake of further liberating Eve, of a scriptural nuance I have thus far slighted. Whereas the God of Israel displays the animals before Adam *in order* that he might name them (and so, by implication, might rule over them), the Bible observes of Eve (rather more noncommittally) only *the fact* that Adam christens her. This subtle distinction, wire-drawn in Genesis to aery thinness, becomes explicitly dichotomized in *Paradise Lost*. On the one hand, Milton's God summons the creatures "to receive / From [Adam] thir Names" "In sign" of their "fealty" and "low subjection" (VIII, 342–45) to him; but on the other hand, the naming of Eve has a quite different symbolic purport: for whereas the beasts approach Adam "cow'ring low / With blandishment," while "each Bird" likewise "stoop'd on his wing" (350–51) in awe-struck deference to him, Eve's advent is replete with the lofty dignity of a Catullan epithalamion:

> On she came,
> Led by her Heav'nly Maker, though unseen,
> And guided by his voice, nor uninform'd
> Of Nuptial Sanctity and marriage Rites:
> Grace was in all her steps, Heav'n in her Eye,
> In every gesture dignity and love.   (484b–89)[44]

This is a far cry indeed from its source's laconic notice "[God] brought her unto the man"; it is also the harbinger of a radically modified onomastic ritual: left breathless by Eve, this "fairest . . . / Of all [God's] gifts" (493–94), Adam declares,

> *I now see*
> Bone of my Bone, Flesh of my Flesh, *my Self*
> Before me; *Woman is her Name*, of Man
> Extracted.   (494b–97a, emphasis mine)

Here, where Genesis has "This *is now* bone of my bones," as if Eve's Adamic origin somehow depended upon her husband's perception thereof, Milton writes "*I* now *see* / Bone of my Bone," subtly transforming the biblical Adam's power into the more modest recognition of Eve's autonomy. The point is reinforced in what follows: in Genesis, Adam legislates his wife's name ("she *shall* be called Woman"); Milton, however, substitutes the far less dictatorial "Woman in her Name," which amounts, again, to a simple acknowledgment that Eve's nature is such-and-such. Finally, Adam's merely recognizing what his prototype virtually creates (in imitation of the biblical God's creating a world out of words) is mediated by his addition of the phrase "my Self" to Genesis ii, 23a: "my equivalent," he means, if not indeed "my equal." Milton's Adam — as we learn in Book IX — will never demand submission from such an unfallen "help meet," much less seek to subjugate her after the fashion of a mere brute.[45]

Two cruxes remain in the account of Eve's creation. The first concerns whether we are to take the phrase "they shall be one flesh" (Genesis ii, 24) literally — especially in the contradictory light of the subsequent verse's grammatical plurality ("*they* were *both* naked, the man *and* his wife," ii, 25): (8) does the Bible *really* intend that sexual intercourse in marriage could bridge the chasm that — from Adam on down — has divided *I* from *Thou*? Saint Paul seems to ridicule this interpretation by remarking that even whoremongers could quite readily conform to the Mosaic letter construed as such (1 Cor. vi, 16). Since the letter killeth, Paul elsewhere prefers to read Genesis ii, 24 as an analogue of Christ's intimate oneness with the church (Eph. v, 31–32). But Milton deploys a more complex figurative strategy than Paul's for accommodating the passage to rational exegesis: for him, to read it literally would postulate a metaphysical impossibility, as Raphael's comments on the love of angels imply: "Whatever pure thou in the body enjoy'st," he tells Adam,

> we enjoy
> In eminence, and obstacle find none
> Of membrane, joint, or limb, exclusive bars:
> Easier than Air with Air, if Spirits embrace,
> Total they mix, Union of Pure with Pure
> Desiring; nor restrain'd conveyance need
> As Flesh to mix with Flesh, or Soul with Soul. (VIII, 622–29)

The contrast between angelic and human sexuality could not be more pointed: neither flesh nor human soul can love as angels do; Genesis ii, 24 cannot mean what it says.

Milton therefore makes Adam adjust the language of Scripture to suggest a figurative reading of "they shall be one flesh":

> for this cause [man] shall forgo
> Father and Mother, and to his wife adhere;
> And they shall be one Flesh, one Heart, one Soul.
>
> (VIII, 497–99)

Adam's appositional glosses imply precisely that human dimension to Eve's personality in the absence of which the animals could not be what she decidedly is for him — a companion "fit to participate / All rational delight" (390–91). The first of them also mediates the contradiction between the Bible's "one Flesh" and Milton's "one Soul," for the "Heart" is the fleshly tabernacle of the human spirit: "Marke in my heart, O Soule, where thou dost dwell, / The picture of Christ crucified," cries Donne in a relevant sonnet.[46] Adam and Eve cannot be "one Flesh" per se, but neither are they consigned to the apparent doom of their biblical counterparts, namely, to be "the bifurcated halves of a primal self . . . trying to recapture [its] impossible primal unity" (Alter, p. 31). Through the holiness of their hearts' affections — by loving one another as God loves them — Milton's unfallen man and woman can become, as Adam says, "one Heart, one Soul." But in what sense?

Various passages in *Paradise Lost* IV make it clear that by "one Soul" Adam means simply that he and Eve — whether "Imparadis'd in one another's arms" (IV, 506) or not — can aspire without impediment to a marriage of true minds. Admittedly, given Milton's traducianism, Adam might appear to intend "one Soul" literally; but the most likely evidence, his plaintive lament "Part of my Soul I seek thee, and thee claim / My other half" (487–88), sounds suspiciously like a Petrarchan lover's sigh-blown quotation of some learned precedent from an *ars amatoria;*[47] moreover, Milton elsewhere assures us that Adam and Eve are merely of one mind — "unanimous" (736), a word that literally translates the phrase "one Soul." Buoyed by their unanimity, Adam wittily and punningly mimics it when he blends the cognates *part* and *partner* with the homonyms *sole* and *soul* into the solution sweet of denominating Eve the "Sole partner and sole part of all [the] joys" of Eden (IV, 411). Finally, in the first human instance of love at first sight, Adam desiderates his newborn wife "by my side / Henceforth an individual solace dear" (485–86). Editors often gloss the word *individual* etymologically as meaning "inseparable," but of course it also equivocally suggests precisely the opposite — "existing as a single, separate, thing or being." Adam naturally does not intend this meaning, but he experiences the full force of his *double entendre* in Book IX when he accedes, correctly if ambivalently, to Eve's desire to tend the garden alone; for she cannot be an individual *solace* without first becoming a separate individual. In such wise does Milton construe the Bible's dictum "they shall be one flesh."

Let us turn now to the last crux in Genesis ii, 18–25, (9) the sexual naiveté implicit in the notice that Adam and Eve were naked but knew not shame (ii, 25). This brief verse is more an appendage to than the climax of the creation of Eve, part of a separate etiology deployed to fore-shadow the fall and to account for fallen man's newly acquired knowl-edge of good and evil in terms of his concomitant sexual awareness (iii, 7, 10–11). Milton, on the contrary, believes that man acquired only "guilty shame: dishonest shame / Of Nature's works, honor dishonor-able" (IV, 313–14) by eating the fruit: his Adam and Eve are sophis-ticated prelapsarian adults whose informed sexuality Milton memorializes in the celebrated epithalamion "Hail wedded Love" (750–70): they love unashamedly not because they think not of sex but because, being "Virtue-proof" (V, 384), "they thought no ill" of it (IV, 320). Why, then should the Bible suggest that they think of it not at all?

For Milton the answer may derive from the vagaries of oral for-mulaic poetry as he probably understood them. Raphael apprises Adam of what "was done / From the beginning, that posterity / Inform'd by thee might know" (VII, 637–39), but we may presume that Adam, once fallen, would have been inadequate to the task. Is it not likely that behind Genesis ii, 25 lay a tale of prelapsarian human sexuality that, eroded by time and the human proclivity for fictionalizing history, was recorded finally as "they were both naked, the man and his wife, and were not ashamed"? Given the evidence I have discussed thus far, Mil-ton appears to have regarded all of Genesis as at best a highly elliptical and at worst a badly botched vestige of some such Ur-text as Raphael's narrative. Our poet, gifted protégé of the all-knowing "Spirit" who "Wast present" at the creation (I, 17–22), presumes to reconstruct that Ur-text, recording, among other things, the exemplary matrix whence issued Genesis ii, 25.

Milton does so, moreover, precisely where a reader of Genesis would expect him to—when Adam appends to his redaction of ii, 18–24 the quite innocent (but ominously foreboding) confession that his passion for Eve inclines him to uxoriousness (VIII, 523–59). Since precisely this tendency will occasion his fall (IX, 997–99), Raphael takes the opportunity, if not to rebuke Adam, at least to remonstrate "with contracted brow" (VIII, 560) against his inappropriate submissiveness to an inferior (561–78). Then, to drive the point home, the angel arbitrarily (and incorrectly) hy-pothesizes that the issue at hand is sexual passion, an assumption he seizes upon to castigate Adam for supposedly regarding intercourse as the *ne plus ultra* of earthly bliss:

> But if the sense of touch whereby mankind
> Is propagated seem such dear delight
> Beyond all other, think the same voutsaf't

> To Cattle and each Beast; which would not be
> To them made common and divulg'd, if aught
> Therein enjoy'd were worthy to subdue
> The Soul of Man, or passion in him move. (579–85)

Since Genesis i enjoins both man and beast to be fruitful and multiply, and since both creatures reproduce sexually, the naked unashamedness of ii, 25 might be taken to imply less a childlike innocence than a virtual parallelism between human and brute sexuality. Indeed Raphael concludes with a kindred observation: "carnal pleasure" is essentially bestial, he tells Adam, "for which cause / Among the Beasts no Mate for thee was found" (593–94). Apart from its impact on Adam (to which I shall attend in a moment), the angel's rebuke is a corrective commentary on Genesis that cautions *us* not to construe ii, 24 as meaning that human love and bestial lust are equivalent.

Adam is said to be "half-abash't" (595) at Raphael's well-intentioned but misplaced reprimand. The word *abash* derives from a Middle English verb (*abaisen*) that means "to gape in surprise" or "to be dumbfounded," and Adam is indeed astonished at the affable archangel's unwontedly austere and not at all sweetly "contracted brow"; but *abash* also means "to inflict with a sudden loss of self-confidence and a growing feeling of shame," emotions inappropriate to unfallen man. That is why Milton writes "*half*-abash't": he means "abash't etymologically speaking," for Adam is surprised, yes, but disconcerted, no, at Raphael's censure, for he has nothing to be ashamed about, as his spirited self-defense (596–611) amply demonstrates. Milton thus completes his apologetic expansion of Genesis ii, 18–25 by speculating that verse 25 derives from the transformation of "half-abash't" into the litotes "not ashamed." It is a fit conclusion to his account of Eve's creation, and the glory of it all is that the poet shapes his defense of Scripture without a trace of defensiveness: Genesis is never mentioned in the course of Adam's and Raphael's colloquy, for it is hardly *their* concern to practice hermeneutic apologetics; meanwhile the biblical reverberations of the episode will be discerned by the learned reader of *Paradise Lost* as waves of implication that continue the task of making Genesis safe for Miltonic orthodoxy.[48]

VIII. A SECOND CONCLUSION: GENESIS I, 31–II, 3

Let us return now briefly to the first creation account and to its concluding verses:

[i, 31] And God saw every thing that he had made, and, behold, it *was* very good. And the evening and the morning were the sixth day.

[ii, 1] Thus the heavens and the earth were finished, and all the host of them.

[ii, 2] And on the seventh day God ended his work which he had made; and he rested on the seventh day from all his work which he had made.

[ii, 3] And God blessed the seventh day, and sanctified it: because that in it he had rested from all his work which God created and made.

This passage accounts etiologically for the cult practice of celebrating the Sabbath, whose observance it "invests with all the reality of creation itself" and "represents . . . as a fundamental law of the world order."[49] But the four verses also contain at least two cruxes: (1) they imply that God finished creating on day six but assert that he ended "on the seventh day"; and (2) they say that God rested on the Sabbath, implying that an omnipotent Deity can somehow experience fatigue.[50] Raphael eliminates the first difficulty by fiat, declaring that "The Sixt [day], . . . of Creation *last* arose" (VII, 449, emphasis mine; cf. 568, 601). He later makes the same point less obtrusively by reversing the sequence of Genesis i, 31–ii, 1:

> [ii, 1] Here finish'd [God], [i, 31a] and all that he had made
> View'd, and behold all was entirely good;
> [i, 31b] So Ev'n and Morn accomplish'd the Sixt day.　　　(548–50)

Raphael now takes up the matter of God resting; first, preveniently: day six was "accomplish'd," true,

> [ii, 2a] Yet not till the Creator from his work,
> Desisting, though unwearied, up return'd
> Up to the Heav'n of Heav'ns his high abode.　　　(551–53)

The phrase "though unwearied" (an echo of Isaiah xl, 28) says it all, of course, although its connection to Genesis ii, 2b–3 becomes apparent only some forty lines later: "on Earth the Seventh / Evening arose" (581–82), when the Son, resituated now at the right hand of the Father, "sat him down" (584–88),

> [ii, 2b] and from work
> Now resting, [ii, 3a] bless'd and hallow'd the Sev'nth day,
> [ii, 3b] As resting on that day from all his work.　　　(591b–93)

This passage subtly concludes Milton's reworking of Genesis i–ii by adjusting the Authorized Version one last time: where the biblical God hallows the Sabbath "*because* that in it he had rested from all his work," Milton writes "*As* resting on that day." Does God repose on the Sabbath? In the *Christian Doctrine* Milton affirms it: "If it is said that God rested, let us not deny it" (YP VI, p. 135); and *Paradise Lost* VII, 591–92 ("and from work / Now resting") certainly agrees; but if we construe "As" in the next line as introducing a simile, it is only *as if* Messiah seeks refreshment from labor. It is a strange way to conclude an account that has otherwise, and with a zeal approaching fanaticism, made intricate seem straight.[51]

IX. CONCLUSION

Source analysis of the sort I have essayed is risky in at least two respects. For a given literary motif there is first of all the problem of specifying exactly what the author's source is. Does Milton's conception of Sin in *Paradise Lost* II derive from Spenser, from Ovid, from Hesiod, or from a handbook of mythology?[52] Second, the comparativist may draw unwarranted inferences about compositional processes and authorial intentions from his inventory of source modifications. The work of Allen H. Gilbert is paradigmatic of the pitfalls confronting one who would speculate, in the absence of draft manuscripts, about the stages by which a poem got put together, and the leap from what an allusive author modifies to why he adjusts his sources will smack to many of the intentional fallacy.[53]

The very existence of these dilemmas nevertheless adds credibility (and, I hope, a certain urgency) to the task of studying Genesis and *Paradise Lost* comparatively. On the one hand, verbal parallels demonstrate to a moral certainty that Milton's source for the creation is the Bible in the Authorized Version.[54] Moreover, I would assert (with the previous pages at hand to back me) that it is in source analysis (if anywhere) that critics relying primarily on textual evidence can hope to speculate least speculatively on matters of composition and intentionality. James Sims has accounted for the divagations between Milton's and the Authorized Version's accounts of the creation as resulting from "the work of composing poetry from the prose of Genesis" (p. 33). I would argue on the contrary that they proceed from the more profound, programmatic, and problematic determination to order the cacophanies of Scripture in the service of a theology that is rational root and branch. In that determination, and in some of the methods by which he proceeds, Milton reveals himself to be astonishingly like the modern practitioners of higher biblical criticism.

By affiliating themselves with a modification of the Graf-Wellhausen hypothesis, the editors of *The Interpreter's Bible* have managed to rationalize essentially all the cruxes in Genesis i–ii. The inconsistencies between the two creation narratives, chronological and otherwise, become trivial upon the assumption of composite authorship. As for the trouble-

some irrationalities of Genesis ii, 4b–25, modern exegesis has elegantly
disposed of them by rewriting the received text in a manner not unlike
Milton's reliance upon interpolation, paraphrase, and linear rearrangement. On the assumption that the primordial narrative from which Genesis ii is presumably redacted must have made logical sense, the editors
have sought to construct a hypothesized *Ur*-text by deleting eleven verses
as impertinent late additions. I cannot pause to rehearse the rationales
offered for their various emendations,[55] but it will be instructive to repeat the editors' reconstructed version of the creation of woman, for it
strikingly resembles the Miltonic recension that I analyzed above:

[ii, 18] And the LORD God said, *It is* not good that the man should be alone;
I will make him a help meet for him. [ii, 21] And the LORD God caused deep
sleep to fall upon Adam, and he slept; and he took one of his ribs, and closed
up the flesh instead thereof. [ii, 22] And the rib, which the LORD God had taken
from man, made he a woman, and brought her unto the man.

The mere deletion of verses 19–20, which *The Interpreter's Bible* justifies on seven separate grounds (I, 497–99), has the parsimonious consequence of eliminating the hints of divine inadvertency and implicit misogyny that characterize the received text. Milton, more cautious than
the modern exegetes whose methods he anticipates, would not boldly
excise verses from Sacred Scripture; but as we have seen, he produces
the same rationalizing effect by relegating ii, 19a to Book VII and by
positioning ii, 18 between verses 20 and 21. If I may hazard a general-
ization from this typical coincidence, Milton is a higher biblical critic
without a well-formed documentary hypothesis on which to ground his
reconstructive efforts.

What, finally, are we to make of Milton's redaction of Genesis? I
am awed by the poet's zeal for logic and stupefied by his skillfully accomplishing such an apparently effortless interfusion of contradictory sources.
But in the end, his rage for order may have been gratified at too great
a price, for the harmonies Milton desiderates seem to distort the biblical
world view beyond recognition. Robert Alter has provocatively suggested
that the authors of Genesis deliberately and artfully juxtaposed the two
creation accounts, not because they piously and inartistically regarded
their inherited materials as canonical and so unalterable, but because they

had certain notions of unity rather different from our own, and because the fullness of statement they aspired to achieve as writers in fact led them at times to
violate what a later age and culture would be disposed to think of as canons of
unity and logical coherence. The biblical text may not be the whole cloth imagined by pre-modern Judeo-Christian tradition, but the confused textual patch-

work that [proponents of the Graf-Wellhausen hypothesis have] often found to displace such earlier views may prove upon further scrutiny to be purposeful pattern. (*The Art of Biblical Narrative*, p. 133)

It is just possible that the radical discontinuities of Scripture represent the conscious intention of a final redactor rather than a slipshod concomitant of composite authorship. If Alter is right, Milton may have been more consumed with the lust of logic than smit with the love of sacred song, and his version of Genesis might be less an uncommon work of art than the common gloss of a theologian. God knows I hope not.

University of Texas, El Paso

NOTES

1. John Milton, *Considerations touching the Likeliest Means to Remove Hirelings out of the Church*, in the *Complete Prose Works of John Milton*, ed. Don M. Wolfe et al. (New Haven: Yale University Press, 1953–82), VII, p. 303, cited hereafter as YP.

2. The process begins explicitly at *PL* X, 1028–40, and continues throughout the remainder of the epic. See Georgia B. Christopher, "The Verbal Gate to Paradise: Adam's 'Literary Experience' in Book X of *Paradise Lost*," *PMLA*, XC (1975), 69–77.

3. According to the documentary hypothesis, to some form of which most modern biblical scholars subscribe, the Pentateuch comprises four or more disparate sources woven together into a more or less organic whole by a final redactor or redactors. Among many excellent accounts, the work of E. A. Speiser is brief, lucid, and accessible to the non-specialist. See *Genesis: Introduction, Translation and Notes* (Garden City, N.Y., 1964), pp. xx–lii.

4. *PL* I, 26, in *John Milton: Complete Poems and Major Prose*, ed. Merritt Y. Hughes (New York, 1957). This edition is cited throughout.

5. Irene Samuel, "The Regaining of Paradise," in *The Prison and the Pinnacle*, ed. Balachandra Rajan (Toronto, 1973), p. 116.

6. For a useful account of Renaissance attitudes toward Genesis, see Arnold Williams, *The Common Expositor: An Account of the Commentaries on Genesis, 1527–1633* (Chapel Hill, N.C., 1948). Williams does not, however, attempt sustained exegesis of *Paradise Lost* in the light of the commentaries. James H. Sims, *The Bible in Milton's Epics* (Gainesville, Fla., 1962), has a useful taxonomy of echoes of Genesis in *Paradise Lost*, but he too eschews close comparative analysis. Dennis Burden, *The Logical Epic* (London, 1967), and J. Martin Evans, *"Paradise Lost" and the Genesis Tradition* (Oxford, 1968), have written substantive analyses of Milton's departures from the received biblical text, but both are concerned chiefly with cruxes in the fall of man.

7. Gen. i, 1. I cite the Authorized Version throughout. Although Milton read Hebrew and Greek and had access to other versions, *PL* VII echoes chiefly the A.V. See Harris F. Fletcher, "The Use of the Bible in Milton's Prose," University of Illinois Studies in Language and Literature, XIV, no. 3 (1929); and Sims, *The Bible in Milton's Epics*.

8. See the *Christian Doctrine*, YP VI, pp. 299–325.

9. Milton writes "the Heav'ns" for Genesis' "the heaven" to distinguish the visible sky and its inhabitants from the Empyrean, the home of God that Milton elsewhere identifies as the "Heav'n of Heavens" (*PL* III, 390).

10. Echoing the concept of primary matter elaborated by Aristotle, *Physics* I, esp. chaps. 5–7.

11. The same point is implied at the end of the War in Heaven when Raphael remarks that "strict Fate had cast too deep / [Hell's] dark foundations" (VI, 869–70): for *fate* in *Paradise Lost* is the spoken will of God (VII, 173).

12. In the *Christian Doctrine* Milton translates as *incubabat* (brooded) the Hebrew word that the King James Version translates as *moved* (perhaps on the precedent of Jerome's Vulgate, which has *ferebatur*). See YP VI, p. 304.

13. According to Uriel, however, the separation of the elements occurred after God created light; Raphael reverses Uriel's chronology.

14. In *PL* many phenomena lay claim to being the "first of things": the Greek God "*Titan*" is said to be "Heav'n's first born" (I, 510), a lie exploded when Milton, confirming Raphael's opinion, invokes "holy Light, offspring of Heav'n first-born" (III, 1). But elsewhere Milton calls Night the "eldest of things" (II, 962), and Adam and Eve speak of "Air, and ye Elements, the eldest birth / Of Nature's Womb" (V, 180–81). Milton's Samson, on the other hand (who has read Genesis), believes with Raphael that "Light is the prime work of God," his "prime decree" (*SA* 70–85). I am not certain how to adjudicate these apparently conflicting claims. According to the translation of Gen. i, 1–3 favored by Speiser (*Genesis*, pp. 3, 11–13), the Bible indeed declares light to be the first creature produced in the six days' work, but Milton, as we have already seen, describes heaven and earth as antedating light. Perhaps he regarded the unlighted universe as a container and light as the first fully differentiated "thing" called forth from the "Matter unform'd and void" (VII, 233) of the just-circumscribed world.

15. *Physics* IV, 10–14, esp. chap. 11.

16. See Williams, *The Common Expositor*, pp. 52–53.

17. I omit discussion of Milton's brief but fascinating elaboration of Gen. i, 6–8 (at *PL* VII, 261–75). Kester Svendson has definitively analyzed Milton's transformation of the biblical firmament into the entire "expanse of liquid, pure, / Transparent, Elemental Air" that the Ptolemaic cosmology of *PL* extends "In circuit to the uttermost convex / Of this great Round" (VII, 264–67). See *Milton and Science* (Cambridge, Mass., 1957), p. 60. I also omit Milton's recension of Gen. i, 9–10 (at *PL* VII, 276–309): it is an entirely straightforward elaboration of biblical verses that the poet found unproblematic.

18. The first creation account is thought to be a redaction edited by the priests of Jerusalem (and hence is referred to as the "P" version), while the second narrative is attributed to an entirely different source (identified as "J," after the tetragrammaton *YHWH*, vocalized as *Yahweh* or *Jahweh*, which "J" habitually uses to identify God).

19. Milton's treatment of Gen. i, 11–13 and ii, 5–6 may be schematized as follows:

Gen. i, 11–12a	=	*PL* VII, 309b–28a
ii, 5b	=	331b–33a
ii, 6	=	333b–34a
ii, 5a	=	334b–37a
i, 12b–13	=	337b–38

20. Hughes, in a note at line 331, repeats the relevant biblical verses but omits the crucial word *for:* the misleading effect of his omission is to disguise Milton's taking issue with the logic of his source.

21. Milton's treatment of Gen. i, 20–25a and ii, 19a may be schematized as follows:

Gen. i, 20–23	=	*PL* VII, 387–448*
i, 24	=	450b–56a
ii, 19a	=	456b–58
i, 25a	=	456b–58
i, 25a	=	459–92

*I have reserved lines 449–50a for discussion below in section VIII.

22. Thus they translate, "Now the serpent was more subtle than any other wild animal that the LORD God had made."

23. Raphael's correction is "unwitting" because the Bible does not exist from his point of view. The same is true at IX, 560, where Eve knows the "Serpent" to be the "subtlest beast of all the field."

24. Milton recognizes this when he writes of the second half of day six, "There wanted yet the Master work, the end / Of all yet done" (VII, 505–06), where "the end" means "the last" but also "the purpose or object" of all previously created things.

25. In VII, 387–448, describing the creation of sea beasts and fowl on the fifth day, Milton is similarly scrupulous in following the sequence given in Gen. i, 20–23.

26. For a defense of Raphael and God in the present context see my "More Theirs by Being His: Teaching Milton to Undergraduates," *MQ*, XI (1977), 4–9.

27. At *PL* VII, 249, 309, 337, 352–53, 395, and 549 and 556–57 (both of which repeat i, 31).

28. Satan finds the animal fast asleep and possesses him without disturbing his repose (IX, 182–91). Being unaware of what is happening to him, the serpent can hardly assent to it.

29. This interpretation is recorded by Williams, *The Common Expositor*, pp. 60–61. The problem with it is that while he does not bless the earth animals, the God of Genesis recognizes that they are good (i, 25b).

30. In a note at X, 83–84, Hughes glosses *Conviction* as "formal proof of guilt." If he means that the serpent's guilt is so obvious that formal declaration of it would be supererogatory, Hughes has in my opinion missed Milton's point.

31. It is possible to construe *unable* (165) as modifying *Serpent* rather than *God*; since, however, God is the adjudicator throughout the passage, any transferring of guilt would appear to be exclusively his prerogative.

32. For the range of relevant connotations, see *OED*, s.v. *sly*, A.l.a and 3.b; *insinuate*, 1.c; *fatal*, 1 and 6.a; *fate*, 3.a and 4.b; and *guile*, 1.

33. Milton's treatment of Gen. i, 24–25 and iii, 1a may be schematized as follows:

Gen. i, 24	=	*PL* VII, 450b–56a ("Cattle," "Creeping things," and "Beast of the Earth")
i, 25a	=	456b–59 (beast of the earth)
	=	460 (cattle)
	=	461a (beast of the earth)
	=	461b–63a (cattle)
	=	463b–74 (beast of the earth)
	=	475–76a (creeping things – "Insect or Worm")
	=	476b–79 (insects)
	=	480–81a (worms)
	=	481b–84a (serpentine worms)

	=	484b–89a (ants)
	=	489b–92a (bees)
	=	492b–94a (insects and worms)
iii, 1a	=	494b–97a (the serpent)
i, 25b	=	497b–98 (periphrastically)

34. Ernst Häublein, "Milton's Paraphrase of Genesis: A Stylistic Reading of *Paradise Lost*, Book VII," in *Milton Studies*, VII, ed. Albert C. Labriola and Michael Lieb (Pittsburgh, 1975), p. 119.

35. Speiser disposes of these implications by boldly translating the relevant verse, "I will make man in my image, after my likeness," a decision he justifies as follows: "Heb. employs here plural possessives. . . . Yet no other divine being has been mentioned; and the very next verse uses the singular throughout; cf. also ii 7. The point at issue, therefore, is one of grammar alone, without a direct bearing on the meaning. It so happens that the common Heb. term for 'God,' namely Elohim . . . is plural in form and is so construed at times" (*Genesis*, p. 7n26).

36. In the *Christian Doctrine* Milton writes that "*God is said to have created man in his own image, after his own likeness,* Gen. i. 26, and not only his mind but also his external appearance" (YP VI, 135).

37. Milton's treatment of Gen. i, 26–29 and ii, 7–9a, and of ii, 16–17, may be schematized as follows:

Prolegomenon	=	*PL* VII, 505–16a
Gen. i, 26a	=	516b–18
i, 26	=	519–23
i, 27a	=	524
ii, 7a	=	524–26a
i, 27a	=	526b–28a
ii, 7b	=	528b
i, 27b	=	529–30a
i, 28	=	530b–34
ii, 8	=	535–38a
ii, 9a	=	538b–39
i, 29	=	538b–39
	=	540–42a
ii, 16	=	540–42a
ii, 17	=	542b–47

38. Elsewhere, however, Raphael echoes Milton's view (IV, 295–311) that Eve is ontologically subordinate to Adam: see, for example, VI, 909 and VIII, 560–94.

39. Milton's second treatment of Gen. i, 26–29 and ii, 7–9, and of ii, 15–17, may be schematized as follows:

Gen. i, 26–27	=	*PL* VIII, 253–91
ii, 7	=	253–91
ii, 15a	=	292–318
ii, 8	=	292–318
ii, 15b–16	=	319–22
ii, 17a	=	323–26
ii, 9b	=	323–26
ii, 17	=	327–37
i, 28–29	=	338–41

40. Robert Alter, *The Art of Biblical Narrative* (New York, 1981), pp. 27–32 (on

the creation of Eve) and pp. 141–47 (on inconsistencies between the account of her creation and the details of chapter i).

41. In *The Common Expositor*, Williams argues that in the Renaissance, commentators believed that biblical Hebrew signifies naturally by, among other things, etymological transparency: the commentators "proved" this "by the names in Genesis. Thus, *Adam*, the name of the first man, means 'man.' *Eve* means 'life.' *Cain* means 'from' or 'by the Lord,' so that only in Hebrew does Eve's statement at the birth of Cain, 'I have gotten a man from the Lord,' make any sense." These features in Hebrew enabled the commentators to conclude, in Williams' words, that "In the beginning man was given a perfect language to go with the perfect nature in which he was created" (p. 228). They were at least partly right, as modern exegesis has demonstrated. Thus, for example, at Gen. ii, 7, where "Yahweh God formed man from clods in the soil," there is a play on the words *adam* ("man") and *dama* ("soil" or "ground"). As Speiser has argued, "This should not . . . be mistaken for mere punning. Names were regarded in ancient [Semitic] cultures not only as labels but also as symbols, magical keys as it were to the nature and essence of the given being or thing. . . . The writer or speaker who resorted to 'popular etymologies' was not interested in derivation as such" (*Genesis*, p. 16n5). Milton would agree.

42. Notice that Genesis says nothing about Adam naming the fish — as if, in a departure from i, 26–29, man does not have dominion over these creatures of the sea. Milton eliminates this silent inconsistency by having God assure Adam that he has hegemony over the

> Fish within thir wat'ry residence,
> Not hither summon'd, since they cannot change
> Thir Element to draw the thinner Air.   (VIII, 346–48)

43. Cited in J. B. Pritchard, ed., *Ancient Near Eastern Texts Relating to the Old Testament* (Princeton, 1969), p. 68.

44. Cf. V, 358–60:

> Nearer [Raphael's] presence *Adam* though not aw'd,
> Yet with submiss approach and reverence meek,
> As to a superior Nature, bow[ed] low.

Unlike the animals vis-à-vis himself, Adam is not awestruck at Raphael's appearance, for both he and the angel are rational creatures; but like the animals the first man bows in submission to his decided superior. That Eve does not analogously curtsy to Adam suggests that she is not *qualitatively* inferior to her husband: they share the same (human) nature. But see also note 38.

45. At IV, 295–311, Milton says that Eve's hair "impli'd / *Subjection, but* requir'd with gentle sway" (307–08, emphasis mine). The adversative conjunction *but* negates the pejorative implications of *Subjection* — as does the oxymoron at IX, 376–77, wherein unfallen Eve has the last fatal word prior to separating from her husband against his wishes if not his will: "So spake the Patriarch of Mankind [Eve's father, no less!], *but* Eve / Persisted, *yet* submiss, *though* last, repli'd" (emphasis mine). The oxymoronic nature of Eve's unsubmissive submission is experienced more elegantly still in the contradictory descriptions that she (IV, 449–91) and Adam (VIII, 484–520) give of their nuptials: both accounts are true, though Eve attributes to native narcissism what Adam perceives as sweet reluctant amorous delay. He *will* not interfere with her freedom of choice.

46. John Donne, "What if this present were the worlds last night?" (2–3), in *The Complete Poetry of John Donne*, ed. John T. Shawcross (Garden City, N.Y., 1967), p. 343.

47. Williams has suggested a possible traducian implication of this passage; see *The Common Expositor*, p. 87.

48. Milton's treatment of Gen. ii, 18–25 may be schematized as follows:

Gen. ii, 19b	=	*PL* VIII, 338–56
ii, 20	=	352–444
ii, 18	=	444–51
ii, 21	=	452–68
ii, 22a	=	469–77
ii, 22b	=	478–90
ii, 23	=	491–97a
ii, 24	=	497b–99
ii, 22b	=	500–522
ii, 25	=	523–611
ii, 24	=	612–29

49. See *The Interpreters Bible*, ed. George Arthur Buttrick et al. (New York, 1952), I, p. 489.

50. Doubtless the notion of God resting at all found its way into Genesis on account of its central importance in the *Enuma Elish*. There, too, though for reasons of their own, the gods rest before, during, and after the creation of heaven, earth, and man. See Pritchard, *Ancient Near Eastern Texts*, pp. 60–72.

51. Milton's treatment of Gen. i, 31–ii, 3 may be schematized as follows:

Gen. i, 31b	=	*PL* VII, 449–50
	=	504
ii, 1	=	548
i, 31a	=	548–49
i, 31b	=	550
ii, 2a	=	551–53
i, 31a	=	554–57
ii, 2a	=	558–81
i, 31b	=	568
ii, 2	=	581–92
ii, 3	=	592–634
i, 31b	=	601

52. See my "'Real or Allegoric': The Ontology of Sin and Death in *Paradise Lost*," *ELR*, VI (1976), 317–35.

53. Allen H. Gilbert, *On the Composition of "Paradise Lost": A Study of the Ordering and Insertion of Material* (Chapel Hill, N.C., 1947).

54. See the sources cited in note 7.

55. For the full account see *The Interpreter's Bible* I, pp. 491–501.

MILTON REVISES
THE READIE AND EASIE WAY

Stanley Stewart

I N *T H E* *Censure of the Rota* (1660), one of the more valuable contemporary examples of Milton criticism, an anonymous writer pretending to be James Harrington, whose own idea of a "Grand Councel"
differed from Milton's, expressed serious reservations about his prose
style. Specifically, *The Readie and Easie Way to Establish a Free Commonwealth* suffered from a pronounced lack of candor: "you fight al-
wayes with the flat of your hand like a Retorician," the critic complained,
"and never Contract the Logicall fist."[1] It is only fair to say that in March
and April of 1660, this anonymous detraction cannot have been the
weightiest of Milton's worries. Nevertheless, from a critical standpoint,
the accusation is interesting, for, of all his works, *The Readie and Easie
Way* is uniquely aimed at settling, if only for Milton himself, the political issues that had preoccupied him from the time of his earliest writings
on ecclesiastical government. No single work is more critically situated
in the Milton canon, standing as it does at the end of Milton's prose career
and at the beginning of the period of his most vigorous poetic efforts.[2]

   Despite its strategic place in the canon, *The Readie and Easie Way*
has been overshadowed in recent criticism by attention to such earlier
works as *Of Education, Areopagitica,* and *The Doctrine and Discipline
of Divorce.* I mention these works because they share a rhetorical feature germane to the question raised in *The Censure.* They are alike addressed to specific audiences, and the latter two share the purported aim
of exhorting an authoritative body to specific legislative action. In the
closing days of the interregnum, Milton similarly addressed *A Treatise
of Civil Power* and *The Likliest Means to Remove Hirelings* to Parliament. The fact that Milton's last important political statement is not so
directed is noteworthy. For even if we argue that the prefatory paragraph to the first edition of *The Readie and Easie Way* appears to address a seated Parliament ("now sitting more full and frequent," p. 355),
the second seems to appeal to the voters at large ("in the midst of our
Elections," p. 408), on whom the responsibility had fallen to elect those
"Knights and Burgesses" (p. 431) most liable to preserve the values for

which Parliamentary forces had fought and died, no less than to the body actually "to consider freely of the Government" (p. 408).

Apparently, the contemporary critic thought that Milton handled both his subject and his audience too obliquely. In all likelihood he had read only the first edition of the work, and it seems probable, for reasons that we will consider later on, that he would have found the revised pamphlet even less satisfying.[3] He seems to link Harrington and Milton, despite the pretense of Rota opposition.[4] In any event, he thought Milton avoided the key issue of the rights of citizens to elect representatives, and of those representatives subsequently to vote as they saw fit. The two men separated on the role of the peoples' "Consciences," which, as Milton had written, "Christ set free."[5] Harrington favored a succession of Parliaments as an essential feature of political balance, the major virtue of his tripartite system. On the other hand, Milton's revisions gingerly addressed the underlying issue of the prerogatives and limits of citizens and their elected representatives.

Besides shedding light on the justice of the critic's opinion, analysis of these changes may also help to elucidate the shift in Milton's mind as he turned from writing polemical prose to poetry. The revisions of *The Readie and Easie Way*, made during the spring of 1660 (probably in March, as the evidence points toward publication during the first week of April), indicate diminishing interest in certain aspects of the political scene, and concomitant expanding focus on its fictional — or as some prefer to say, its mythical — possibilities. Milton began his career as a controversialist, as (and here the critic's Harrington persona makes sense) a "Retorician." And yet not long after writing and revising *The Readie and Easie Way*, he would characterize the archenemy of God as the supreme master of "persuasive Rhetoric" (*PR* IV, 4). This shift amounts to nothing less than (if I may coin a phrase) "a radical change."

In the following pages I will discuss the ideological and stylistic impact of the changes Milton made in his last important political tract. Harrington considered government the "Soul of a City or Nation,"[6] so it may help to think of these stylistic reservations fictively attributed to him as those associated with one who advocated including the virtues of "the *Democratical* or *Popular*" kind of government (p. 16), namely, one modeled on the Old Testament "Church of God" and selected through the participation "of the *whole people*" (p. 15). Harrington's insistence on the free "*election* or *suffrage* of the people" (p. 23) separated him from many supporters of the Rump, including Milton. And yet his nemesis was not Milton, but Hobbes, whose idea of man's irrepressible self-interest he sought, in words sounding much like those employed in attacking Milton four years later (pp. 10–11), directly to answer. Paradoxically, his words resemble Milton's too, for in *The Tenure of Kings and Magistrates* Milton took vigorous exception to Hobbes on the same point (p. 754). It is not only Harrington, then, whose views strikingly conflict with those of the Milton of the late winter and spring of 1660, but also the Milton of *Areopagitica, The Doctrine and Discipline of Divorce,* and *The Tenure of Kings and Magistrates.*

I

I take it that the critic's contrast between the rhetorician's slap on the face and the polemicist's closed fist implied a veering on Milton's part from the characteristic practices of political controversy. Behind the anonymous critic's wit lies a cogent point concerning the tone of Milton's work, and even its method of argument, in contrast to Harrington's. In *The Common-Wealth of Oceana* (1656), Harrington set forth his own model political structure. Just as Milton meant to respond to the conception of a rota system in *Oceana,* Harrington aimed to counter Hobbes's *Leviathan* (1651). Harrington's utopia was constructed in such a way that "Power [could] never swarve out of the hands of the many" (p. 274). This practically egalitarian effect stemmed "from the root by an equal election or rotation, into the branches of Magistracy or Soveraign power." Disguised as Harrington, the critic indicts Milton for his attitude toward Charles II ("You have slandered the Dead," *Censure,* p. 9); in fact, if Charles were, as Milton argued, a Catholic, "he might long since have procured all the Forces of the Catholique world upon" England (p. 14). And yet it was not in his antipapal views, but in his very idea of government, that Milton's judgment showed its major fault. As expressed in *The Readie and Easie Way,* it left no place for the wishes of the majority of people. In contrast, Harrington's utopia checked the power of aristocracy by those of monarchy and democracy ("of *the Senate debating and proposing, of the People resolving, and of the Magistracy executing,*" p. 27). Marked as it was by an "Arbitrary unlimited power" (*Censure,* p. 13), Milton's "Free Commonwealth" drew this critic's harshest remarks.

Accordingly, Harrington's known republican bent serves to heighten the critic's attack on Milton. For this fictive Harrington argues — and not without verisimilitude — that Milton's idea of a "Free Commonwealth" was, with respect to the people's vote, intrinsically equivocal: "For though you bragge much of the Peoples Manageing their own affaires, you allow them no more share of that in your *Utopia* (as you have ordered it) then only to set up their throates and Baul . . . once in an Age, or oftner, as an old Member drops away" (p. 14). But as he elsewhere complains, and in this we find an important area of Milton's unease, Milton's argumentative faults owed much to allegiances shared with such zealots as the

Fifth Monarchy Men. This may have been a less telling point for Milton as March 1660 passed, for he jettisons the harsh remarks in the first edition on those "pretending to a fifth monarchie of the saints" (p. 380). Even the revisions of the prefatory paragraph show Milton moving away from the political concerns central to discussions of the Rota. Consider this ostensibly traditional disclaimer on republishing the pamphlet:

I thought best not to suppress what I had written, hoping

it may perhaps (the Parlament now sitting more full and frequent) be now much more useful then before: yet submitting what hath reference to the state of things as they then stood, to present constitutions; and so the same end be persu'd, not insisting on this or that means to obtain it. (P. 355)

that it may now be

of much more use and concernment to be freely publishd, in the midst of our Elections to a free Parlament, or their sitting to consider freely of the Government; whom it behoves to have all things represented to them that may direct thir judgment therin; and I never read of any State, scarce of any tyrant grown so incurable, as to refuse counsel from any in a time of public deliberation; much less to be offended. If thir absolute determination be to enthrall us, before so long a Lent of Servitude, they may permitt us a little Shroving-time first, wherin to speak freely, and take our leaves of Libertie. And because in the former edition through haste, many faults escap'd, and many books were suddenly dispersd, ere the note to mend them could be sent, I took the opportunitie from this occasion to revise and somwhat to enlarge the whole discourse, especially that part which argues for a perpetual Senat. (Pp. 408–09)[7]

Understandably, commentary on this passage has focused on the dates of composition, the first edition being written before, at General

Monck's insistence, Parliament disbanded for elections to fill the seats of the "secluded Members," the second during those elections. But if we look at other aspects of the two versions we find that each emphasizes different concerns. In the first edition Milton implicitly addresses "the Parlament," since he permits its publication on the basis of that body's "more full and frequent" meeting. And he also emphasizes, matter-of-factly, that Parliament should open itself to full discussion of history as well as of proposed constitutions, without precluding any possible "means" to pursue "the same end."

The emphasis of the expanded version is aimed partly to include a wider audience. The revised preface implicitly addresses not only the "free Parlament" Milton hopes the people will elect, but the people who will do that electing. Further, if a hortatory implication lay submerged in the first edition (i.e., in the form of a challenge to the Rump not to preclude any "means" from consideration), in the second it is emphasized. Milton knows and tells the reader what it "behoves" a "free Parlament" to hear, and in so doing he justifies revision and reissue of the work. If an internationally known scholar can recall no government nor "any tyrant" unwilling to listen to advice at the appropriate time, it follows that Milton should at the very least be heard on this important subject. The revised prefatory passage, then, is more self-assertive than the first.

But it is more than merely self-assertive and hortatory. In the second edition Milton introduces an entirely new context. After providing an almost obligatory justification for a second edition (the first was hurried, full of errors, and so on), he proceeds to delineate what the first edition refers to as "the state of things" in far from matter-of-fact terms. He not only raises doubts about the motives of future temporal leaders ("If thir absolute determination be to enthrall us"), but he also suggests a liturgical and historical context in which England's choice should be understood. Slavery is no longer only a political concept, but one construed in relation to the corporate life of the church. With its twin associations of the children of Israel wandering for forty years in the wilderness, and of Christ's fasting for forty days and forty nights, Lent conjures a sense of possible relief ("a little Shroving-time first"), if only in free speech. But, more deeply, in the spurt of publications and their implied exploration of fresh and liberating ideas, Milton's allusion to the Christian calendar reminds this wider audience of the triumphant end of every Lenten season in observance of the Resurrection. The new preface begins with just a hint of the old Miltonic faith in books: "I know they are as lively and as vigorously productive as those fabulous dragon's teeth; and being sown up and down, may chance to spring up armed men"

(*Areopagitica*, p. 720). More than a routine apology for a second, enlarged edition, this prefatory address to the reader provides a biblical context in which the choice facing the country must be considered. The narratives brought to mind are relevant and rich, and, as we shall see, they shift the rhetorical stance of the speaker from argument to prophecy.

This construing of present circumstances in the context of biblical narrative is evident in the first major addition to the work, which follows a remark on the favorable response England's revolt had earned abroad. It is noteworthy that, while considerably expanding the passage, Milton also deletes specific references to the two French cities that had experienced the most serious disorders in reaction to news from England. The revision elaborates upon the thinking behind England's earlier commitment to kingship, which never entailed the sacrifice of "true religion" or liberty. As evidence, Milton reminds the reader of "the *Irish* massacre" (p. 410) and of its support from the Roman See. Of their English forebears, Milton writes:

> They made not thir covnant concerning him with no difference between a king and a god, or promisd him as *Job* did to the Almightie, *to trust in him, though he slay us:* they understood that the solemn ingagement, wherin we all forswore kingship, was no more a breach of the covnant, then the covnant was of the protestation before, but a faithful and prudent going on both in the words, well weighd, and in the true sense of the covnant, *without respect of persons,* when we could not serve two contrary maisters, God and the king. (P. 411)

While Milton seems to attack the motives of the Royalists who fled to Oxford, and so to justify those who remained in Parliament as members of the Rump, he also lays the basis of the commonwealth ("the end of all Government") in the higher mandates of natural law, "which is the only law of laws truly and properly to all mankinde fundamental" (pp. 412–13). The only recourse of a proper government, then, transcends such legalisms as supported the claims of crypto-Royalists then gaining strength in London and in the countryside as well. For beyond the prerogatives of Englishmen resided the august claims of "evangelic rules," which Milton firmly distinguishes from "meer positive laws, neither natural nor moral" (p. 413). In effect, by absenting themselves, the so-called "secluded Members" ignored the moral imperative of this higher law, and so were responsible for the "anarchie and confusion" that followed (p. 414).

In *The Censure* we read that "the Parliament of *England* . . . never consisted of a pack'd Party of one House, that by fraud and covin had disseaz'd the major part of their Fellows, and forfeited their own right, by abetting the ejectment of the whole House of Peers, and the greater part of their own" (p. 5). With this objection in mind, we find it more than coincidental that Milton's first major addition emphasizes the issue, not of peoples' votes, but of the intentions they reflect: "suppose bad intentions in things otherwise welldon; what was welldon, was by them who so thought, not the less obey'd or followd in the state; since in the church, who had not rather follow *Iscariot* or *Simon* the magician, though to covetous ends, preaching, then *Saul*, though in the uprightness of his heart persecuting the gospell?" (pp. 414–15). Again, biblical allusion casts the political situation in a perspective calculated to challenge the claims of the corporate body over the individual conscience. As in *Paradise Lost*, so here Milton expresses the intense conflict between the individual conscience and the worldly arbiters of right and wrong: "for on Earth / Who against Faith and Conscience can be heard / Infallible?" (*PL* XII, 528–30). On the face of it Milton writes as if in response to the popular view that the "right" majority always seems preferable to the "wrong" minority, even when the former's actions proceed from venal impulses. And yet, in a more generous temporal perspective, fidelity to conscience (or "evangelic rules") contradicts the impulses (and "suffrage") of the many, "there being in number little vertue" (p. 415). Indeed, Milton links the actions of the many with *"sacrilege"* and "blood-guiltiness" (pp. 418, 419). If Englishmen fail to grasp the spiritual meaning of the opportunity before them, they will justify their "enemies, who will now think they wisely discernd and justly censur'd both [them] and all [their] actions as rash, rebellious, hypocritical and impious" (p. 422).

II

Before we turn to the additions that would greatly enlarge Milton's work, it may be well to look at one notable deletion, this to demonstrate how Milton sought to deemphasize the topical concerns of the immediate political situation. Because of the importance of this revision, I quote at length:

> I doubt not but all ingenuous and knowing men will easily agree with me, that a free Commonwealth without single person or house of lords, is by far the best government, if it can be had; but we have all this while say they bin expecting it, and cannot yet attain it.
>
> > Tis true indeed, when monarchie was dissolvd, the form of a Commonwealth should have forthwith bin fram'd; and the practice therof immediatly begun; that the people might have soon bin satisfi'd and delighted

with the decent order, ease and benefit therof: we had bin then by this
time firmly rooted past fear of com-
motions or mutations, and now flour-
ishing: this care of timely setling a
new government instead of the old,
too much neglected, hath bin our mischief. Yet

I answer, that
the cause therof may be ascrib'd with most reason to the frequent distur-
bances, interruptions and dissolutions which the Parlament hath had partly
from the impatient or disaffected people, partly from som ambitious leaders in the Armie; much contrarie, I beleeve, to the mind and approbation
of the Armie it self and thir other Commanders,
when they were
                                    once undeceivd, or in thir own power.

Neither ought the small number of
those remaining in Parlament, be
made a by-word of reproach to them,
as it is of late by the rable, whenas
rather they should be therefor hon-
ourd, as the remainder of those faith-
full worthies, who at first freed us
from tyrannie, and have continu'd
ever since through all changes constant to thir trust; which they have de-
clar'd, as they may most justly and
truly, that no other way they can dis-
charge, no other way secure and con-
firme the peoples libertie, but by
setling them in a free Commonwealth. And doubtless, no Parlament
will be ever able under royaltie to free
the people from slavery: and when
they go about it, will finde it a la-
borious task; and when they have don
all, they can, be forc'd to leave the
contest endless between prerogative
and petition of right, till only dooms-
day end it: And

Now is the opportunitie, now the very season wherein we may obtain a
free Commonwealth and establish it for ever in the land, without difficulty or much delay.

The Parlament have voted to fill up their number: (Pp. 364–67)	Writs are sent out for elections, and which is worth observing in the name, not of any king, but of the keepers of our libertie, to summon a free Parlament: which then only will indeed be free, and deserve the true honor of that supreme title, if they preserve us a free people. Which never Parlament was more free to do; being now call'd, not as heretofore, by the summons of a king, but by the voice of libertie. (Pp. 429–31)

It would be easy to overlook the first major deletion here because the changes involve a measure of expansion as well. The latter amounts to a concession of mistakes made by the Rump ("Tis true . . . Yet"). The omitted section, on the other hand, is an explicit attack on the idea that "a free Commonwealth" is logically dependent on "free elections." Milton was well aware of the many broadsides and pamphlets calling for free and open elections which had burgeoned on all sides as Monck made his slow and circumspect way from Scotland.[8] Their unified theme was for the restoration of "the secluded Members." By associating a fully seated Parliament (i.e., large numbers of people) with "the rable," and the Rump with "the remainder" of the faithful opponents of tyranny, Milton implied that any enlargement of that body would entail a lapse in faith and worthiness. Indeed, the only honorable reward for the "faithfull worthies" who remained after years of struggle would be the establishment in England of "a free Commonwealth."

Then too, Milton deletes the pessimistic argument that, should the moment pass unseized, no other would ever occur when Parliament, under a monarchy, could throw off the shackles of "slavery." Rather, until the end of time, the land must suffer a ceaseless "contest" between the claims of king and subjects. Originally, Milton crisply stated that the Parliament had "voted to fill up their number." The revised passage emphasizes the legal authority ("the keepers of our libertie") under which the election had been called. And Milton's concern here is more than legal nit-picking. The added sentences lay down the challenge of a definition. Since "not any king . . . but the keepers of . . . libertie" in answer to the "voice of libertie" had summoned Parliament, it was unthinkable that its members could be "addicted to a single person" (p. 432).

In tandem, the deletion and addition show Milton subduing his thesis that a unique and irrecoverable opportunity confronts England to establish a "free Commonwealth," and developing in its place a prescriptive definition of that entity. The Parliament will be free if and only if it conducts itself in such a way as to "deserve the true honor of that supreme title." The inevitably circular drift, which seems to have irritated *The Censure*'s author, can be schematized in this way: (1) a free Parliament must preserve "a free people"; (2) monarchy precludes freedom; (3) therefore, a free Parliament cannot restore the monarchy. The poignance of Milton's view was not lost on Harrington's witty impersonator, who perceived Milton's bias, not only against Charles, but also against the Parliament, insofar as its freedom entailed the vote. (For how can a body be "free" if it is constrained to choose only among alternatives approved by Milton?) And yet a certain poignance emerges from the clarity with which Milton expresses, in ostensibly logical form, mutually exclusive articles of faith: (1) the "free Parlament" is the highest authority; (2) the highest authority is "evangelic rules." Hence, the unaddressed and unresolved tension in Milton's work between the authority of Parliament and that of "evangelic rules." In fact, as the author of *The Censure* cleverly observes, Milton is uncomfortable with Parliament — with the thing itself, and the word, too: "And therefore very prudently you would have the Name Parliament abolished, because it signifies a Parly of our Commons with their Norman Kings" (*Censure*, pp. 13–14). The sentence to which Milton's self-appointed adversary refers is the first to follow the addition that we have been discussing, and unlike the reference to the radical movements in Paris and Bordeaux, it survives the changes made for the second edition.

III

Most of the expansion Milton imposed on *The Readie and Easie Way* derives from three inserts (pp. 409–20, 437–43, 449–55), the first two of which introduce entirely new material. A third is so enlarged that it only remotely resembles the original version. The first insert follows revision of this sentence:

> The Parliament of *England*, assisted by a great number of the people who appeerd and stuck to them faithfullest in defence of religion and thir civil liberties, judging kingship by long experience a government
>
> | unnecessarie,
>   burdensom
> expensive, useless |
> and dangerous, justly and magnanimously abolishd it; turning regal bondage into a free Commonwealth, to the admiration and terrour of our

| | emulous
                                  neighbours [.]
, and the stirring up of *France* it self,
especially in *Paris* and *Bourdeaux*, to
our imitation. (Pp. 355–56)

For at least two reasons the changes here require attention. First, Milton replaces the judgment that monarchy is "expensive" and "useless" with the more general claim that it is "unnecessarie." Though kingship remains a dangerous burden, the economic issue is muted by a broader, metaphoric accusation. Further, just as Milton broadens his indictment he also broadens the notion of England's "neighbours" by omitting references to the French cities which had played the most notable parts in the response to English events (see Ayers's note, p. 356).

There follows an insert of a hundred lines (YP VII, pp. 409–20) in which Milton discusses the commitment Englishmen had made to "*preserve the Kings person*," reiterating the familiar argument that Charles had conspired with the Irish and other rebels to reestablish the Roman religion. As for those excluded members of Parliament, they had, as we have seen, failed to follow "the law of nature" (p. 412), which is tantamount to those "evangelic rules" recognizable only to a "free conscience" (p. 414).

This argument is all-important in that Milton's idea of Christian liberty goes hand in hand with the low esteem in which he holds the democratic vote, with its consequent rotation of members. "The best affected" people in government did not waste time counting noses, but rather attended to the "waight" of the reasons advanced by those who vote. Once again, Milton construes the issue in a biblical context. The trouble with the simple "throates and Baul" is that the process renders the superior, reasonable opinions no better than unworthy, irrational ones: "who had not rather follow *Iscariot* or *Simon* the magician, though to covetous ends, preaching, then *Saul*, though in the uprightness of his heart persecuting the gospell?" (pp. 414–15). Not only does this addition further define the vote in a context of the Christian imagery introduced in the revised preface, but it isolates passages calculated to emphasize a charge of greed against those who sought to accommodate the restoration of a Stuart to the throne. Judas Iscariot, Simon Magus; Charles I, Charles II— like father, like son. And yet the rhetorical question implicates the majority in Parliament and in England with the "covetous" simony of these villains, and the lesser number with St. Paul's "uprightness" of heart. In this way he reintroduces the economic issue deleted from the prefatory paragraph, but in a specifically religious context. Only the virtuous prefer with St. Paul "libertie" of conscience to economic well-being. As James Egan writes, "the 'fit audience' capable of perceiving the full implications of *The Readie Way* was small indeed."[9]

In his second lengthy insert (pp. 437–44) Milton deals directly with the objections expressed in *The Censure* that his system of government by its permanence was prone to "growing too imperious" (p. 437).[10] Milton appeals to history to disprove the notion that, in practice, oligarchies ("great men") were more inclined to excess than "the common sort" (p. 438). The truth is that either popular government failed to meet the needs of the many, or, worse still, "brought them to such a licentious and unbridl'd . . . power." Between these two horrors Harrington's system of "annual rotation" (p. 440) suspended the nation with unwieldiness and a host of associated ills, not the least of which was seen in its proclivity to be "incontinent of secrets" (p. 441). In a remark reminiscent of *Areopagitica*, Milton offers as the alternative to the "rude multitude" (p. 442) the "voices [of] the worthiest":

To make the people fittest to chuse, and the chosen fittest to govern, will be to mend our corrupt and faulty education, to teach the people faith not without vertue, temperance, modestie, sobrietie, parsimonie, justice; not to admire wealth or honour; to hate turbulence and ambition; to place every one his privat welfare and happiness in the public peace, libertie and safetie. (P. 443)

Given this list of virtues it would not be amiss to think of Milton's great admiration for Spenser. We are moving here beyond the art of statecraft to art itself: "so we be still going on by degrees to perfection" (p. 444). Or to put the same thought another way, as Milton's anonymous critic observed even of the first edition of *The Readie and Easie Way*, which lacks the present passage, Milton's *"Utopia"* does not burden itself with too much thought of the practical world.

Indeed, as we learn from the third insert, Milton is impatient with the intrusions of that world, which sometimes conflict with his imaginative aims. The longer version (this revision is more an expansion than an addition) is not only more complex than the original, but it is also not based, as is the earlier version, on speculation. It takes its rise in a series of rhetorical questions suggesting the strangeness of any impulse to reenter slavery (p. 448). No less an authority than Aristotle taught that monarchy could not survive in the presence of "able and worthie men united in counsel to govern" (p. 449), and England had many such men.

Part of this section voices Milton's oft-repeated practical objections to Charles's restoration. He envisions a reign of terror with an unmanageable increase in lawsuits, denouncements, accusations, and revenges. His moral answer to legalistic insistence on the "right of . . . election" (p. 455) is to insist that during the struggle the majority had forfeited the claim to that "right," and, further, that the "libertie" attained in that historical undertaking could not be jettisoned. Those who had fought, seeking "nothing but thir own just libertie," were thereby endowed with the right "alwaies . . . to keep it."

And yet the most telling aspect of this insert is not Milton's view of the inconveniences of restoration, but the manner in which he elaborates upon his biblical theme. Milton rejects his adversaries' argument that Scripture merely countenances republican sentiments:

This is not my conjecture, but drawn from God's known denouncement against the gentilizing *Israelites;* who though they were governd in a Commonwealth of God's own ordaining, he only thir king, they his peculiar people, yet affecting rather to resemble heathen, but pretending the misgovernment of *Samuel's* sons, no more a reason to dislike thir Commonwealth, then the violence of *Eli's* sons was imputable to that priesthood or religion, clamourd for a king. They had thir longing; but with this testimonie of God's wrath; *ye shall cry out in that day because of your king whom ye shall have chosen, and the Lord will not hear you in that day.* (Pp. 449–50)

As this passage shows, Milton does not permit his practical and theoretical statements to pass as an unqualified admixture, but rather insists that his conception of the future is no mere matter of opinion. The "providence" of God decrees that England had been saved from captivity. We are reminded of the distinction — so important to an understanding of *Paradise Lost* — between the "ordain'd" and "permissive will" of God (*PL* III, 665, 685), as Milton attempts to preempt the issues of law and suffrage by arguing that Englishmen were on the verge of undoing the "wondrous acts" through which God's "providence" had been revealed. Not "conjecture," then, but Scripture revealed the truth of England's situation. God ordained the commonwealth for his "peculiar people": "Some I have chosen of peculiar grace / Elect above the rest"; "And one peculiar Nation to select / From all the rest" (*PL* III, 183–84, XII, 111–12).

IV

Although Milton jettisons his near-defense of those "pretending to a fifth monarchie of the saints" (p. 380), his revisions nonetheless show him moving toward the likes of Baxter, Eliot, Rogers, and Stubbe, that is, more and more toward a belief in a "true, spiritual religion" whose lineaments can be seen in "the scriptures." Barker argues that the deletion of this segment of about twenty-eight lines is "profoundly significant."[11] Apparently, Milton came to see that the passage only reiterated what, in the revised version, was more amply treated in less particular, less tendentious terms, and that, I would think, it also disrupted a continuing discussion of "libertie of conscience" (pp. 379–83, 456–57).

Again, the deletion exhibits Milton's move away from particulars toward biblical allegory. Indeed, the discussion of liberty and civil rights, now uninterrupted by reference to the Fifth Monarchy Men, extends to the closing sentences of the work, where Milton imposes on *The Readie and Easie Way* what are, for me, the most emphatic, revealing changes of all. Not only do the changes continue to deemphasize topical concerns, but they also amplify the author's association with Old Testament prophecy. Consider the differences:

Thus much I should perhaps have said though I were sure I should have spoken only to trees and stones; and had none to cry to, but with the Prophet, *O earth, earth, earth!* to tell the very soil it self, what

| God hath determined of *Coniah* and his seed for ever. (P. 388) | her perverse inhabitants are deaf to. Nay though what I have spoke, should happ'n (which Thou suffer not, who didst create mankinde free; nor Thou next, who didst redeem us from being servants of men!) to be the last words of our expiring libertie. (Pp. 462–63) |

But I trust I shall have spoken perswasion to abundance of sensible and ingenuous men: to som perhaps whom God may raise of these stones to become children of

reviving libertie; and may

| enable and unite in thir noble resolutions to give a stay to these our | reclaim, though they seem now chusing them a captain back for *Egypt*, to bethink themselves a little and consider whether they are rushing; to exhort this torrent also of the people, not to be so impetuos, but to keep thir due channell; and at length recovering and uniting thir better resolutions, now that they see alreadie how open and unbounded the insolence and rage is of our common enemies, to stay these |

ruinous proceedings;

| and to this | justly and timely fearing to what a precipice of destruction the deluge of this epidemic madness would hurrie us through the |

general defection of a misguided and abus'd multitude.

Again, the most obvious difference may be that of length, the revised passage being almost twice as long as the original, but the longer text is no mere dilation upon a constant theme. As Robert Ayers points out, Milton retains the quotation from Jeremiah while dropping the allusion to Coniah. Presumably, the original figure suggested a too-accurate analogy between Charles and Coniah, who was punished for his lack of fidelity to the Covenant by exile from the promised land. Further, and this is as important, Coniah was also deemed unworthy to be in the line of high priests, with which Milton associates not only Christ, but his own prophetic vision.

On the other hand, what an author preserves may be as important as what he takes out, and in the same passage Milton does keep Jeremiah's reference to the trees and stones. Perhaps, as Hughes suggests (p. 898*n*), he had the New Testament text in mind; but the allusion to Jeremiah is the more relevant context. By dropping the topical reference, Milton intensifies the emphasis on the prophet who cried out to the children of Israel: "Hear now this, O foolish people, and without understanding; which have eyes, and see not, which have ears, and hear not" (Jer. v, 21). The expanded passage elaborates, first, the perversity of the prophet's audience, who were deaf to the voice of prophecy. In the expanded version, Jeremiah's dilemma becomes Milton's, and the seer is constrained to affirm the inevitable stroke of history, should his audience not heed his warning: "Hear, O earth; behold, I will bring evil upon this people, even the fruit of their thoughts, because they have not hearkened unto my words, nor to my law, but rejected it" (vi, 19).

In *Christian Doctrine*, Milton often cites Jeremiah in contexts touching Jehovah's relation to Israel. For example, in arguing that, since man's actions were created free, it follows "that God made no absolute decrees about anything which he left in the power of men,"[12] he recalls the words of Jehovah in the eighteenth chapter of Jeremiah to prove that God could "reverse" his "decree" when a "nation did not keep the condition upon which the decree depended." And Jeremiah proves a consistent context to show that God's decree with respect to men rests wholly on men's keeping of the covenant: "Jer. xxvi.3: *if it should happen that they are obedient and that each man turn from his evil path, so that I repent the harm I intend to do them because of the depravity of their behaviour.*"

Understandably, then, the same context figures in Milton's discussion of predestination and freedom of the will, with their concomitant theological concept of reprobation. Again, God decrees nothing except man's freedom. This is what Jeremiah means by his figure of *"reprobate silver,"* which typifies Jehovah's rejection of an apostate people (vi, 30), for in the same prophet, Milton points out, we soon read that "God says to the same people: *amend your ways and actions, and I will cause you to dwell in this place"* (p. 191). The will, then, remains free even after all the effects of the Fall have been considered. Otherwise, we would not read in Jeremiah that God called out to Israel even when that nation would not answer: " — but why, if he had only been speaking to incapable blockheads?" (p. 396) For Jeremiah as Milton construed him, faith — "FIRM PERSUASION" (p. 471) — is the key: *"every one of them shall know me . . . and that I pardon their iniquity and remember their sin no more"* (pp. 471–72).

Further, in Jeremiah we find precedence for Milton's theme, in *The Readie and Easie Way*, of a remnant of the faithful preserved during the time of the nation's captivity (p. 487), a theme which bears also on another of Milton's interests in his last important prose treatise, namely, that of the true priesthood. In the chapter "Of Justification," Milton recalls God's promise to the faithful. He will unseat those unworthy to succeed to the throne of Judah, and he will reward those who observe the covenant: *"because I will pardon them whom I make a remnant"* (Jer. i, 20). In the words of St. Paul, Milton found the authority for his idea of Christian liberty: *"I will make a new Covenant with the house of Israel"* (Heb. viii, 8, 9), words which he linked to Jeremiah's prophecy (xxxi, 31–33 [p. 522]).

Milton suggests here not only a comparison between an apostate Israel and a backsliding England, but between two prophets in two similar historical situations. Jeremiah preached at a time just after the Law had been rediscovered during work on Solomon's temple in Jerusalem. Likewise, from Milton's point of view, the Rump had taken the divine initiative in offering Englishmen a unique opportunity to renew the bond between God and man. Like Jeremiah, Milton sees an honored nation turning a deaf ear to God's Law and its back on generations of its own descendants.

In this connection, Robert A. Ayers's annotation seems preferable to Hughes's. Milton's excision of the reference tò Coniah, as Ayers points out, tends to erase the emphasis on Charles, and, we might add, even on Milton's leitmotif of the "single person." In place of the allusion to Coniah's shortcomings to himself and his seed, we find the only prayer in either version of *The Readie and Easie Way*. This parenthetical utterance is a petition to the Father and the Son — to the creator of man as a free moral agent, and to the redeemer of mankind from the bondage of enforced service — for divine intervention. Implicitly, the City of Man is irreparably fallen, so the speaker invokes the reign of "King Jesus."[13] Milton's anonymous critic grasps the drift of Milton's thought in this direction: "you rest Scripture most unmercifully, to prove, that though Christ said, His Kingdome was not of this world, yet his Common-wealth is" (p. 10).

The biblical allusiveness of the April text, then, is both less historically topical and more thematically amplified. The Old and New Testaments, the Law and the Gospel, establish the means of man's redemption in time. But the prophet prays for his listeners because they have heard the Word but not heeded it. God created man free. This much is familiar to all Milton readers: "To force our Consciences that Christ set free" ("On the New Forcers, p. 145). By the gift of his Son the Father renewed that trust for all time. But men are constrained to choose. Though they may reject, they cannot ignore the attribute of freedom (reason) lodged in the will as a gift. Like the Fallen Angels, men cannot elude responsibility: "I form'd them free, and free they must remain, / Till they enthrall themselves" (*PL* III, 124–25).

The original version stressed the recurrent theme in leftist prose of opposition to the rule of "a single person." Coniah's disobedience led to God's curse upon him and his seed: "Thus saith the Lord, Write ye this man childless, a man that shall not prosper in his days; for no man of his seed shall prosper upon the throne of David, and ruling any more in Judah" (Jer. xxii, 30). In the revised edition, Milton turns his focus on the relation of the prophet to the people at large. In this way, he is like John Eliot, who in *The Christian Commonwealth* [1659] reminded his readers that God's people had been commanded to "enter into Covenant with the Lord . . . Whereby they [were to] submit themselves to be ruled by the Lord in all things, receiving from him, both the platform of their Government, and all their Laws."[14] The Coniah allusion too easily shifted blame to the "single person" of Charles II, who, late in March, Milton had reason to believe would ascend the throne. Milton retains the prophet's words, but his prayer places the issue within a larger context of both the Old and New Testaments. The revised text omits the question of the unregenerate seed of Coniah, and stresses instead the onus thrust upon an unfaithful people, who in Jeremiah's time had lusted after false gods.

V

I have tried to show that, in revising *The Readie and Easie Way*, Milton did more than expand upon arguments advanced in the first edition. He did that, of course, but much more. He also enriched the tract by reinterpreting the political situation in biblical terms. And he amplified his own voice by inviting associations of it with prophetic models.

With this important shift in mind, we must adjust our notion of the "early" and "later" political tracts. In particular, in *The Development of Milton's Prose Style*, Thomas Corns points out that *The Readie and Easie Way* deserves comparison with Milton's more successful early political writings, but he bases that favorable judgment almost entirely on a word-count analysis of adjectival uses, since the more admired works tend to employ a larger percentage of adjectives.[15] But as we see in the example at the beginning of section 3 above, in revising his work Milton sometimes reduces the number of adjectives (trading the intensives "expensive" and "useless" for "unnecessarie"), and, as elsewhere, deletes even aptly derisive adjectives applied to the "secluded Members."

The word-count approach, useful as it may be, nonetheless omits consideration of the question of how words that may be counted are in fact used. Milton's revisions remind us of the tone of the "national digression" in *Areopagitica:* "Methinks I see in my mind a noble and puissant nation rousing herself like a strong man after sleep, and shaking her invincible locks" (p. 745).[16] The emphasis in the revised work is on the seer, whose prophetic vision distances him from the hurly-burly of the immediate (and depressing) political situation. In this way, the anonymous critic of *The Censure of the Rota* is less justified in his view that Milton was veering from the characteristic practices of political controversy than he would have been had he been talking about the second rather than the first edition of *The Readie and Easie Way*.

In the second edition, Milton aims at a more consistently metaphoric approach to his audience. He remains a combatant in the "wars of truth," but after the revision he engages in a more cosmic battle than before, one in which the history of God's people in the distant past is more relevant than the latest casting of the "throates and Baul" in Westminster. In the context of this revision, the audience is asked to think about right and wrong, not in relation to the emerging, legalistic (and Hobbesian) notion of consent of the governed, but in relation to the covenant ordained by God for his people throughout history, from the Old Testament past to the New Testament dispensation, which extends as far into the future as any prophet can see. This story the prophet knows directly only through prayer and faith. And it is one to which Milton, newly exiled from the world of active politics, would now address himself to a different audience, in a different mode and form, but in a prophetic voice, which seems, for all its differences, to have a familiar ring.

University of California, Riverside

NOTES

Unless otherwise indicated, all books published before 1700 bear a London imprint. I have regularized the spelling of *i* and *j*, *u* and *v*, expanded contractions, ignored meaningless capitals and small capitals, and silently corrected obvious printer's errors.

1. *The Censure of the Rota Upon Mr Miltons Book, Entituled, the Ready and Easie way to Establish A Free Common-Wealth* (1660), p. 13, in William Riley Parker, *Milton's Contemporary Reputation* (Columbus, Ohio, 1940); see also Parker's comments on the authorship of this work, p. 282. Parker calls *The Censure of the Rota* "the most pointed and significant criticism" (p. 55).

2. Only *Brief Notes Upon a Late Sermon*, Milton's rejoinder to Griffith's *Fear of God and the King*, comes after the second edition of *The Readie and Easie Way*. On the dating of these two works, see Robert W. Ayers's comments in *The Complete Prose Works of John Milton*, ed. Don M. Wolfe et al. (New Haven, 1953–82), VII, pp. 345–46, hereafter designated YP. All quotations from both versions of *The Readie and Easie Way to Establish a Free Commonwealth* will be from this edition. When the texts being compared overlap, that of the second edition will be followed.

3. See Ayers's full discussion of the dating of the first and second editions, YP VII, pp. 345–346, 399–400. Keith W. Stavely writes that "the publication dates of *The Readie and Easie Way* are more significant for the analyst of Milton's rhetoric than are those of any other of Milton's pamphlets" (*The Politics of Milton's Prose Style* [New Haven, 1975], p. 98).

4. As Emile Saillens points out, Milton's plan as outlined in *The Readie and Easie Way* owes much to Harrington's (*John Milton: Man, Poet, Polemist* [Oxford, 1964], p. 226). See also Barbara K. Lewalski, "Milton: Political Beliefs and Polemical Methods, 1659–60," *PMLA*, LXXIV (1959), 191–202.

5. *John Milton: Complete Poems and Major Prose*, ed. Merritt Y. Hughes (New York, 1957), p. 145; hereafter, unless otherwise indicated (see n. 2), all citations from Milton in my text will be from this edition.

6. James Harrington, *The Common-Wealth of Oceana* (1656), p. 11; hereafter, citations from this work in my text will be from this, the first, edition.

7. In order to emphasize the differences between the first and second editions, I employ the somewhat uneconomical opposing-column format. Overlapping texts will be centered. As in this example, variants will be presented with the first edition on the left and the second on the right.

8. This point could be documented from many examples, but John Gauden's sermon, published on February 28, was typical of the Royalism gripping London in the wake of General Monck's arrival. In this sermon, preached at St. Paul's before a distinguished company which included Thomas Aleyn, the lord mayor, Gauden offered "Thanksgiving unto God for restoring the Secluded Members" (*Slight Healers of Publick Hurts* [1660], title page). Ironically, like Milton, he calls also for a time of plain dealing and free speech (pp. 2–3), but his metaphor is all-important. England suffers from a disease, with poor treatment by "*fallacious Physitians*, and cruel Phlebotomists" (p. 13); the cure will be England's return to "one *Soveraign*" (p. 59). See also *A Letter Sent from the Commissioners of Scotland to . . . Lord General Monck* (March, 1660).

9. James Egan, *The Inward Teacher: Milton's Rhetoric of Christian Liberty* SCN Editions and Studies, II (University Park, Pa., 1980), p. 86. For an extensive discussion

of Milton's attitude toward the majority, see also Hugh M. Richmond, *The Christian Revolutionary: John Milton* (Berkeley and Los Angeles, 1974), ch. 4.

10. Barbara K. Lewalski writes that Milton revised his work "apparently in answer to a clever Royalist attack disguised as a Harringtonian criticism" ("Milton: Political Beliefs," p. 197), but as she also notes, *The Censure* was published on March 26. Rhetorically, it makes little difference whether Milton was responding to actual or only anticipated objections.

11. See Lewalski's discussion of the relation between Milton's late tracts and the "less fanatical millenarians" (ibid., p. 201). Arthur Barker, *Milton and the Puritan Dilemma* (Toronto, 1942), p. 279.

12. *Christian Doctrine*, trans. John Carey, ed. Maurice Kelley, YP VI, p. 155. And in *The Doctrine and Discipline of Divorce*, Milton writes: "He who wisely would restrain the reasonable soul of man within due bounds, must first himself know perfectly how far the territory and dominion extends of just and honest liberty. As little must he offer to bind that which God hath loosened, as to loosen that which he hath bound" (Hughes, p. 699).

13. In *A Holy Commonwealth* (1659), Richard Baxter concedes the Royalist postulate that the sovereign must be one, but that sovereign must be God (pp. 16–17). Christ, he writes, "*is established the King of the redeemed, and the Administrator General*" (p. 47). Accordingly, "*The people as people are not the Soveraign Power*" (p. 63).

14. John Eliot, *The Christian Commonwealth* [1659], pp. 1–2.

15. Thomas N. Corns, *The Development of Milton's Prose Style* (Oxford, 1982), p. 23.

16. See Ernest Sirluck's rhetorical analysis of *Areopagitica*, YP I, pp. 170–78, esp. p. 171. Richmond, *Christian Revolutionary*, comments on the connection between these two works (p. 151).

THE DOUBLING OF THE CHORUS
IN *SAMSON AGONISTES*

Kathleen M. Swaim

S*AMSON AGONISTES* is riddled with doubleness from its smallest
details to its largest issues. In terms of action, for example, Samson's
birth was twice annunciated by an angel; an amorous Samson was betrayed by two women; the Officer enters twice to call Samson to the feast
of Dagon, himself a bi-form idol, and receives two contradictory responses; two shouts signal the opening and closing of Samson's entertain-
ment of the Philistines. At the smallest level, doubleness appears in the
ironies of such charged diction as "guiding hand," "ransom," and "father's
house."[1] According to one Hebrew etymology, even Samson's name, "there
a second time," implies the doubleness to be worked out in the career
of the strong man given a second chance to redeem himself and to serve
as God's champion through a second definition of "strength."[2]

One effect of such doubleness is that many commentators have experienced *Samson Agonistes*, and especially its conclusion, as variously
puzzling rather than fully satisfying, and some of the best recent criticism has recognized in these dissatisfactions both an artistic design within
the play itself and the author's strategy operating upon his audience. For
Stanley E. Fish it is a matter of "Question and Answer" and for Christopher Grose of "Discovery as Action."[3] Because *Samson Agonistes* lacks
an equivalent of the narrators of the diffuse and brief epics, the guiding
principle of the value scheme it shares with them must be sought elsewhere. The standards of both positive and negative moral value do not
in *Samson Agonistes* align with readily identifiable representatives. The
misguided Dalila and Harapha provoke not so much condemnation as
careful distinctions between what is valid and invalid in those aspects
of Samson they mirror so exactly, and the limitations of mind of the theo-
retically sympathetic Manoa severely limit our receptiveness to his character. Even the Philistines, as Fish notes (pp. 257–59), arouse a variety
of sympathies. The reader's problem, like the hero's problem, is com-
pounded in that the evidence points so regularly not toward but away
from secure identification of those principles. Even syntactically, as John
Carey points out (p. 337), an extraordinary number of questions are asked

in *Samson Agonistes*, including for example six in Samson's first speech, and although questions may sometimes point toward their answers, they do not articulate them.

To my mind the most original and illuminating work of recent criticism of *Samson Agonistes* is Anne Davidson Ferry's exploration of language as a device of characterization and a vehicle of action in the play. In her examination of the play's silences, although she is citing absent evidence, she provides a reader's solution to a reader's textual problem. For her the poem's highest value is placed not "upon articulation, but upon unutterable truths, inexpressible meanings," for which Milton found an answerable style "which seems to reach for its effects beyond the realm of articulation and therefore expresses truths which seem to escape the limits of human language itself." Samson's fall, for her, is "a violation of his proper relation to language," and to regain heroic stature he must restore in himself the "fort of silence" which it was his divinely imposed task to guard. Samson's progress toward that goal is marked by his increasing imperviousness to the speech of others and the increasing reticence of his own use of words. Finally, in her view, we seem to hear even Samson's silences; "We come to know Samson by what is *not* said."[4]

One nearly inevitable result of thematic values that defy articulation and a poetic that depends upon the meaning of silences is a fragmentation of the literary criticism of *Samson Agonistes*. The problems are exacerbated by the remarkabale incidence and centrality of abstract nouns in the play (see Carey, p. 338). Commentators have tended to deal with confinable problems and areas of textual evidence; thus the high proportion of embattled attention to Milton's preface, Aristotelianism or the lack of it, tragedy or purgation and the lack of it, and the surprisingly imaged Phoenix and other similes in lines 1687–1707. I am particularly concerned that commentators on the conclusion have tended to focus separately on the figures in the simile sequence, or on Samson's agon, or on the role of the Chorus, but have neglected the significance of Milton's connections between these textual units. Thus one of my secondary purposes is, in the words of *Areopagitica* (Hughes, p. 742), pursuing the golden rule in literary criticism, to gather up limb by limb these dissevered pieces into a homogeneal whole.

In particular it is my present purpose to address a variety of kinds of structural and thematic doubleness in *Samson Agonistes* and to establish a context for reading the second semichorus of lines 1687–1707, with its poetically heightened but logically elusive array of dragon/villatic fowl, eagle, and Phoenix/holocaust similes. In this climactic instance of choral bifurcation into balanced semichoruses, the Chorus duplicate the psychic alteration the offstage hero has undergone and mediate that change for the poetic audience. Their transcendence of their prosaic norms into a burst of poetry parallels Samson's transcendence into silence. The themes and artistry of the poem wonderfully coincide at this juncture of the metaphysical and the metaphorical, controlling and unifying the various lesser instances of doubleness throughout *Samson Agonistes.*

Like Milton's two epics, *Samson Agonistes* is governed by the epistemological distinction between experience and faith, the data of this world and the imperatives of the transcendent. Experience sees as valid only the individual ego and what is and has been. It defines by sense perceptions, materiality, and history; its psychic condition is despair. Faith, however, is "the evidence of things not seen"; validity here, through exercises of patience and transcendence, resides in aligning the self with the divine plan, however incomprehensible. Such alignment both negates and fulfills identity; it transcends both reason and rational discourse. I have felt free to draw relevant citations from *Paradise Lost* and *Paradise Regained* to explicate these central themes and thus to take on something of the missing narrator's guiding role.

For most of the play Samson operates exclusively and fruitlessly in the experiential mode, a psychic orientation which Manoa reinforces and in which the Chorus collude. Prophesy is restricted to the historical past, and in general, as Ferry has pointed out (pp. 144–48), words are handled to a remarkable extent as if they were physical entities. Samson's despairing rehearsals of his own history lead only to self-pity and self-condemnation, a sense of desolation and "Heav'n's desertion" (632), and a sense of the failure of his championship and of the divine plan. But between the first and second visits of the Officer a significant reversal occurs. Martin Mueller describes it as a shift from sluggishness to suddenness of action, from dominant Philistine whim to dominant decisiveness by God and Samson, from a causal nexus of probability and necessity to a teleological nexus. For Roger B. Wilkenfeld, at this point ritualistic past events and heroic future events collapse into each other, freeing Samson from his past and preparing for the obliteration of temporal distinctions as Samson is transformed into a new salvific myth. For Marcia Landy, it is an occasion for the reader, the Chorus, and Samson to sort out crucial differences between the double perceptions that have heretofore pervaded *Samson Agonistes.*[5]

Another way of describing the change is in terms of language usage, not merely in Ferry's silence but also in the verbal strategies which establish the characteristics of Samson's new voice. From the Messenger's account of Samson's final moments readers infer a revitalization of the hero's faith, but in the only direct evidence — Samson's three speeches at lines 1381–89, 1399–1409, and 1413–26 — our inferences derive from an alteration of the mode of Samson's speech rather than from the content. Between the first and second appearances of the Officer we are told of Samson's "rousing motions" (1382), which reverse his decision and reverse his temporal orientation from past to future and his psychic orientation from experience to faith. The hero turns from the secure rational data of his achieved past to the uncertainty of the future before him; this turning is also a draining of insistence upon both control and selfhood. In the words of Raymond Waddington, Samson progresses "from self-knowledge to God knowledge."[6] Verbally, on the one hand Samson re-mans his "fort of silence" and on the other hand resumes the role of riddler he played in his youth.

The essential characteristic of Samson's new mode of speech is its doubleness, and that is conveyed by more than silence. Ferry describes Samson's "apparently calculated inscrutability," his outward lies which the reader receives as a shared secret of Truth, and his now intentional metaphorical meanings (pp. 169–70). To the language of unspecified referents also noted by Ferry, including "some," "something," "nothing," "aught," and "some" (p. 169), should be added several complementary speech practices. Now Samson's future orientation is couched in careful conditionals which imply an alternative or an alternative certainty: "If there be aught of presage in the mind" (1387). Moreover he articulates what he will not do — dishonor Hebrew law or stain his vow — but he does not articulate what he will do. He sees that this day will be remarkable (the future tense is significant) within the alternatives of "By some great act, or of my days the last" (1389); but, as Low has demonstrated, in the issue the day is memorable on both accounts, a synthesis transcending mortally recognized antitheses. Samson's third speech, his last onstage, continues the terms of the first in the conditional of "Happ'n what may" and "I cannot warrant," the negation of "Nothing dishonorable, impure, unworthy," and the alternatives of "The last of me or no" (1423–26). In a sense Samson has returned to the riddling speech of his youth, but the earlier experiential terms of the riddle's answer (honey, lion), and the earlier arrogance of the presentation, have been replaced by the "intimate impulse" of faith in fulfillment of divine promises. The altered speech demonstrates a release from monolithic historical fact and from insistence on rationality.

In Samson's second or middle speech, however, a new note is struck, and its name is irony. This doubly directed use of language distinguishes between the expedient, for its experiential audience onstage, and the transcendent, for its fit audience of divine omniscience and Christian readers and interpreters.

> Masters' commands come with a power resistless
> To such as owe them absolute subjection;
> And for a life who will not change his purpose?   (1404–06)[7]

Samson owes absolute subjection to only one master, the God of the chosen people. Divine motions have become commands within the law which Raphael explicates in "Freely we serve, / Because we freely love, as in our will / To love or not; in this we stand or fall" (*PL* V, 538–40). As in the conclusion of *Paradise Lost, life* becomes redefined to signify "A gentle wafting to immortal Life" (XII, 435), and *death* is "to the faithful . . . the Gate of Life" (XII, 571). Again Samson insists on what he will not do—"in nothing to comply / Scandalous or forbidden in our Law" (1408–09)—but now the positives are available, at least by indirection, in Samson's full control of ironic distinctions and thus of doubleness. Samson can handle what is susceptible to language with rhetorical skill, and he can convey what transcends language through meaningful silence. As Radzinowicz describes the occasion, Samson here achieves freedom from contingency and change (pp. 345–46), but it is also freedom from the constraints of language and law. These freedoms are two aspects of the New Dispensation of the Logos.

One further speech of Samson's is reported by the Hebrew Messenger to the Chorus and Manoa, and in this Samson continues to speak in his new ironic voice and builds on his previous expression. Now he distinguishes precisely the extent to which he has performed in obedience to the Philistine commands, an obedience that is carefully linked to the past and to the dictates of reason. His newly defined self and will, attuned to God and emphatically in the present, are asserted in "Now of my own accord" (1643).[8] He will offer illustration of his newly defined strength, a strength greater than the earlier physical prowess (1644), a strength defined not in Old Testament or Philistine terms but in terms of the new dispensation within which "suffering for Truth's sake / Is fortitude to highest victory, / And to the faithful Death the Gate of Life" (*PL* XII, 569–71). His trial "with amaze shall strike all who behold" (1645) — words that echo the triumph over the Adversary in *Paradise Regained:* "But Satan smitten with amazement fell" (IV, 562). The Philistines are, we might say, damned and annihilated by the limitations of their verbal capacities, which imply also a confinement of understanding to the things of this world.

When we turn from a consideration of Samson's career as verbal action, informed by and issuing in various forms of doubleness, to a consideration of the climax as represented in the Chorus of Danites, some additional operations of doubleness in *Samson Agonistes* emerge. Doubleness may be seen in the two different ways that the characters other than Samson are handled. In the first and more frequently recognized of these, the characters sharing episodes with Samson are seen as mirrors or extensions of the hero's mind and thought, who serve unconsciously to facilitate his growing understanding and selflessness by presenting aspects of the hero that can thus be seen, evaluated, and transcended. Manoa, Dalila, and Harapha perform these clarifying functions. Raymond Waddington explicates the process concisely in describing the effect of Manoa (whom Waddington equates with despair) on his son: "The quality of repeating what Samson knows or has said, but saying it in another voice, without Samson's hedge of equivocation, and so sharpening the articulation, crystallizing it, defines Manoa's function. . . . Manoa thus externalizes Samson's attitudes and the structure of the episode becomes a dialectic between Samson and Samson as he evaluates, qualifies, and corrects the stances in his soliloquy and assertions to the Chorus" (p. 270).[9] The second doubling function of characters in *Samson Agonistes* is as imitators of his experience who, because they operate in a less intense psychic and passionate mode, can clarify to the audience what is inarticulate and transcendent in the hero's experience. Manoa is sometimes seen as providing such a parody or even a counterpointing subplot (Mueller, pp. 247–50), and for Nancy Y. Hoffman "Manoa is the human parallel, at times the human antithesis, always the human continuum, of the more distant, mythic Samson."[10]

But more frequently it is the Chorus who are seen as undergoing suffering and changes of mind that parallel Samson's own. Jon Lawry has traced in detail the evidence that the Chorus parallel Samson's agon and growing self-awareness from their first entrance and throughout the play; Joan S. Bennett provides a theologically subtle analysis of the parallels between Samson's and the Chorus's guilt, piety, "carnal vision," and the like; for John Huntley, Milton explores the redemptive process at the extraordinary level in Samson, at the ordinary and sufficient level in the Chorus, and at the insufficient level in Manoa; and Mary Ann Radzinowicz applies the design in linguistic detail to the concluding lines of *Samson Agonistes*.[11] In these discussions a supplementary distinction is frequently drawn, between the Chorus as actors in relation to Samson and as vicarious spectators in relation to the reading audience. None of the commentators, however, has explored the parallelism of character and psychic action in relation to the climactic semichoruses of *Samson Ago-*

nistes, or has recognized that the Chorus's experience and victory are significantly verbal and poetic activities that should be measured against Samson's transcendence into silence.

The pervasive doubleness of *Samson Agonistes* emerges with special force in the Chorus's reenactment of the hero's climax. Throughout, the Chorus's misunderstandings of Samson and his fall and mission and the Chorus's vacillations have been closely akin to Samson's own. The Chorus become something like an extension of Samson's mind, a recognition faculty as characters approach and a reflective and interpretive faculty when they depart. It is in general the Chorus's task to expatiate upon a word or motif arising in a preceding speech, and their fulfillment of this assignment gives to their role an echoing quality. My present argument is that those echoes are not merely a matter of diction, but are more largely in the second semichorus a matter of altered expression and vision analogous to Samson's transcendence into silence. The Chorus of survivors of Samson's transcendence makes its own creative leap forward, but that leap is one of poetry reflecting Samson's leap of faith.

When we turn to the two climactic semichoruses that signal the poetic culmination of *Samson Agonistes*, patterns of doubleness are given special application. Even at the simple level of structure, the previously unified expression of the Chorus is now divided into two balanced semichoruses, reflecting two groups or two movements of the Chorus. Thematically, the first semichorus is in the experiential mode, the second in the mode of faith or poetry. Anthony Low has likened the two semichoruses to "a diptych or a pair of wings," adding, "on the one side is pictured the fall of the Philistines into darkness and final blindness; on the other Samson rises out of ashes into sudden flames of illumination" (p. 101).[12]

The semichoruses are introduced by a unified choral unit of nine lines in which the explicit emphasis is primarily upon the historical or experiential or what we might call the prosaic. Samson's Old Testament motivation of revenge is celebrated (cf. Judges xvi); the experiential is rendered most severely in the choral acknowledgment that greater numbers are slain in Samson's death than in his life; and the crisis of humanistic tragedy is focused upon Samson's self-slaying and within the Sophoclean formula of "tangl'd in the fold / Of dire necessity" (1665–66). Even in these lines, however, readers schooled in Christian paradox may draw inferences with faith-full possibilities from the balancing of "Living or dying" (1661), the revenge that is "dearly bought" yet "glorious" (1660), and the self-slaughter that is victorious. Further, the typological capacities of such readers enable them, unlike the Chorus, to see the transcendent in Samson's having "fulfill'd / The work for which thou wast fore-told / To *Israel*" (1661–63). For such readers the "Not willingly" of line 1665 signifies Samson's transcendence of his own earlier wilfulness and his submission to fulfilling the divine will. In this introductory unit the Chorus follow through on their previously established role as responders to Samson's career and as mediators to the more expansive understanding of the reading audience whom they represent on stage.

The two interpretative options of experience and faith are developed separately in the two succeeding semichoruses. The first, lines 1669–86, examines the Philistine situation experientially and attaches their frenzy of self-destruction to their excesses of self-indulgence and misguided worship of Dagon, a worship that is radically blinding and self-ruinous in the mode of the Nativity hymn; they are internally blind to the truth and light and "living Dread" of Israel. This semichorus proceeds in the verbal mode established previously as normal for this Chorus of Danites; it is at once lyrical and philosophical, given to avuncular generalizations on the follies of human nature and grounded in a generalized piety toward their retributive God who has been vindicated by Samson's destructive act. At this point the Chorus's interest is in experiential matters and their expression is prosaic.[13]

In the second semichorus, lines 1687–1707, however, the Danites (or half the Danites) act out the process of revelation. Both their vision and their voice shift from experience to faith, from prose and the past to poetry and the future. Their characteristic weighing of paradoxes or of thesis and antithesis on a horizontal scale shifts to a perception of synthesis and a perception and ascension of a vertical scale. Formulaic generalizations give way to progressive revelations of uniqueness and specificity. Prose transmutes to poetry, and their new awareness is set forth in imagery that transcends its own capacity for expression. Milton's deployment of the concept of vengeance provides a miniature of my point. Low makes the very interesting observation that vengeance is not mentioned in *Samson Agonistes* until after Samson's death (p. 187). The very experiential (and even numerical) issue of vengeance, with its foundations in the Old Dispensation of the Old Testament, is stressed by the very experientially oriented and prosaic Manoa, but vengeance is cited only to be transcended by the Chorus. As Low adds: "the Semichoruses rejoice more at the assertion of God's will and the rebirth of Samson's faith and greatness than at the destruction of the Philistines that must inevitably accompany these goods" (p. 189).

A great many learned and interesting points have been made by scholars glossing the facts, implications, and traditions of the individual images within the second semichorus and using those glosses to illuminate the themes of *Samson Agonistes*. Among the themes explicated may be mentioned: immortality (A. S. P. Woodhouse), pollution and purgation (Martin Mueller), remedy and ransom (Lee Sheridan Cox), allegorized metamorphosis and therefore spiritual ascent and transcendence (Raymond Waddington), metaphorical triumph over self (Mary Ann Radzinowicz), freedom (Roger B. Wilkenfeld), and spiritual rebirth into "the 'new creature' (related to Christ)" (Albert R. Cirillo).[14]

Despite the helpfulness of all this to those of us who operate within the dispensation of literary criticism, the criticism has invariably failed to heed the essential fact that the poetic lines containing the imagery are voiced by the Chorus and are therefore important evidence of their characterization and participation in the whole shape of the dramatic poem. Further, few, if indeed any, commentaries on *Samson Agonistes* fail to mention the Phoenix, testifying indirectly to the climax of the second semichorus as the climax of the whole poem, but even when the Phoenix is examined within the context of the other bird and fire imagery, critics seem not to notice that both the imagery sequence and its syntax elude the alignments of straightforward logic. T. R. Henn describes the Phoenix image as a "long decorative excursion," on the one hand "cumbrous and artificial" and on the other hand facilitating an "expansion and realignment of Samson's death into a mythology of its own"; for Martin Mueller we have here an increase in tension and perplexity caused by the revelation of the teleological design whose end will "remain shrouded in mystery forever"; and for Roger B. Wilkenfeld the image suspends temporal perspectives and establishes a new emblem for Samson and his achievement of freedom, replacing the old emblem of the motionless blind man in chains. One critic who has explored the relations of the concluding imagery to the artistic mode of the poem as a whole and to its hero's apotheosis is Lynn Veach Sadler. In her view the imagery, especially of the "ev'ning Dragon," is "apocalyptic in the manner of Revelation." For her Revelation is confined to a biblical text and manner, but, as I shall show, revelation is also a psychic and spiritual action which the Chorus here undergoes.[15]

The sudden burst of visual imagery in the second semichorus must be measured against the visual norms of *Samson Agonistes* as a whole as well as against the speech normal to the Chorus. Anthony Low says of Manoa's speech at lines 1708–14 what is sometimes suggested of the expression of *Samson Agonistes* in general, that "it seems deliberately to avoid using concrete imagery," and that it proceeds with "deliberate vagueness" and "a kind of hypnotic circling about" (pp. 218–19). *Sam-*

son Agonistes' heavy dependence on abstract nouns, in John Carey's view, throws the play's sparse imagery into bolder relief (pp. 338–39).[16] Although he does not link the verbal and poetic development to the character and psyche of the Chorus, Martin Mueller describes the overall verbal design concisely: "Milton's drama is so intellectual that it often approaches the nature of a debate, but in the end it transcends the limits of the intellect and beyond these limits direct expression must yield to metaphor. The decisive discontinuity in *Samson Agonistes,* the change from reason to faith, is accompanied by a change from argument to image" (pp. 242–43). The imagery participates in the "controlled turbulence" Balachandra Rajan sees as the overall shape of *Samson Agonistes:* in this "an equilibrium is deliberately imperilled so that a richer, more inclusive equilibrium can be achieved through the process of disorientation" (p. 143). But Mueller finds Milton "silent" in *Samson Agonistes* on the raptures of heaven, celebrated in ecstatic language as inexpressible in his other works (pp. 239–40), and Mary Ann Radzinowicz sees the progress of Milton's whole poetic career as a shift in emphasis from the youthful role of poet as rhapsode to the mature role of poet as sage (p. 359). My point is that in *Samson Agonistes* the rhapsodic and inexpressible voice is given to the Chorus. With the second semichorus a light breaks in upon them in Huntley's account (p. 144); they become, in Summers' words, "rapt" and "inspired by a sense of purpose beyond their conscious knowledge" (p. 173); and for Radzinowicz resemblances between Samson and the images proceed "with breathtaking swiftness" (p. 177).

These are terms which describe revelation, in both its normal and its theological uses. The intertwined patterns of the imagery of the second semichorus clearly present the Chorus as undergoing such a process of revelation, particularly when — as rarely happens in the commentaries — the images are viewed not in isolation but as a sequence. In the most prominent imagery, that of birds, the sequence proceeds from the "tame villatic fowl" (numerous and domestic), to the Eagle (with its Jovian echoes of regal power and its greater rarity), to the Phoenix (with its uniqueness, mystery, and transcendence of time and mortal norms). The sequence includes several reversals. The initial bird image attaches to the Philistines, the others to Samson. The first is experientially based and immediate, the others soar. As the "blindness internal" of the Philistines in the first semichorus reverses at the hinge of the semichoruses to the "inward eyes illuminated" of the erstwhile blind Samson, so the images shift from emphasizing the Philistine point of view (radically experiential as Matthew Arnold can attest) and the destructive aspects of the event to emphasizing the creative transcendence of Samson's achievement and, through him, of God's. Initially in the image sequence Samson is likened to "an ev'ning Dragon," the enemy of Dagon's reductionist, experiential worshippers, the domestic fowl. The Eagle image concisely asserts divine Hebraic retributive justice. What had seemed (note "as seem'd," 1698) a logically reliable reading of the fate of virtue gives way in content and in expression to the mysterious power and unique vitality of the emerging Phoenix. The Chorus's correction of the initial error of attribution sparks secure and multiplying illumination.

Ferry has drawn in some detail the contrast between the Chorus as characters who *see* and Samson as a character who *feels,* and the Chorus's revelation is thus dominantly visual (p. 141). Northrop Frye's account of *Samson Agonistes* as "a kind of visual anti-play" in contrast to the visual mode of Greek tragedies may be cited to develop a related argument. Like Ferry, Frye sees Samson as living "in a kind of seance-world of disembodied voices," but for Frye the shift of metaphors from the eye to the ear is linked with a distinction between pagan and biblical traditions, the biblical transferring "visual metaphors to an envisioned future state." Frye distinguishes also between the visual image as centripetal and the revelation of the Word as centrifugal, that is "a command, the starting-point of a course of action" (pp. 150, 149, 146–47).[17] The nonvisual Samson receives his "rousing motions" through a kind of *listening* to divine command; his verbal result is silence. But the visual Chorus enact their analogue in the terms appropriate to their lesser condition as community rather than uniquely touched individual, as survivors and mediators rather than annihilated sufferers. Their new course is no less centrifugal, but their action or issue is heightened verbal expression. Such expression is pagan (as opposed to Frye's biblical) only in the sense, for example, that the "Mighty *Pan*" of the Nativity hymn is pagan. Here, as throughout his career, Milton uses mythology as an experiential vocabulary, a kind of shorthand, for the inexpressible.

As the Chorus visualize a sequence of bird images, they are led from an experiential, rationally valid assessment of the Philistines as "tame villatic Fowl" to an unexperiential revelation of the reason-transcending Phoenix. The latter vision is imposed upon them (as grace is an imposition) rather than willed or controlled; that imposition occurs at the characteristically Miltonic coincidence of the realms of imagination and grace. Their normative present vision of immediately preceding events (the destruction of the Philistine temple/henroost) is transcended, and their visual metaphor envisions a future state, as experience gives way to the epistemology of faith. Their centripetal imaging shifts to centrifugal imagining as transcendent possibilities open before them. The change is a matter of chronological orientation from past to present, but more importantly it is from moral ambiguity within the image to a special typological kind of clarity, openendedness, and transcendence. Unlike the Dragon, which may be read in terms of moral polarities (Satan or Christ), the double-nesses within the Phoenix image all move in the same direction, toward Christian mystery, carrying the individual perceivers (whether Chorus or reading audience) as far upward as their imaginative capacities will stretch. In this poetic crisis the various doublenesses throughout *Samson Agonistes* come into complete focus.

In lines 1697–1706 the Chorus lose control of both their syntax and their imagery as this power and mystery emerge in their perception, and what is revealed to them is no less than the paradox of the New Dispensation. If we turn for guidance to other Miltonic articulations of this critical issue — and given the limitations imposed upon *Samson Agonistes* by its dramatic form, we must turn elsewhere — we find the Chorus's revelation articulated precisely in Adam's testament of Book XII of *Paradise Lost:*

> Henceforth I learn, that to obey is best,
> And love with fear the only God, to walk
> As in his presence, ever to observe
> His providence, and on him sole depend,
> Merciful over all his works, with good
> Still overcoming evil, and by small
> Accomplishing great things, by things deem'd weak
> Subverting worldly strong, and worldly wise
> By simply meek: that suffering for Truth's sake
> Is fortitude to highest victory,
> And to the faithful Death the Gate of life.   (XII, 561–71)

There too the divisiveness that is the inevitable postlapsarian inheritance is resolved by the special doubleness of Christ as paradox, whose incarnation unifies the alternatives of experience or faith. As in *Paradise Lost* Michael had taught Adam to acknowledge his "Redeemer ever blest" (573), so the example of Samson teaches the Chorus of Danites the true meanings of providence, strength, victory, and death/life. Given the unique psychology of Adam, whose edenic form has not yet lost "All her Original brightness" (I, 592), Milton couches Adam's testimony in a lean and spare style appropriate to the Logos and savior of *Paradise Regained*, a style that would be admired in the circles of the Royal Society; for his quite different dramatic purposes in *Samson Agonistes* Milton couches the analogous testimony of the Chorus (who literally provide a *stylization* of the fallen audience of readers) in a poetically heightened expression that transcends rational, visual, syntactical, and in sum experiential categories. He is thus demonstrating those powers he attached to the poet in *The Reason of Church Government,* "beside the office of a pulpit," to be "more doctrinal and exemplary to a nation" (Hughes, p. 669). He fulfills his poetic and spiritual mission to fallen, "soft," modern temperaments: "Teaching over the whole book of sanctity and virtue through all the instances of example, with such delight to those especially of soft and delicious temper who will not so much as look upon Truth herself, unless they see her elegantly dressed" (Hughes, p. 670). In concluding his testimony Adam acknowledges having been taught "by his example whom I now / Acknowledge my Redeemer ever blest" (XII, 572–73). That Redeemer is in *Paradise Regained,* however, "above example high" (I, 232), and must be mediated by Samson who is exemplary to the nation of chosen but fallen interpreters. Radzinowicz has argued that throughout *Samson Agonistes* Milton "plays on repetitions of the words *example, experience, prophecy, image, test, trial, spectacle, event,* and *occasion*" (p. 107). In general Samson is not so much an example as an illustration, in the senses which, according to the *OED,* dominate sixteenth and seventeenth-century usage — the action of making or fact of being lustrous, luminous, or bright. As the *OED* explains, the history of *illustration* parallels that of *illumination,* with "spiritual enlightenment" as the primary sense. The fiery transcendence of Samson will enflame the breasts of those who will turn their minds to his career with imaginative and spiritual revitalization.

In the eleven lines on the Phoenix, the Chorus attempt to express their newly revealed awareness, and they both fail and succeed. They succeed in their breakthrough to new vision and expression, and they fail in that, unlike Samson's, their breakthroughs are into mortal rather than transcendent categories. Their success is limited in that, chronologically and typologically, the fullness of the Christian event and logos lies so far in their future that they must look far forward to it rather than achieve it. In the words of Hebrews xi, 39, these Danites "received not the [full Christian] promise," but they have learned from Samson, who "obtained a good report through faith."[18] The monument proposed for Samson will mediate his "good report" as promissory to future generations who, like the Chorus at present, will find their imaginations and their faith inflamed for future spiritual action. The reliance of all the characters in *Samson Agonistes* upon Samson's history and upon experiential history more generally will be transcended as it is subsumed in the larger Christian time scheme of promise and apocalypse. The Danites come to proceed, as Samson himself does, in the mode of future-oriented faith rather than achieved experience. And the Danites both succeed and fail in that their mode of expression has been transformed from prose to poetry, from adage to image. New salvific imagination and dispensation have become operative within them, but their achievement of poetry falls short of Samson's achievement of silence. Whereas Samson's language in his final speeches distinguished between what can be experientially articulated and silence, negating the former categories and implying the latter through controlled irony, the Chorus with their lesser psychic transformation — but also their experiential survival — attain only to self-transcending and reason-transcending poetry. The second dimension of their speech is not ironic but iconological and typological. The shift in their mode of speech and vision shows that they have been put in touch with transcendent mystery; their very loss of control over the sequence of images and their own syntax testifies to the operations of revelation within them.

The second sequence of images, relating to fire, develops related points and will serve to place *Samson Agonistes* within the teleological framework of Milton's other poetry. Initially Samson's "fiery virtue" is "rous'd / From under ashes into sudden flame" (1690–91). At the second stage fire images become regally and cosmically focused in the thunderbolts of line 1696. At the third stage the fire-consumed sacrificial tomb of the Phoenix's holocaust becomes an ashy womb teeming with new life, new inspiration, and new modes of action and time.[19] Death of the old body gives birth to new fame, new inspiration. In this reversal of incarnation, experiential body is separated from transcending spirit. To the limited experiential and backward-looking consciousness of Manoa — he cannot tell one father's house (his own) from another father's house (God's) — this new dispensation appears primarily in terms of Samson as a monument or memory locus:

> Thither shall all the valiant youth resort,
> And from his memory inflame thir breasts
> To matchless valor, and adventures high.   (1738–40)

For Manoa such teaching will be straightforward and historical, even simplistic, but as Radzinowicz notes, "to the Chorus the lesson lies in the giving of the lesson" (p. 178). For those for whom memory is an act of faith, putting them in touch with the promises to be fulfilled, rather than an act of experience, for those operating with and within a Christian framework, for typological exegetes and potential poets and readers, Samson's act and new definition of the nature of action will have enormous transcendental results. New vision looks forward to, in Milton's terms, that occasion when

> The World shall burn, and from her ashes spring
> New Heav'n and Earth, wherein the just shall dwell
> And after all thir tribulation long
> See golden days, fruitful of golden deeds,
> With Joy and Love triumphing, and fair Truth.
>
> (*PL* III, 334–38)

It is a time when "God shall be All in All" (III, 341), and when, following the Covenant of Noah's rainbow, "fire [shall] purge all things new, / Both Heav'n and Earth, wherein the just shall dwell" (XI, 900–01), and when God will

> dissolve
> *Satan* with his perverted World, then raise
> From the conflagrant mass, purg'd and refin'd,
> New Heav'ns, new Earth, Ages of endless date
> Founded in righteousness and peace and love,
> To bring forth fruits Joy and Eternal Bliss.   (XII, 546–51)

The biblical and Miltonic passages developing these images and concepts could be arrayed at great length, but the point need not be belabored. From Milton's earliest poetry to his latest "the world's last session" is anticipated, "And then at last our bliss / Full and perfect is, / But now begins" (Nativity hymn, 163, 165–67), and that beginning is with the fiery virtue flaming in the spirit of the valiant, aspiring, imaginative individual believer.

Also drawing upon the data of Milton's other late poems, we can see that the Chorus of Danites in *Samson Agonistes* must be numbered with, and may be measured by, those other Miltonic characters who are touched by the transforming process of revelation. The process is available in *Paradise Lost* in the dialogue of Father and Son in Book III which Irene Samuel has traced with such care. That dialogue moves "from its presumably fixed beginning to an unforeseen end," arriving "by tremendous leaps at a resolution unimaginable except to Omniscience at the outset."[20] It is illustrated also by the good angels in Book VI, who "each on himself reli'd, / As only in his arm the moment lay / Of victory" (238–40), and who act faithfully without needing to see the motives or consequences of their actions beyond the fulfillment of their submission to the divine will. It is available to Michael in Books XI and XII, who is revealing to Adam what is in the process of being revealed to himself: "reveal / To *Adam* what shall come in future days, / As I shall thee enlighten" (XI, 113–15). And it is reconstituted even more applicably at the climax of

Paradise Regained, when, immediately following Christ's climactic standing at Book IV, line 561, the witnessing narrator's poetic energies flood
imaginatively upon him and issue in the Oedipus and Hercules similes.
The sudden flow of poetry in the *Paradise Regained* similes is a precise
equivalent of the sudden flow in the climactic semichoruses of *Samson
Agonistes,* and the agency of this poetic act, the redeemed narrator of
Paradise Regained — who also mediates the hero's spiritual transcendence
through "pagan" poetry — is the precise analogue of the Chorus of surviving Danites in the dramatic poem which Milton paired with the brief
epic in the volume published in 1671.

In their final speech, also the last lines of *Samson Agonistes,* the
Chorus speak in the muted tones characteristic of the survivors of Shake-
spearean tragedies: practical matters are susceptible to verbalizing on such
occasions (and this the very practical Manoa manages with a vengeance),
but it is too soon to capture in words the full meaning of the experience,
even if divine silence could ever be translated into mortal language. (The
libraries of interpretation of Shakespeare's and Milton's themes argue
powerfully that the task is inexhaustible.) Several conclusions from the
evidence and criticism I have cited may, however, be drawn, and they
bring into rounded perspective the various doublenesses operating
throughout *Samson Agonistes,* particularly the junctures of metaphorical and metaphysical, poetic and spiritual, verbal and transcendent,
pagan and Christian, experiential and faith-full.

Following the semichoruses, the Chorus of Danites in *Samson Agonistes* have only one additional speech, and this has been frequently and
wisely commented upon by the critics. Though its opening is founded
upon a recapitulation of the characteristic endings of Euripides, the speech
translates into the radical formula of Christian prayer, "Thy will be done,"
and celebrates the Christian principles of the uncontrollable divine intent and God's illustration of his faithful champion — *illustration,* as noted
above, in the sense of both chosen example and illuminated/luminous occasion. The final lines are these:

> His servants he with new acquist
> Of true experience from this great event
> With peace and consolation hath dismist,
> And calm of mind, all passion spent.

The final line signifies, as Radzinowicz observes, "not a void or blank
of mind" but rather "a vivid, energetic recognition of a truth." The final
lines are sometimes described as forming a sort of sonnet or as themselves
a "sweet lyric song" (pp. 357–58, 64–65.)[21] Anthony Low finds here Mil-

ton's most notable achievement of what he calls "transcendent poetry," and it is so because the earlier experiential language has been purified or redeemed: "Because of what has gone before, Milton has reached a point where 'peace' *means* peace, and doesn't simply state it; 'calm' transmits calmness" (p. 220, italics his). The *peace* anticipated for Israel earlier was merely a literal matter, like the "No War, or Battle's sound" of the Nativity hymn (53), rather than "the perpetual peace" (7) or "universal Peace" (52) of the New Order, or the "peace from God, and Cov'nant new" of *Paradise Lost* XI, 867. In his youthful exploits Samson had been "The Image of [God's] strength" (706) under the Old Dispensation, but in his sacrificial death and memorialized monument Samson functions as an image of the "strength sufficient and command from Heav'n" (1212) of the New Dispensation. Samson is a redeemer of language and will communicate as Milton believed the Bible to communicate, through its "written Records pure" which are "not but by the Spirit understood" (*PL* XII, 513–14). The analogues of such "written Records" in *Samson Agonistes* are Samson's "Acts enroll'd / In copious Legend, or sweet Lyric Song" (1736–37), but the "sweet Lyric Song" takes on new meaning when it is recognized as encapsulating the poetic act of the second semichorus. As Low observes, "heart will speak to heart and soul to soul, the only way Milton thought goodness could be spread — not by force or by institutions, but by persuasion and example, resulting in the free choice of the 'paradise within'"; Samson achieves the status not of eidolon but of true image, "a saving image, a revelation of [God's] face" (p. 104).

The New Dispensation effected by Samson's victory is not merely a matter of redeemed language, but more largely a matter of literary transformation, the transformation of the metaphysical into the metaphorical and even the mythical. For John C. Ulreich, Jr., "the Miltonic image is a paradox, a re-union of the mind with objects, of what is inwardly vital with what is outwardly fixed and dead," and "figurative meaning is a product of mythic consciousness." For him Samson's spiritual problem was a loss of such participation, a dissociation from metaphorical awareness, especially of the meaning of his blindness, which gives way to rediscovery and a conscious re-creation of symbolic meaning in his sacrifice of himself.[22] The reader's process is similar. As Ferry describes it, the facts of Samson's career "have all finally been transformed from facts of unique individual experience into metaphors for the human condition," in particular "a universally applicable metaphor for the final step toward the 'rest' which is the goal of all men" (pp. 175–76). Samson's transformation has become for Wilkenfeld "a mythical event by obliterating temporal distinctions" (p. 165). The "calm and sinless peace" of the final lines of *Samson Agonistes*, with its echoes of Christ in *Paradise Regained* (IV, 425), completes the Miltonic scheme of spiritual action, and spiritual action for Milton resides essentially in the redemption of experience into what is here "true experience." This is a verbal as well as a value transformation. Samson's achievement, like Christ's which he typifies, is to purge what I have been calling the experiential by realigning it within the transforming perspective of achieved faith, and such realignment resolves the pervasive and perplexing doubleness of the fallen human condition. The salvation which Samson offers is not for "servile minds" (1213), confined to the killing letter of the Old Dispensation or of the unredeemable imagination, but for those through whom "the Spirit giveth life." Radzinowicz summarizes: "It is the truth itself of experience which is the poetic object of delight. The theology of expanding revelations to free men capable of growth is matched in Milton's last great poem by a poetics of changed consciousness" (p. 363). Overall we may say of *Samson Agonistes* as an inspirational construct what John Shawcross says of Samson's action: "The action is not useless; it is just that fit audiences are few."[23]

University of Massachusetts, Amherst

NOTES

1. All Milton citations are from *John Milton: Complete Poems and Major Prose*, ed. Merritt Y. Hughes (New York, 1957). Anne Davidson Ferry discusses "guiding hand" and double meanings in *Milton and the Miltonic Dryden* (Cambridge, Mass., 1968), pp. 153–57. In *Toward "Samson Agonistes": The Growth of Milton's Mind* (Princeton, 1978), Mary Ann Radzinowicz lists a number of words with significant double meanings (p. 23) and distinguishes between two meanings of *delivered* (p. 93). Anthony Low provides detailed discussion of various kinds of doubleness throughout the dramatic poem in *The Blaze of Noon: A Reading of "Samson Agonistes"* (New York, 1974), chap. 4, "Irony: Reversal and Synthesis." On what Low calls the "irony of alternatives," see also Joseph H. Summers, "The Movements of the Drama," in *The Lyric and Dramatic Milton*, ed. Summers (New York, 1965), pp. 157–59. It is hard to believe from the plethora of recent commentary that as recently as 1954 Don Cameron Allen could speak of "the slight critical literature on this poem" (*The Harmonious Vision: Studies in Milton's Poetry* [Baltimore, 1954], p. 82).

2. *The Poems of John Milton*, ed. John Carey and Alastair Fowler (London, 1968), pp. 330–31; and Radzinowicz, *Toward "Samson,"* p. 99n.

3. Stanley E. Fish, "Question and Answer in *Samson Agonistes*," *Critical Quarterly*, XI (1969), 237–64; Christopher Grose, "'His Uncontrollable Intent': Discovery as Action in *Samson Agonistes*," in *Milton Studies*, VII, ed. Albert C. Labriola and Michael Lieb (Pittsburgh, 1975), pp. 49–76. See also E. W. Tayler, "Milton's *Samson*: The Form

of Christian Tragedy," *ELR*, III (1973), 306–21, especially on the play's "proleptic genius," "binocular vision," "double vision" (p. 311), and "relentless" ironies (p. 217).

4. Ferry, *The Miltonic Dryden*, pp. 130, 148, 159, 164, 165, 149 (italics hers). On the reader's (as distinct from the characters') processing of the double language, see also pp. 150–57. See also Marcia Landy, "Language and the Seal of Silence in *Samson Agonistes*," in *Milton Studies*, II, ed. James D. Simmonds (Pittsburgh, 1970), p. 176; and Low, *Blaze of Noon*, pp. 107, 109. None of these critics links the language issues with Christ the Word or notes that the Samson chapters in Judges immediately follow the chapter on the pronunciation of *Shibboleth*, an incident touched on in *SA* 289.

5. Martin Mueller, "Pathos and Katharsis in *Samson Agonistes*," *ELH*, XXXI (1964), reprinted in *Critical Essays on Milton from ELH* (Baltimore, 1969), pp. 234–52, esp. p. 237; Roger B. Wilkenfeld, "Act and Emblem: The Conclusion of *Samson Agonistes*," *ELH*, XXXIII (1965), 162–65; and Landy, "Language and the Seal of Silence," p. 191. For Grose, this is the point of Samson's real victory, when Samson "has actually heard what the Chorus could not bring itself to say" and when reason is rejected ("'His Uncontrollable Intent,'" pp. 61–63).

6. Raymond Waddington, "Melancholy Against Melancholy: *Samson Agonistes* as Renaissance Tragedy," in *Calm of Mind: Tercentenary Essays on "Paradise Regained" and "Samson Agonistes" in Honor of John S. Diekhoff*, ed. Joseph A. Wittreich, Jr. (Cleveland, 1971), p. 278.

7. In contrast, Low stresses the practicality and "tactical necessity" of Samson's "equivocations" and flatly denies that Samson is here resorting to silence (*Blaze of Noon*, p. 107, and see pp. 74–76). Irene Samuel also generally deplores the critical tendency "to substitute our guesses for what the poet gives" ("*Samson Agonistes* as Tragedy," in Wittreich, *Calm of Mind*, p. 248).

8. Contrasting Milton's version of Samson's final speech with the vengeful mode of Judges, Ferry notes the absence from Milton's version of "any form of prayer, or declaration of faith, or hymn of praise, any claim by Samson to be God's instrument, or hint of his restored sense of divine favor" (*The Miltonic Dryden*, p. 171).

9. Low carries the design a bit further in *Blaze of Noon*, p. 47. For Georgia Christopher, Samson's conversations with others serve as doses of homeopathic medicine ("Homeopathic Physic and Natural Renovation in *Samson Agonistes*," *ELH*, XXXVII [1970], 361–73).

10. Nancy Y. Hoffman, "Samson's Other Father: The Character of Manoa in *Samson Agonistes*," in *Milton Studies*, II, ed. James D. Simmonds (Pittsburgh, 1970), p. 195.

11. Jon Lawry, *The Shadow of Heaven: Matter and Stance in Milton's Poetry* (Ithaca, 1968), pp. 358 ff., esp. pp. 358–61, 373–74, 389–96; Joan S. Bennett, "Liberty Under the Law: The Chorus and the Meaning of *Samson Agonistes*," in *Milton Studies*, XII, ed. James D. Simmonds (Pittsburgh, 1978), pp. 146 ff.; John Huntley, "A Revaluation of the Chorus' Role in Milton's *Samson Agonistes*," *MP*, LXIV (1966), 145; Radzinowicz, *Toward "Samson Agonistes,"* pp. 63–65. Although she refers only to the Chorus at lines 183–86, Marcia Landy notes what I am exploring more largely, that "the Chorus translates Samson's psychic condition into physical terms" ("Language and the Seal of Silence," p. 182). See also Low, *Blaze of Noon*, p. 124, and chap. 6 passim.

12. Additional distinctions are drawn by Lawry, *Shadow of Heaven*, pp. 394–95; Radzinowicz, *Toward "Samson Agonistes,"* pp. 362–63; and Arnold Stein, *Heroic Knowledge: An Interpretation of "Paradise Regained" and "Samson Agonistes"* (Hamden, Conn., 1965), p. 199.

13. For similar views, see Balachandra Rajan, *The Lofty Rime: A Study of Milton's*

Major Poetry (Coral Gables, Fla., 1970), p. 131; Summers, "Movements of the Drama," p. 167; and Louis L. Martz, "Chorus and Character in *Samson Agonistes*," in *Milton Studies*, I, ed. James D. Simmonds (Pittsburgh, 1969), p. 121.

14. A. S. P. Woodhouse, "Tragic Effect in *Samson Agonistes*," *UTQ*, XXVIII (1958–59), 205–22, reprinted in *Milton: Modern Essays in Criticism*, ed. Arthur E. Barker (New York, 1965), pp. 458–59; Mueller, "Pathos and Katharsis," pp. 243, 245–46; Lee Sheridan Cox, "Natural Science and Figurative Design in *Samson Agonistes*," *ELH*, XXXV (1968), reprinted in *Critical Essays on Milton from ELH*, p. 275; Waddington, "Melancholy Against Melancholy," pp. 279–80; Radzinowicz, *Toward "Samson Agonistes,"* p. 177; Wilkenfeld, "Act and Emblem," pp. 162, 166–67; and Albert R. Cirillo, "Time, Light, and the Phoenix: The Design of *Samson Agonistes*," in Wittreich, *Calm of Mind*, pp. 228–29.

15. T. R. Henn, *The Harvest of Tragedy* (London, 1956), p. 264, cited in Wilkenfeld, "Act and Emblem," p. 166; Mueller, "Pathos and Katharsis," pp. 246, 240; Wilkenfeld, "Act and Emblem," pp. 166–67; Lynn Veach Sadler, "Typological Imagery in *Samson Agonistes*: Noon and the Dragon," *ELH*, XXXVII (1970), 205. Grose speaks of the outcome as "at least vaguely apocalyptic in its nature" ("'His Uncontrollable Intent,'" p. 50); on the relation of *Samson Agonistes* to Revelation, see also Northrop Frye, "Agon and Logos: Revolution and Revelation," in *The Prison and the Pinnacle*, ed. B. Rajan (Toronto, 1973), pp. 150–54. Lee Sheridan Cox, in "The 'Ev'ning Dragon' in *Samson Agonistes*: A Reappraisal," *MLN*, LXXVI (1961), 577–84, argues for a winged dragon, rather than snake, as *dragon* is usually glossed, and stresses the "flexibility of the visual image" (p. 581) in focusing on Samson as "the seeing one" and the "relation of vision and power, flight and judgment" (p. 584). For Carey, *Poems of John Milton*, p. 341, "the snake in the henroost" undercuts the eagle and Phoenix images.

16. See also Christopher Ricks, *Milton's Grand Style* (Oxford, 1963), p. 54. Carey summarizes the imagery of *Samson Agonistes* on pp. 339–43, as does Cox, "Natural Science and Figurative Design," pp. 253–76. See also Carey, "Sea, Snake, Flower, and Flame in *Samson Agonistes*," *MLR*, LXII (1967), 395–99. Duncan Robertson, "Metaphor in *Samson Agonistes*," *UTQ*, XXXVIII (1969), 319–38, defends *Samson Agonistes* against critical claims of a lack of metaphor, but his argument is largely confined to such matters as the relation of physical strength to virtue, hair to strength, body to prison, and military to moral defeat.

17. For other distinctions between visual and auditory, see Landy, "Language and the Seal of Silence," pp. 177 ff.

18. Hebrews xi has been frequently cited by commentators on *Samson Agonistes* in a variety of connections. See especially Low, *Blaze of Noon*, pp. 179–81, and Radzinowicz, *Toward "Samson Agonistes,"* p. 287.

19. Mueller reads the holocaust as Samson's healing purification by fire, "the burnt offering Samson makes of himself" ("Pathos and Katharsis," pp. 245–46); but see Carey, *Poems of John Milton*, p. 400n1702.

20. Irene Samuel, "The Dialogue in Heaven: A Reconsideration of *Paradise Lost*, III, 1–417," *PMLA*, LXXII (1957), 601–11, reprinted in Barker, *Essays*, pp. 240–41.

21. See also Wilkenfeld, "Act and Emblem," p. 168; and Mueller, "Pathos and Katharsis," p. 251. However, numerous commentators have found that, in Frye's words, "the Danites see only as far as the old dispensation allows them to see" ("Agon and Logos," p. 162); similarly Bennett, "Liberty Under the Law," pp. 159–60, for whom the Chorus show only "a blinded piety." For Grose, "'His Uncontrollable Intent,'" p. 66, the final moral of the Chorus "seems in its diffuseness to cover almost any conceivable phenomenon."

22. John C. Ulreich, Jr., "The Typological Structure of Milton's Imagery," in *Milton Studies*, V, ed. James D. Simmonds (Pittsburgh, 1973), pp. 80–81.

23. "Irony as Tragic Effect: *Samson Agonistes* and the Tragedy of Hope," in Wittreich, *Calm of Mind*, p. 304.